LIPPMANN, LIBERTY,
AND THE PRESS

LIPPMANN, LIBERTY, AND THE PRESS

by
John Luskin

The University of Alabama Press
University, Alabama

To: A.R.L.

PREFACE

Grants from the University of Alabama Research Grants Committee and a sabbatical free from teaching supported preparation of this manuscript. Access to the Walter Lippmann Collection in the Yale University Library greatly expedited gathering of the source material.

The Yale collection contains most of the books and magazine articles written by Lippmann or making mention of him. It also includes a file of New York *World* editorial pages from 1924 to 1931, with an indication of the authorship of each editorial, and indexed volumes of all of Lippmann's "Today and Tomorrow" columns.

More than forty large black boxes of Lippmann's correspondence and unpublished papers are stored in a library vault, but they are flagged with red signals warning that they are not yet accessible to researchers. The Edward M. House Papers and the Henry L. Stimson Papers, also at Yale, contain Lippmann letters which are a valuable supplementary source.

It may seem strange that the papers of Lippmann, a Harvard graduate and overseer, are at Yale. The collection was initiated by Robert O. Anthony, an Amherst alumnus who admired Lippmann and began in 1931 to save and file the then new "Today and Tomorrow" columns. In 1946 Anthony's collection, expanded to include books and hundreds of magazine articles, had grown so large that Lippmann and Anthony sought an institutional home for it. The Yale Library was chosen because its archives department specialized in similar private collections.

Help and encouragement in producing this manuscript came

also from many people: Mrs. Katherine Blackstock, secretary of the Historical Manuscripts and Archives Department at the Yale Library; Mrs. Vernice Washburn, executive secretary of the University of Alabama Research Grants Committee; Morgan L. Walters, director of the University of Alabama Press; Mrs. Mary Ann Green, a University of Alabama graduate student; my brother, Stanton Luskin; and especially my wife, who worked with me during every stage of the project.

JOHN LUSKIN

June 1972

CONTENTS

Lippmann, Liberty,
and the Press

Chapter I

HARVARD, SOCIALISM, AND BOHEMIA

IN MARCH OF 1909, WALTER LIPPMANN WROTE ENTHUSIASTICALLY that "the old dogmas . . . the old individualism" were crumbling under the onslaughts of socialistic thought and that *laissez faire* was being "reluctantly relinquished" in favor of collective action.[1] Sixty years and some ten million words later, he wrote that "the excessive promises made since a liberal majority came into being in the first part of this century" had inevitably produced unhappiness, bitterness, and reaction in a majority of the American people.

He had come to believe, he said in January of 1969 as he approached his eightieth birthday, that the "critical point was passed when the liberal reformers promised not only the redress of specific grievances but universal and utopian glories." Woodrow Wilson's promise to make the world "safe for democracy," Franklin Roosevelt's promise to rid it of fear, the world-wide guarantees against Communism made by the Truman, Eisenhower, Kennedy and Johnson administrations were in large part, he said, "to speak bluntly, pernicious bombast which, as the applause dies down, can only mislead friend and foe alike." The time had come, he said, "for the American people to face the facts of life . . . to accept the fact that there are no universal remedies for the hardness of the human condition on this planet."[2] George Santayana, who taught Lippmann at Harvard, used to tell his philosophy classes: "A youth who is not an anarchist is a knave; an old man who is not a conservative is a fool."[3] Lippmann was never an anarchist, though for a short time he was a Socialist, which was generally considered to be as bad, and whether as he advanced in years he became a conservative has long been a question for debate. Many of his friends who stayed to his left believed that he had turned reactionary and reproached and upbraided him for what they considered to be his desertion of liberal causes or candidates.

But the question of liberal-or-conservative has become moot, and Lippmann's critics, who, especially in the 1930's and 1940's were numerous and often savage, are either silent or dead. By the time he was seventy Lippmann had become mythological—a living legend who was called the greatest journalist of his time—who like the New York *Times* was the Fifth Estate of the press, *sui generis* and irreplaceable.[4]

Myth-making, however, as Lippmann himself has pointed out, obscures the facts and blurs the record. The legend of John F. Kennedy transcends his accomplishments as President, Lippmann said, though he conceded that he was "glad of the legend and I think it contains that part of the truth which is most worth having."[5] So the legend of Lippmann, whom one of his colleagues described as descending *on* Olympus and another characterized as far more important than the transitory Presidents who serve in Washington and then retire to Independence, Northampton, Palm Springs, Johnson City, and Valhalla, may surpass his achievements.[6]

But the achievements have been monumental—author of 21 books; editor of the New York *World* and director of its great editorial page; associate editor of the *New Republic* in its infancy; syndicated columnist whose views were published by newspapers in nearly all the world's big cities for more than 35 years; contributor to scholarly journals and to the most popular magazines.

He has won two Pulitzer Prizes, has been awarded the Presidential Medal of Honor, and has received decorations from foreign governments. From 1926 to 1965 he received honorary degrees from nineteen universities, including California, Chicago, Columbia, Harvard, Michigan, and Wisconsin.

Every President from Woodrow Wilson to Richard Nixon either has personally sought his advice or has attended to it in his columns. Foreign ministers and even prime ministers have called on him as soon as they have called on the White House and the State Department. In fact he has been described as "a solitary counterpoise to the State Department," and one official in the department has said that "it was common for meetings of the Policy Planning Staff . . . to open with a discussion of why Walter Lippmann was wrong in his column this morning. There could have been no greater tribute."[7]

The point at which Lippmann decided to become a journalist—if indeed he ever consciously decided to become one—is uncertain. Some of his friends anticipated a career in politics for him, as Governor of New York, Secretary of State—even President. His education, preparing for Harvard and at Harvard, might easily have impelled him toward university teaching as a philosopher, economist, political scientist, or classicist.

During Lippmann's last year at Harvard, while he was serving as assistant to Santayana, Lincoln Steffens visited the campus in search of "young blood" for *Everybody's,* the muckraking magazine which he helped edit. Some of the professors made lists for him of their most promising students, and when Lippmann's name appeared on all the lists, Steffens tentatively offered him a job. But first, he suggested that Lippmann should get some experience as a reporter; so during the Spring of 1910, his last months at Harvard, Lippmann worked part-time for the *Common,* a liberal Boston weekly paper. The job bored him, spending, as he described it, "all day in the office, reading newspaper clippings, and trying to restate the facts as colorlessly as possible." Soon after graduation he asked Steffens for a job, saying that "money does not happen to be an important consideration at this time."[8]

From that point on, except for four months as executive secretary to the Socialist Mayor of Schenectady, N.Y., in 1912, and government and Army service during World War I, Lippmann has spent all his life writing for newspapers and magazines and working on his books.

Though, as he told Steffens, he had no need to be well paid—his parents were more than moderately well-to-do—he has been paid well enough to lead a life of quiet luxury. When he sold his Washington house in 1967 and bought a fourteen-room apartment on Park Avenue in New York, one of his fellow columnists wrote: "Walter Lippmann's house, which he just sold, was only a little smaller than Grand Central Station and could easily accommodate 300 diplomats, senators and such people without infringing the fire laws."[9]

The most intimate account of Lippmann's boyhood and his

days at Harvard has been written by his classmate Carl Binger, who became a famous psychiatrist. Lippmann's parents, Jacob and Daisy Baum Lippmann, were born in New York, children of German-Jewish immigrants. Jacob was a clothing manufacturer and real estate broker. Daisy was a graduate of Hunter College. With his parents and his maternal grandmother, Walter, an only child, lived first in a brownstone house on Lexington Avenue, then a four-story brick house on East 79th Street, and finally in a big stone house on East 80th Street, which was Lippmann's home until 1917.

His three elders saw to it, Binger says, that Walter had "every advantage." They were prosperous enough to live well in New York, to send the boy to a private school, and to take him to Europe on the best steamships for summer holidays. The school was Dr. Julius Sachs' School for Boys at 32 West 59th Street, where from 1896 to 1906 Lippmann impressed a succession of teachers with his industry and precocity.

"I don't suppose," Binger says, "he ever got less than an A on any examination in his life." He knew French irregular verbs as well as M. Porret, his teacher; he could translate Ovid at sight, and he was the only boy in school unterrified by the course in Greek which the bearded Dr. Sachs taught.

Walter wanted to play on the football team, but his mother preferred that he take piano lessons. He did become a fairly good tennis player, and was a member of the debate team, which was coached by Arthur Garfield Hays, later distinguished as a civil liberties lawyer. With Binger, Walter edited the school newspaper and he became editor of its magazine. His stories in the magazine, Binger recalls, "sang songs of social significance." One dealt with a child's grave next to Grant's Tomb and another with a poor old woman who sold apples at Fifth Avenue and 23rd Street.[10]

The New York of Lippmann's childhood bore no resemblance to the city of today. The horseless carriage had yet to come, and there were no tall buildings to break the skyline. The closest to a skyscraper in 1896, the year Lippmann entered school, was the 16-floor home of the New York *World*, which Joseph Pulitzer, who had come to New York from St. Louis in 1883, had built on Park Row.

From their offices on the eleventh floor, where the city room was located, and high up under the golden dome where Lippmann

was later to work as editor, the men of the *World* could survey
all of Manhattan, look across the river at Brooklyn, and gaze
out to sea. New Yorkers in 1896 had a profusion of newspapers
to read. Only 9,000 of them bought the New York *Times*. That
year Adolph Ochs from Chattanooga purchased the paper and
started it toward the pinnacle of success and esteem. More than
200,000 people bought the morning *World,* which of the three
Pulitzer papers—morning, evening, and Sunday editions—was
always THE *World.*

In 1895 William Randolph Hearst came east from San Francisco
and purchased the *Journal,* an evening paper which soon began
stridently and successfully to offer Pulitzer his greatest competition. The *Herald* of James Gordon Bennett, Jr., attracted 140,000
subscribers. Horace Greeley's once great *Tribune* was surviving
under Whitelaw Reid and, like the *Sun,* was still in the race with
70,000. Readers whose interest was sports found it satisfied in
the *Telegram* (100,000), and the intellectuals, 25,000 of them, sub-
scribed to E. L. Godkin's *Post,* which had become, as A. J. Liebling
has phrased it, "a symbol of the unpopularity of virtue."

In the late 1890's the *World* transcended them all. In 1955 Liebling interviewed a former *World* reporter, who recalled the days
of glory. "Being a newspaperman gave you stature then," says
Ned Brown. "Everywhere except in society. It didn't cut any
ice there. But elsewhere a first-string reporter on any recognized
paper—especially one of the *World's*—had a lot of prestige. *Civis
Romanus erat.* He was a citizen of no mean state." (Like Lippmann,
Ned Brown worked for the *World* the last day it was published
in 1931. He was a writer specializing in boxing.)

But the character of the *World's* early journalism—except for
its editorial page—was of a kind which revolted Lippmann when
from the tower room of the *World* he watched it practiced in
the tabloids during the 1920's.

The boys of Dr. Sachs' school would not have known the boys
from the lower East Side who found the trunk of a man's body,
wrapped in oilcloth, floating in the East River in the Summer
of 1897. But unless the *World* and the *Journal* were prohibited
in their homes, they read about them. The search for the identity
of the victim and for his killer was described in hundreds of
columns of space in both papers and typified the popular journalism of the time. Reporters interviewed the former chief of the

United States Secret Service, who told them the killer was probably a Sicilian, because the torso was wrapped in red oilcloth and Sicilians loved bright colors. A palmist deduced for the *World* that the victim had a domineering disposition and must have made enemies. Handwriting experts, spirit mediums, and a phrenologist also contributed their solutions—the phrenologist being slightly handicapped by the failure of the man's head to emerge from the river. A pathologist interviewed by the *World* capped all the speculations by saying that the murderers were cannibals. (It developed that there were two killers, a woman who grew tired of her lover, and a new boyfriend who helped her cut him up.)[11]

The *World's* dignified editorial page, irritated by criticism of the paper's sensationalism, declared that in offering a prize of $500 in gold to any reader who sent in a correct solution of the crime the paper was acting simply as a minister of justice. Thirty-four years later on the last night that the *World* went to press, with Lippmann as its editor, there was long debate in the news room whether the biggest headline on Page One should be above the story of a woman found murdered in Central Park or above the story of the death of the *World*. The death of the institution got top billing. News evaluation is a delicate and intricate problem.[12]

No picture of Pulitzer, though in the 1890's he was one of the great men of his time, decorated young Lippmann's room at home. Top billing there, Carl Binger recalls, was given to a bust of Napoleon and a picture of Napoleon's retreat from Moscow. There were also pictures of frescoes from the Sistine Chapel.

Charles Eliot of the five-foot bookshelf fame was president of Harvard in 1906 when Lippmann left New York for Cambridge, the month he became seventeen. Abbot Lawrence Lowell, who was to succeed Eliot in 1909 and whose role in the Sacco-Vanzetti case Lippmann was later to defend in *World* editorials, taught a course in government. The star of first magnitude on the faculty was William James, and the most luminous of the others were Santayana, Ralph Barton Perry, and Josiah Royce—all in the Philosophy Department—and Barrett Wendell, George Lyman Kittredge, and Charles Townsend Copeland, in English. Alfred North Whitehead, William Ernest Hocking, and John Livingston Lowes came during the next generation.

Lippmann earned his bachelor's degree in three years *(cum*

laude), but did not take it until the end of his fourth year in 1910. His sphere of concentration (the term "major" was not used) was philosophy, and he stayed on for the fourth year principally to assist Santayana. President Eliot's famous free elective system was in force, and Lippmann sampled almost everything available except mathematics and the natural sciences. (In later years he deplored his ignorance of physics and biology.) He studied Latin, German and Italian, history and government, the fine arts, and economics. Charles Taussig, who was later one of Franklin Roosevelt's advisers on fiscal policy, taught one of Lippmann's three courses in economics.

Every Harvard class includes men who become famous, and 1910 was the year of a bumper crop. Besides Lippmann and Carl Binger, there were T. S. Eliot, John Reed, Heywood Broun, Robert Edmond Jones, Alan Seeger, and, less often mentioned, Bronson Cutting, who went to New Mexico for his health and established a political empire there.

Lippmann wrote for the *Advocate,* for *Harvard Illustrated,* and for the *Monthly,* became president of the newly-organized Socialist Club, and worked at Hale House, a settlement for underprivileged children in Boston. He lived in Weld Hall, a barracks-like building whose rooms were without private baths or central heating.

Ibsen and Shaw, Wells and Wilde were the literary vogue, and Beatrice and Sidney Webb, Lincoln Steffens, Upton Sinclair, and Ida Tarbell provided the ideas and the information for discussion of the evils of capitalism. Henri Bergson, whom Lippmann greatly admired, came from France to lecture; and from England, to teach a course in government, came Graham Wallas, whose ideas stimulated Lippmann to write his first book, *A Preface to Politics.*

On week-ends in the Spring and on holidays, Carl Binger remembered, he and Lippmann and some of their classmates visited Ralph Albertson at his farm north of Boston. Albertson, like Mayor George R. Lunn of Schenectady, for whom Lippmann was to work, was an ordained minister turned Socialist. Faye, one of Albertson's three daughters, became Lippmann's first wife in 1917. And as head of the committee that published the Boston *Common,* Albertson was Lippmann's first employer.[13]

Lippmann's published reminiscences of his Harvard years center on Santayana and Copeland. In one of Santayana's classes, he recalled twenty years after he sat in the class, a student who

had drifted away from the argument began drawing a picture
instead of taking notes. Pride in his craftmanship led him to show
his creation to his neighbor. As the picture passed down the aisle,
Lippmann remembered, it caused "enough commotion to recall
Mr. Santayana from the realm of essence. When the scandal was
exposed, it turned out to be a picture of the platonic heaven
with philosophical angels sitting on banks of clouds, and in the
middle of them Mr. Santayana with his hat and cane. Mr. Santayana had arrived in heaven to congratulate the angels on their
perfection."[14]

Copeland, or Copey, as he was always called, was one of a succession of famous Harvard English professors who tried to teach
students to write prose and verse—others were LeBaron Russell
Briggs, Bernard De Voto, Robert Hillyer, and Archibald MacLeish.
Copeland's teaching was "a little mad . . . as genius is so often
mad," Lippmann said twenty-five years after he was graduated.
Reading one's work aloud to Copeland, Lippmann said, was "like
a catch-as-catch-can wrestling match . . . You could fight back but
eventually he stripped you to your essential self. Then he cuffed
the battered remains and challenged them . . ."[15]

Harvard's discussion clubs—there were dozens of them, ranging
from the Circolo Italiano to the Methodist Club, the Socialist Club,
and the Pierian Sodality—were too anemic to suit Lippmann the
undergraduate, and he proposed in 1910 that they be reorganized
into fewer combinations of larger groups. It was a wholesome
sign, he said, that the Divinity Club had invited the Socialist Club
to a joint meeting. And he added exuberantly, "A joint meeting
of the Christian Scientists and the Philosophical Club would be
a stirring affair."

The political apathy of his fellow undergraduates distressed
Lippmann. "We move in political darkness," he wrote in 1909.
"Rather we sit in political darkness . . . Our consciences are not
social; we are 'hopelessly private persons.' " Then echoing Santayana's observation about anarchists and conservatives, he said
that "it is decidedly ridiculous for young men to be conservative . . .
Men who are 'orthodox' when they are young are in danger of
being middle-aged all their lives." Like Horace Greeley nearly
a century before him, he wrote in defense of the suffragettes and
ascribed their failure to win the vote to "the great dulling mass
of people who don't care."[16]

Although enthusiasm for political reform did not permeate the Harvard classes, a few zealots did care. "If anyone taking a bird's-eye view of Cambridge at one o'clock in the morning were to see five or six groups of excited Harvard men gesticulating wildly on various street corners," Lippmann wrote in *Harvard Illustrated,* "let him know that the Socialist Club held a meeting that evening." The Socialist Party polled ten million votes throughout the world, he noted, and was "infinitely more comprehensive than Christianity . . ."

"He who listens carefully enough will hear at Harvard heresies about private property which ten years ago would have been denounced by the public press as leading straight to atheism, to free love, and all the other horrors that terrified ignorance can conjure up."

The sterility of political and economic theory as it was presented and discussed in the classroom—"for all the world like scholastic philosophers arguing about the nature of 'substance' "—dismayed the twenty-year-old Lippmann. The test of capitalism vs. Socialism must be pragmatic, he insisted. "Socialism stands or falls by its fruits in practice. If it can be shown . . . that private enterprise is more beneficent, then the Socialist case collapses. And good riddance to it."[17]

Three years later Lippmann expounded his ideas about political pragmatism in *A Preface to Politics,* after his disillusioning experience as a member of the Socialistic city administration in Schenectady. But his disenchantment did not stem, as has been supposed, from observing socialism in practice, but rather from the Schenectady Socialists' failure to practice socialism.

The Schenectady venture followed a year and a half of work for Lincoln Steffens on *Everybody's,* beginning in the Summer of 1910. Lippmann was not enthusiastic about his work on the magazine. He read and edited manuscripts, helped Steffens as a kind of ammanuensis during interviews and investigations, and after the first few months began to write a few signed articles. Lippmann was grateful for what Steffens taught him about the craft of editing and the art of interviewing, but when the offer of the job in Schenectady came late in 1911, he felt he had been "rescued."[18]

Steffens claimed that it was he, not Copey, who taught Lippmann how to write. The trick, he said, was to "learn under the pressure of conversation to sum up a thought in one sentence. It was this that I taught Walter Lippmann and my other disciples . . . When Lippmann showed me a paragraph, I'd say: 'Good, but just what did you want to say?' He said he meant to say what the paragraph said, but I'd shake my head and wonder, till in a rage he would plunk it all out in one good clean sentence. Then I'd say let's put that sentence into the paragraph."[19]

Steffens gave Lippmann full marks as an interviewer. Writing about the assistance his "cub reporter" gave him during an investigation of Wall Street, he said that Lippmann "asked the men he met for more than I asked them for. He searched them; I know it because he searched me, too, for my ideas and theories."[20] Lippmann acknowledged his debt to Steffens as a teacher of journalism soon after the "Today and Tomorrow" column became a huge success in 1932. "Steffens said that if I wrote a paragraph about a fire down the street," Lippmann recalled, "I must write it with as much care and devotion as if that paragraph were going down in history in one of the anthologies."[21]

Lippmann's first signed article for *Everybody's* was a tribute to William James, published in December of 1910, three months after the philosopher's death. James had a truly open mind, Lippmann said. "And he listened to truth from anybody, and from anywhere, and in any form. He listened for it from Emma Goldman, the Pope or a sophomore . . . I think he would have listened with an open mind to the devil's account of heaven, and I'm sure he would have heard him out on hell."[22]

For the article on James, Steffens collected a bet he had made with his *Everybody's* associates. He wagered that he could train a college graduate to be an accomplished writer in six months. He slipped the James article into type under his own signature and when it was passed for publication, triumphantly changed "By Lincoln Steffens" to "By Walter Lippmann."[23]

By the time his second article for *Everybody's* appeared—an appreciation of Henri Bergson as "The Most Dangerous Man in the World"—Lippmann was in Schenectady with the Socialists. A detailed account of his experiences there and of the socialistic "experiment" is buried in the files of the New York *Call,* a socialist weekly newspaper which was suppressed by the government during World War I. In a series of articles by Lippmann; by Morris Hillquit, the militant socialist lawyer; and by Upton Sinclair, the work of Mayor Lunn and his city government, which included, by the way, Charles Proteus Steinmetz, is condemned and defended. (Steinmetz was the gnomish wizard who presided over the General Electric Company's research laboratories. He served the socialist administration as president of the board of education, and in 1916, when Lunn was elected to his second term as mayor, became president of the city council.)[24]

"Schenectady is a disappointment," Lippmann wrote in the New York *Call* six weeks after he quit in May of 1912 as the mayor's secretary. "Nothing is being done there that twenty reform cities can't duplicate... Power has come too soon and it has come in such a way as to make the Socialists play politics... Although they are called Socialists they cannot be Socialists. They did not go through the long and painful process of educating public opinion until it desired real changes..." Concluding that "reform pretending to be radicalism is deadening," he deplored the absence of "an organized party of genuine radicals to keep the reformers alive..."[25]

Four years later the state executive committee of the Socialist Party came to agree with Lippmann and expelled Lunn from the party as a deviationist. The mayor served out his term, shifted gracefully to the Democratic Party, was elected to Congress and later elected lieutenant governor of New York State.

Morris Hillquit, who remained a thoroughgoing Socialist and sometimes paid dearly for it—once being denied a passport by the State Department—replied to Lippmann's criticism that the Schenectady Socialists suffered from timidity and the lack of a bold plan. The "good government" that Lippmann admitted Lunn was providing proved, Hillquit said, "that the workers of this country are ripe and ready to take over the powers of government." Comrade Lippmann, said Hillquit, was singularly reticent about the details of the "bold plan" he advocated for the Socialists, perhaps because he realized that collective ownership of the industrial system could not be achieved at the municipal level.[26] (Schenectady in 1912 was a fiefdom of the General Electric and American Locomotive Companies. Their influence, especially that of General Electric, over the political and economic structure, and their subtle control of the daily press led to the rebellion which put the Socialists in office.)

A week after the Hillquit criticism, Lippmann was back in the pages of the *Call* with an article entitled "The Shrewdly Good," in which he accused the Socialists of "tip-toe politics" and "Wooden Horse tactics." An electorate "strong enough to undertake any such task as Socialism" could not be fed on pap, he said. "The men and women who are trying to be shrewdly good should come out flatly for the biggest truth they see... nothing but that will save them from little successes..."[27]

Two months later, Upton Sinclair, who had been traveling abroad and had not seen the *Call,* asked for space in the paper to join the controversy. Agreeing with Lippmann that a bold plan was needed, Sinclair offered a simple and flamboyant one. Raise hell and go to jail, he suggested.

"I am quite clear in my own mind that Socialists are far better out of office, agitating the social revolution, than in office constructing new playgrounds and bettering the milk supply."

It was absurd, Sinclair said, that a Socialist mayor and city council could think of nothing better to do than try to run a city government better than capitalist politicians. They could, for example, he suggested, organize a general anti-rent strike. This would lead to conflict in the courts, with the county, with the state... "and perhaps the Socialist mayor would go to jail, which would constitute a splendid piece of propaganda..."

"Let us preach Socialism in our campaigns; and let us practice it when we are in office... Choose some line of conduct that will be bold, clear, and revolutionary; follow it regardless of courts, charters, constitutions, or jails."[28]

It took only four months for Lippmann to grow disillusioned with the Schenectady experiment, but his doubts about it were implicit almost from the beginning of his term as secretary. Writing for the *Masses* after two months in office, he deplored the tendency "to impregnate the movement with half baked people who don't understand Socialism" and the temptation "to play safe" by enticing the voters of the old parties.[29]

The question whether Lippmann himself was ever more than a half baked Socialist seems, taking his own word for it, to require an affirmative answer. But testimony to the contrary is rather profuse. Carl Binger takes pains to say that "he was never a doctrinaire Socialist, nor was he ever enthralled by the dialectics of the party... It is a misreading of Lippmann to think that he has swung in his more mature years from the radicalism of youth to the conservatism of age. He never was a radical."[30]

Interviewed by David Weingast for a book which was published in 1949, Lippmann said that he had been a Socialist for "only a short time" and "never a Marxist." And John Mason Brown, who wrote a series of articles after talking with Lippmann in 1954, said that he had been "a Socialist whose brand was nearer to Sanka than coffee" and "a reader though not a disciple of Marx."[31]

On the other hand, Ernest Sutherland Bates, who published an extremely unfavorable article about Lippmann in 1933, said that Lippmann was one of the most militant members of Branch 1, "the most radical of the Socialist groups in New York City," and that in a municipal election in 1913 Lippmann and ten others rejected their party's program and submitted a more "revolutionary left-wing platform . . ."[32]

If this were true, it was only a temporary aberration, for by October of 1912, when he finished writing *A Preface to Politics,* Lippmann had rejected even the mildest precepts of Socialist dogma, except for a half-hearted hazard that Guild Socialism—"co-management of industry by the state and by the labor union"—might provide the basis for progressive government.[33]

Although his four months in Schenectady left no permanent scars, it was a bruising experience for Lippmann. Except for his work, the dreary, class-conscious factory town offered the twenty-two-year-old little stimulation besides a chance to talk with the young scientists at General Electric and the small group of professors in the liberal arts at Union College. (Union gave Lippmann an honorary degree in 1933 and chose him as its commencement speaker. Lippmann's Harvard classmate, Amos Pinchot, found the speech hilarious. Into five sentences of discussion of the national economy, Pinchot noted, Lippmann managed to squeeze five learned references—to Adam Smith, Friedrich List, Alexander Hamilton, Disraeli, and Bismarck. What were "the sadly perplexed members of Union '33 to do on receipt of these pearls of wisdom?" Pinchot asked. Conclude "that Mr. Lippmann is an extremely erudite man . . . and give nine rahs and a tiger for that great economic quarterback, List '41?")[34]

Lippmann's first massive display of erudition—and many said wisdom—appeared in *A Preface to Politics,* which he wrote in the Summer and early Fall of 1912 after leaving Schenectady. As in later years, he retreated to northern Maine to do some thinking about basic problems beyond the hurly burly of government. The problem he pondered was the one his friend and teacher, Graham Wallas, had posed at Harvard—how to cure the masses of apathy and make them feel that politics was more than "a personal drama without meaning or a vague abstraction without substance."

Quite coincidentally, Alfred Kuttner, a friend who went with him to Maine, was working that summer on a translation of Sigmund Freud's *An Interpretation of Dreams,* and as Lippmann read the translation he began to realize, he said later, "how much Freud had to contribute to the psychology which I had learned at college."

When *A Preface to Politics* was published in 1913, it received almost unanimously favorable reviews, prompted a congratulatory letter from Theodore Roosevelt, and was mentioned by Freud in his magazine *Imago.* What Lippmann derived from Freud was the idea that government had always been repressive—by "taboo," by prohibitions and repressions. What was needed, Lippmann said, was a system to provide real people in a harsh world with "civilizing opportunities" for satisfying human desires and needs. The abstractions of "justice" and "liberty" were all too often equated, he said, with negative law seeking to prohibit and punish evil impulses rather than to redirect them toward desirable goals.

As Charles Forcey has pointed out in *The Crossroads of Liberalism,* Lippmann's book was a *tour de force* in which he incorporated, besides the ideas of Freud and Wallas, those of William James, Santayana, Wells, Chesterton, Nietzsche, Bergson, and Georges Sorel. And in so doing he drew, as well, on his experiences as a writer and editor of *Everybody's* and his work in Schenectady. Although some reviewers deplored "the haze of authoritative references" and "rather juvenile and cocksure pronouncements," nearly all agreed that it was an astonishing book for a man of twenty-three.[35]

Among the pronouncements in the book was a statement of Lippmann's "sincere conviction" that movements for political reform, especially including Socialism, too often placed the blame for the maladies of mankind on convenient scapegoats—5,000 prostitutes corrupting the city of Chicago, John D. Rockefeller and J. P. Morgan perpetuating poverty. "What I object to is the emphasis which shifts the blame for our troubles from the shoulders of the people to those of the 'corrupting interests.' "

Exaggeration of the influence of the "interests" permeated criticism of the operations of the press, Lippmann said. The influence of businessmen was paltry, he said, compared to the influence of the general reader of newspapers and magazines.

"I have worked in the editorial office of a popular magazine . . . I think I am pretty well aware of what the influence of business on journalism amounts to. I have seen the inside working of business pressure; articles of my own have been suppressed after they were in type; friends of mine have told me stories of expurgation." But, he concluded, no pressure of the "interests" was "one-tenth so corrupting, so insidious, so hostile to originality and frank statement as the fear of the public which reads the magazine . . .

"This will anger the farmers, that will arouse the Catholics, another will shock the summer girl. Anybody can take a fling at poor old Mr. Rockefeller [Lippmann took one three years later in the *New Republic*], but the great mass of average citizens (to which none of us belongs) must be left in undisturbed possession of its prejudices." And that was the reason, he said, "why American journalism is so flaccid, so repetitious and so dull."[36]

Lippmann may have underestimated the influence of external pressure, as, for example, it was exerted on *Everybody's*. The year after Lippmann joined the magazine, John O'Hara Cosgrave, its crusading editor, resigned in protest against "unaccustomed pressure" from its proprietors, and "subtle restraints" on *Everybody's* and other magazines brought the muckraking movement almost to a standstill by 1912.[37]

Exploring an issue which has received extensive consideration in the 1960's—a lack of attention in the massive mass media toward problems before they reach the crisis stage—Lippmann probed with precision the causes of the substitution of riots and demonstrations for orderly debate and discussion. Writing in *A Preface to Politics* of the textile workers' strike in Lawrence, Massachusetts, in the winter of 1912, he said, "The wretchedness and brutality of Lawrence conditions had been described in books and magazines and speeches until radicals had begun to wonder at times whether the power of language wasn't exhausted." In the context of riots in the ghettoes and the universities and the rioters' contention that conventional speech and print have lost so much of their vitality that they must be reinforced by "symbolic speech," this sounds topical indeed.

"An impassioned protest from a few individuals, a placid charity," were the only tokens of attention the Lawrence workers received, Lippmann said. But the strike, he pointed out, "touched the most impervious: Story after story came to the ears of hardened reporters who suddenly refused to misrepresent the strikers . . . the newspapers actually printed facts about the situation of a working class population . . . the Lawrence strikers did something more than insist upon their wrongs; they showed a disposition to right them. That is what scared public opinion into some kind of truth telling."[38]

In an article which he prepared for *Everybody's* before his resignation, Lippmann deplored the efforts of the press to secure special benefits through attempting to influence legislation. The American Newspaper Publishers Association was trying to ensure passage of a tariff bill which included a provision for duty-free imports of newsprint from Canada. The president of ANPA had sent a telegram to 300 daily newspaper editors suggesting that they instruct their Washington correspondents to treat the bill favorably.

"There is something peculiarly insidious about the point of view in that telegram," Lippmann wrote. "A democracy must, above all other things, keep the sources of public opinion clean." He applauded an editorial in the Philadelphia *North American* which called the bill "a sham and perversion."[39]

Disillusion with the press, reflected in the phrase about "hardened reporters" covering the Lawrence strike, reappeared in Lippmann's second book, *Drift and Mastery,* published in 1914. "It is well known," of course, he wrote sarcastically, "that newspapers make every effort to enable working men to reach public opinion, and make their appeal not to force, but to the national conscience.

"All civil rights are carefully guarded as in Paterson, Lawrence, and the southern lumber camps. Employers are precise in their desire to secure judges who have no bias whatever. And the voters are an active, intelligent body of imaginative democrats fighting at every step to see that justice is done."[40]

Beginning in 1913 Lippmann became one of the clutter of celebrities and notorieties who frequented Mabel Dodge Luhan's "salon" at 23 Fifth Avenue in New York. In Volume 3 of her *Intimate Memories,* a verbal exudation of 542 pages, she tells of her love affair with John Reed and her association with Lippmann,

Steffens, Margaret Sanger, Isadora Duncan, Bill Haywood, Emma Goldman, Alexander Berkman, and scores of others who made her apartment their home away from home. (A portrait of young Lippmann in her book is inscribed "Mabel Dodge, maker of oases, from Walter Lippmann, Nov. 27, 1915.")[41]

Much of what Mrs. Dodge wrote about her friends of 1913–1916 can scarcely have pleased those who read about themselves when the book appeared in 1936. Mrs. Dodge gave the impression, Clifton Fadiman said in a review, "that the New York bohemia of the times consisted of a group of simple-minded narcists all sweating hard over the business of acting like complex introverts."[42]

Lippmann fared badly in Mrs. Dodge's proliferous prose. "Walter was big and rather fat," Mrs. Dodge wrote. (In the profile portrait he gave to her he looked lean and very ascetic.) "But he had, I was fond of saying, intellectualized his fat so that it shone a little." Like Big Bill Haywood, the labor leader, Lippmann reminded Mrs. Dodge of a Buddha. But unlike Haywood, who had lost an eye in a fight, Lippmann, she observed, was "undefaced."

"Walter was never, never going to lose an eye in a fight," she added. "He might, I thought, 'lose his glow, but he will never lose an eye.' "[43] This comment about Lippmann has often been quoted. In 1939, after Lippmann supported Alfred M. Landon for President, Harold Ickes referred to it and said that Mrs. Luhan might have added that "he would never even break his wooden sword unless he should trip over it in a minuet."[44]

Though the members of Mrs. Dodge's circle may have paid dearly otherwise for her hospitality, which was administered by a butler and a cook, it cost them nothing in cash. This would have been unimportant to Lippmann, but it mattered to many of the others, including John Reed. Once when he was broke, Reed asked Steffens for a loan to pay the rent for his room at 42 Washington Square. In Steffens' view it was corruptive to lend a young man money for practical purposes.

"No regular bills, Jack," he told Reed. "But whenever you want money for some wasteful, idiotic affair . . . then you can come to me."[45] (Later, after her husband, Edwin Dodge, fled the premises, Reed solved the rent problem by moving in with Mabel.)

In this atmosphere of freeloading, freethinking, and freeloving, young Lippmann seemed, according to Mrs. Dodge, only relatively at ease. His suits, usually distinguished-looking dark serges, seemed to belong to "another world than this one he was in," she wrote. Toward her affair with Reed, she found him superciliously tolerant.

"I remember how mad I was one day with Walter," she reminisced. "I had been talking with him about living with Reed, and asking him, who was so wise and well balanced, if *he* thought it was all right . . ."

Presumably referring to the fact that her wealth elevated the affair above the squalid, Lippmann replied, she said: "As you conduct it, yes." But it infuriated her when he added: "Of course you can't live at the *White House* with Reed." That, Mabel said in a tantrum, was precisely what she would do if she wanted to do it.[46]

Reed found Lippmann somewhat supercilious and condescending, not toward his life with Mrs. Dodge, but toward Socialism and the labor movement and toward Reed's growing fame as a journalist. Lippmann's two books and his experience in Schenectady gave him no title, Reed felt, to play "stern father" to his "spoiled child."[47]

Nevertheless Lippmann remained inside the inside circle of the improper bohemians and played a prominent part in some of the revelry—for example, in episodes which might be entitled "An Afternoon at Isadora Duncan's," "Evenings with the Anarchists," and "Psychoanalysis Comes to New York City."

Mrs. Dodge vibrated to Miss Duncan and sought to help in her efforts to teach the children of America how to dance. After watching Miss Duncan and her young girls and a group of children she had brought from Russia to perform in Carnegie Hall, Mrs. Dodge became convinced that a way must be found to permit "a thousand little poor children" to learn to dance as Isadora danced.

At first they thought of the football stadiums at Harvard and Yale as sites for mass performances. Robert Rogers, who was a member of the inner circle, ridiculed this proposal in some verses he sent to Mrs. Dodge:

> "And the old Yale Bowl is an awful hole
> For dancing children's feet . . .
> Mayor Curley is a terror

Whom nothing classic suits ...
He'd think it quite deplorable,
However Isadorable,
To see a thousand kiddies
Cutting up like ancient Greeks."

Lippmann curtly responded to this, Mrs. Dodge said, with a note saying, "Curley is not Mayor of Cambridge and could not interfere." But Rogers' advice prevailed.

The next proposal was to persuade young Mayor John Purroy Mitchel to loan Miss Duncan the New York Armory for her project. "I got Walter interested in it," Mrs. Dodge wrote, "because I knew he would give 'cachet' to the event ..." The event was a visit by the mayor to Miss Duncan's studio and apartment, called the Ark, "a sort of loft that she hung with her vast blue curtains the color of robins' eggs ..."

The visit was a disaster. The "Temple of Beauty and Art," as Mrs. Dodge described it, was furnished with low couches for the girls and a great couch for Miss Duncan. When the mayor came—"a spindling young man," Mrs. Dodge said— Isadora and her splendid girls at first disdained him. Then remembering her duty as a hostess, Miss Duncan tried to lead the mayor to her couch. The mayor escaped the pressure of what Mrs. Dodge called Isadora's "warm body," and retreated to a piano stool. The girls and the other guests sat on the couches. Mrs. Dodge paid special attention to Lippmann during the discomfiture that ensued. "Among the various incongruities," she wrote, "I saw at once that Walter did not look well on that couch."

Retiring to her orange dais, where the little girls (presumably the Russian girls) came running from the corners to sit at her feet on the floor, Isadora demanded that the mayor release from prison a woman who had been convicted of murdering her children. The mayor departed. Marguerite Duncan, Isadora's sister-in-law, took Lippmann, Mrs. Dodge, and the other guests into another "more intimate" room and complained that the police of "this terrible city" had come one night recently asking, "What kind of place is this anyway?"

On the night of the mayor's visit, January 26, 1915, Lippmann sent a note from the Harvard Club which said. "Dear Mabel, I am utterly disgusted. If this is Greece and Joy and the Aegean Isles and the Influence of Music, I don't want anything to do with it. It's a nasty, absurd mess, and she is obviously the last person who ought to be running a school. I want you to let me off the committee . . ."[48]

The afternoon with Miss Duncan made a deep impression on Lippmann, for he wrote about it later in the *New Republic*. On that afternoon in her studio, he remembered, "New York was within an ace of God knows what. For someone had induced Mayor Mitchel to come and sit on a gray divan under an orange light while the girls danced. The idea was that he as the head of the government was to be struck mad by a vision of beauty and that we were all to dance on Fifth Avenue." As Lippmann remembered it, Isadora's insistence that the institution of the family be abolished, rather than that a murderess be freed from prison, caused the mayor to leave the Ark.[49]

The first Evening with the Anarchists occurred before Mrs. Dodge perfected her programs, and it was a fiasco. Later at Lippmann's urging ("Do try and *make* something of it . . . Weed it out and *order* it.") they were more shapely—in the parlimentary sense of the word. Three factions were represented at the first Radical Evening: advocates of blood-in-the-streets, proponents of strikes and sabotage, and devotees of Socialism. Emma Goldman and Alexander Berkman (who had tried to kill Henry Clay Frick, chairman of the board of Carnegie Brothers) were supposed to speak for anarchism; Bill Haywood and Elizabeth Gurley Flynn (later head of the Communist Party in the United States) were on the side of strikes and sabotage; Lippmann and Hutchins Hapgood favored non-violent reform. Amos Pinchot, Max Eastman and others, including Mrs. Dodge and Hippolyte Havel, a chef at Polly's Restaurant nearby, were to cheer and boo from the sidelines.

Haywood, Mrs. Dodge remembered, reclined on a yellow *chaise longue* with two or three girls at his feet. They were young public school teachers, she said, who led their students in pledges to the flag by day and gave their souls to Haywood and their other heroes at night. For whatever reason, Haywood was inarticulate that night. Lippmann tried to be helpful. "In a kind but firm voice he asked him definite questions about the policies of the Industrial Workers of the World," Mrs. Dodge said. But this only made Haywood look sleepy.

When Emma Goldman's turn came, she did little better. Shrewish and scolding, was Mrs. Dodge's verdict. So the verbal contest was forfeited to the moderates. The cook from Polly's summed it up. "You talk like goddam bourgeois," he told them, infuriated that Haywood and Goldman had failed to impress.[50]

The second of the Radical Evenings was exciting, because the press had become alerted to the alliance between the rabble-rousers and the bourgeoisie at 23 Fifth Avenue. Lippmann's role this time was to serve as bouncer, identifying and ejecting reporters who came to crash Mabel's party.

The New York *Times,* then as now a decorous newspaper, viewed with grave alarm the support that Haywood, Berkman, and Goldman were receiving from "intellectuals," from people "of culture and education" who had become "extremists" on behalf of strikers and unemployed. Two events aroused the press, which, as Lippmann had observed, seemed reluctant to be aroused.[51]

One was the trial of Frank Tannenbaum, a young leader of the I.W.W., who went with Emma Goldman to the first of Mrs. Dodge's Radical Evenings. The other was a pageant which John Reed produced in Madison Square Garden to dramatize a strike of textile mill workers in Paterson, New Jersey.

The pageant, as Mrs. Dodge remembered it, grew out of a conversation she had with Haywood, who complained that the New York papers would print "not a damn word" about the Paterson strike. Mrs. Dodge suggested that he "bring the strike to New York" and re-enact it. Reed, whom she had not met before, leapt at her suggestion, went to Paterson and got himself arrested, and after twenty days in jail came back to New York and produced the pageant on June 7, 1913.

Robert Edmond Jones was the director. Margaret Sanger and Mrs. Dodge served on the executive committee. Lippmann and dozens of others helped with arrangements. Reed traveled back and forth to Paterson coaching the strikers—more than 1,000 appeared on stage in New York—in their roles. "One of the greatest touches," Mrs. Dodge wrote, "was teaching them to sing one of their lawless songs to the tune of 'Harvard, Old Harvard!' " The show packed the Garden. Most of the news stories about it estimated the number in the audience at 15,000.[52]

In the winter of 1914, Mrs. Dodge attracted the attention of the press to herself and her Evenings by attending the trial of young Tannenbaum, who was sentenced to a year in prison for leading a group of unemployed into a Catholic church to spend

the night. Mrs. Dodge said she was "flustered" by the publicity
she received, but remembered that Lippmann had told her she
"could always get front-page space and I knew I should do what
I could to help . . ." The capsule descriptions of her in the news
stories about the trial annoyed her—"ardent Socialist," "society
matron," "Red." But most of all, she said, "I had hated being
called a 'sphinx' ! "[53]

While young Tannenbaum was in prison, reading Nietzsche
and Marx and other books which Mrs. Dodge had Steffens bring
to him on visiting days, the labor movement demonstrations continued. After a mass meeting in Rutgers Square which Lippmann,
Steffens, Haywood, Goldman, and Berkman attended, Mrs. Dodge
arranged a post-mortem at her apartment. The Washington *Herald*
reported that two hundred were present, which may not have
been an exaggeration, since Mrs. Dodge could not distinguish
between some of her guests and the hostile newspapermen who
came to look and listen.

The reporters were admitted by a "colored factotum," the New
York *Sun* told readers the next day, and they were asked to leave
by a "heavy set young man" who told them the meeting was private
and that "positively nothing should be published about it."

The young man was Lippmann. So in one of his earliest encoun-
ters with the gentlemen of the metropolitan press, the future
editor of the New York *World* slammed the door on what the
press calls "the public's right to know." But the editor of the
World would have seen no reason to excuse his earlier conduct.
In dozens of editorials and "Today and Tomorrow" columns,
he inveighed later against the invasion of privacy.

But Mabel had misgivings. Though it was she who warned Lippmann that the press had arrived, she thought, she said, "They
are just *people,* too . . . Why should I let Walter interfere?" But
Walter squelched her with a glance, she said, and soon had them
all out and "the door closed on their resentful faces."

The press had observed enough, however, to report that
"I.W.W. Men Starve As Leaders Eat . . . Latter Make Merry in
Dodge's Fifth Avenue Home," and "Red Banner There." Many
of the women wore evening gowns, some of them low cut, and
the men and women alike were smoking cigarettes, the *Sun*
reported. Many of the men were in evening clothes, too, and
some of the reporters, perhaps as disguise, wore white ties. What

puzzled Mrs. Dodge, she said, was, "How, then, did Walter know the newspapermen from the anarchists?"[54]

The "Psychoanalysis Evening" did not attract the press, which was as well, perhaps, since no newspaper of the period could have printed an account of the clinical proceedings. Mrs. Dodge asked Dr. A. A. Brill, whose patient she later became, to speak on Freudian Theory and persuaded Lippmann to act as moderator. She also invited her own doctor to attend, but he indignantly declined and urged her to cancel the meeting.

No record remains of what Dr. Brill said, or Lippmann either. An earlier attempt was made to station a stenographer offstage to make a full account of an Evening. But it backfired, because a literal transcription made the dialogue sound incoherent and "Gertrude Steinish." Whatever Dr. Brill said affronted some of the guests, who stalked out huffily and noisily. Freud according to Brill was too salty even for some of the 1914 *avant garde*.[55]

The temptation to ridicule Mrs. Dodge and her Evenings is almost irresistible because the style of her own descriptions of them is a parody in itself. But a record of the times would be woefully impoverished without her *Intimate Memories,* and indeed nearly every important book about the period relies on what she has written.

Her own influence would also seem to have been considerable, for during an era of great political and social unease she kept the most diverse of important people in intimate contact with each other. Wild men and women like Haywood and Goldman seemed to the intellectuals to be less dangerous close up, and to the I.W.W. the bourgeois capitalists at 23 Fifth Avenue sometimes seemed human. Steffens even said that the fire of Haywood's hatred for capitalism never was fully rekindled after his first invitation to an Evening.[56]

During the Dodge Salon years, Lippmann continued to write for *Everybody's,* for *Metropolitan,* and, beginning in 1914, for the *New Republic* when it first appeared. Some of the articles dealt sympathetically with labor's attempt to unionize and even with the I.W.W.'s encouragement of strikes.

When President Taft created an Industrial Relations Commission after the Lawrence textile strike, Lippmann tried to outline the commission's task. In no other country in the world, he said, was the labor struggle more brutal, with "a record of police brutality and class feeling . . . which has bred in the minds of the workers a fear and contempt for the American Government." To the unskilled working man and woman who made up the overwhelming mass of the labor force "no one but the I. W. W.," he said, "has ever preached one word of hope." Though the I.W.W., which was excluded from membership on the presidential commission, offered no program except rebellion, it was up to the commission, Lippmann said, to determine what other organization should begin to put an end to exploiting the nine-tenths of the working force who were outside the A.F. of L. and the Brotherhoods.

The anarchists, the syndicalists, and the I.W.W., he said, despised mere reformers who sought to improve the industrial system. And, remembering his Schenectady experience, he added, "They say, quite rightly, that reform undermines the revolutionary spirit, and substitutes . . . grudging change." But the Lippmann of 1914 was now and forever more would be committed to the principle of grudging change—to the democratizing and civilizing of labor and capital within the profit system.[57]

Although his defense of the I.W.W., even diluted by his distrust of its methods, was an extremely unpopular position for a "good American" to take in 1914, some of Lippmann's own friends began to distrust him because of what they considered his new conservatism. Overt signs of a rift appeared when John Reed called Lippmann "a renegade" and Lippmann responded with a testy letter which Reed had framed and hung on the wall of his room in Washington Square.[58]

Reed's misgivings about Lippmann were partly personal and partly ideological. He deplored Lippmann's joining the staff of the *New Republic* because the magazine was subsidized by Wall Street money, and he disliked its cool and dispassionate editorials about labor, placing the blame for strikes and violence on workers and management alike.[59]

A month after the *New Republic* began publication, Lippmann contributed an article entitled "Legendary John Reed," which his former classmate regarded as less than kind. It would seem that Lippmann was trying to be sympathetic and understanding but also objective and detached in his sketch about his former classmate. ("Reed has no detachment," he wrote, "and is proud of it, I think.") The ruling passion of Reed's life, Lippmann said, seemed to be "an inordinate desire to be arrested." The jails of England, France, Spain, and New Jersey had housed him. When he joined the staff of the *Masses,* Lippmann said, "they advertised him as their jail editor." For a while, Lippmann said, Reed assumed that "all capitalists were fat, bald, and unctuous . . . that the working class is . . . a fine, statuesque giant who stands on a high hill facing the sun." But when "his sympathies marched with the facts, Reed was superb," Lippmann added. "Whatever John Reed could touch or see or smell he could convey." However, he continued, half-admiringly, "There is no line between the play of his fancy and his responsibility to fact."[60]

It may have been—perhaps Freud or Brill could have told him—that Lippmann was responding to some verses Reed had written about him in *The Day in Bohemia,* published the previous year, for Lippmann quoted two lines of them at the close of his article. Of Lippmann, Reed had written:

> —calm, inscrutable,
> Thinking and writing clearly, soundly, well;
> All snarls of falseness swiftly piercing through,
> His keen mind leaps like lightning to the True;
> His face is almost placid,—but his eye,
> There is a vision born to prophecy!
> He sits in silence, as one who has said:
> "I waste not living words among the dead!"
> Our all-unchallenged Chief! But were there one
> Who builds a world, and leaves out all the fun,—
> Who dreams a pageant, gorgeous, infinite,
> And then leaves all the color out of it,—
> Who wants to make the human race, and me,
> March to a geometric Q.E.D.—
> Who but must laugh, if such a man there be?
> Who would not weep, if Walter L. were he?[61]

The "renegade" letter, the reply, the verses, and the article were the work of men in their mid-twenties. Even so, they were too mature to feud for long. Lippmann made the first conciliatory move. "I wrote Jack the other day that I thought it was nonsense for us to quarrel and that I was sorry I'd hurt him," Lippmann told Mrs. Dodge. "He replied at once, reciprocating."[62] Later, when Reed was dangerously ill and had to undergo a serious operation in Johns Hopkins Hospital, Lippmann went down to Baltimore to see him.[63]

Whether or not Reed's characterization of Lippmann influenced the judgment of others, some of Lippmann's friends took a similar view. When Hutchins Hapgood wrote that "God doesn't manifest himself *at all* in Walter Lippmann," Bayard Boyesen, a novelist who frequented the Dodge Salon, responded by saying that Hapgood was right if he was speaking facetiously. Lippmann could "explain (in a rather cocksure fashion) everything, because he leaves out everything essential," Boyesen said. Robert Rogers, a classmate of Lippmann's and Reed's, found Lippmann too idealistic, too trustful that humanity was educable. "How is Walter going to quench this fundamental and illogical passion in us all?" he asked. But except for Hapgood, who disliked Lippmann rather intensely, it was Lippmann the Thinker that they distrusted. Lippmann himself they liked.

Writing of "a fine visit from Walter," Rogers said, "I have never seen him happier or nicer." And Mrs. Dodge found in Lippmann what she called "an antidote" for her passionate friends and lovers. "He was 'Harvardized,' well-bred, and in possession of himself," she said. "There was no incontinence there, no flowing sensuality. Rather a fine poise, a cool understanding, and withal the high humor in the world shining in his intelligent eyes."

As his friend Rogers reported, Lippmann was in high spirits in the Fall of 1914. Whether it was "the book or a regular job or the responsibility of finishing up the incomplete work of the Creator, I don't know," Rogers said.[64] The book was *Drift and Mastery,* completed in July, and the regular job was associate editor of the *New Republic,* which began publication in November. From this time on, Lippmann never ceased to be working on a book and to be regularly employed.

His circle of friends and acquaintances ranged far beyond the people who gravitated to Mrs. Dodge. He visited Theodore Roosevelt at Oyster Bay, and he was one of the group of young men who met frequently in Washington at the home of Justice Oliver Wendell Holmes, Jr. Holmes found them charming and amusingly earnest. Felix Frankfurter, who was teaching at Harvard, and Herbert Croly, Philip Littel, and Francis Hackett, all of whom helped edit the *New Republic,* were in the group.[65] Lippmann brought *Drift and Mastery* for Holmes to read. "Some of our young men here write books well worth reading," Holmes, who was then seventy-three years old, wrote to his friend Leonard Einstein. But he added that "they seem to go more into social questions than aesthetics or philosophy." Sometimes he joshed them about their zeal to improve the condition of mankind. "You young men seem to think that if you sit on the world long enough you will hatch something out," he said. "But you're wrong."

Holmes found the *New Republic,* "rather solemn," but he welcomed "an occasional flattering reference to this old man" from his young friends who wrote for it. Einstein replied that he liked the new magazine, though it was "a bit Evening Posty passed through a college settlement." He enjoyed Lippmann's articles on American politics, but, he said, "his diplomatic opinions are somewhat amateurish." Lippmann was "a born writer," Holmes told Einstein later, praising *Public Opinion,* which, he said, "opens most bitingly."[66]

Lippmann's admiration of the judge was unbounded. When Holmes retired in 1933 at ninety, Lippmann said that he epitomized the life well led. He was, Lippmann said, not only a great judge but a great philosopher. "I have no doubt that his prose is the purest American writing of our time, and . . . his wisdom . . . will be cherished as a tonic to the will of man above any thus far uttered on this continent."[67]

In his own quest for political truth, Lippmann turned in *Drift and Mastery* away from philosophy and toward science as a panacea to improve the human condition. Only by means of the common discipline of scientific method could men in conflict derive "from the same set of facts . . . the same set of conclusions," he said, and thus produce a peaceful and equitable solution of economic and social problems. The theme of "disinterestedness," which later permeated *A Preface to Morals,* began to emerge. The managers of industry were becoming professionals, he said, no longer motivated by greed, conscious that their prosperity depended on prosperity for all.

Drift and Mastery was an optimistic and affirmative book. The work of the muckrakers and the Haywoods was finished, Lippmann said. Now the struggle must be against "the chaos of the new freedom." Others were not so confident, either that the old struggle was over, or that human desires could be disciplined by scientific method. A reviewer in the *Nation* asked, "But how shall we know 'Science' when we see her? . . . If she is to deal with 'facts,' she must be able to assure us that they *are* facts and not fancies, and they . . . must be facts for all men."[68]

Lippmann's own confidence in industrial democracy, which, one would assume, must be based on agreement between labor and management about the facts, was somewhat shaken before the ink on the pages of *Drift and Mastery* was dry. Writing in the *New Republic* and the *Metropolitan* about the testimony of John D. Rockefeller, J. P. Morgan, and others before the Industrial Relations Commission, Lippmann accused industry of moral bankruptcy. Morgan, Rockefeller, and the others, he said, admitted they abdicated responsibility to hired managers who were interested only in profit, propitiating labor just enough to keep it "above the line of revolt."[69]

Both *A Preface to Politics* and *Drift and Mastery* dealt only with domestic problems. When he wrote the books, Lippmann said twenty years later, he could not imagine a war which would disrupt the foundations of society and frustrate his own attempts to give meaning and significance to the maelstrom of events which shook the world. Since the beginning of World War I, he said in the preface to *The Good Society*, "The scheme of the future has been less clear to me . . . I have found myself writing about critical events with no better guide to their meaning than the hastily improvised generalizations of a rather bewildered man."[70]

The story of his bewilderment—"the man who claimed he was not bewildered would write himself down a fool"—he began to tell in the *New Republic* three months after the war started. His work for the new magazine brought him in contact with Colonel Edward M. House, Woodrow Wilson's principal adviser, with the President, and led to his involvement as a wartime propagandist, as a member of the Inquiry which prepared for the peace conference, and as an adviser at the conference. Though he found these experiences disillusioning, they led to his life-long commitment to try as a journalist to help educate public opinion.[71]

Chapter II

THE NEW REPUBLIC, WAR, AND PUBLIC OPINION

THE INSTANT INFLUENCE AND PRESTIGE OF THE *New Republic* IN 1914 were remarkable, considering that tainted Wall Street money financed it and fewer than 25,000 subscribers paid to read it. After a few months of publication it became difficult to see how a discussion of public affairs had been possible before the magazine existed. "After a hundred weeks... it seemed a hundred years old," Irwin Edman remembered.[1]

As Lippmann saw it, the *New Republic's* purpose was "to explore and develop and apply the ideas which had been advertised by Theodore Roosevelt when he was the leader of the Progressive Party" in the 1912 presidential campaign. Actually it was not so simple as that, because the Progressive movement was overshadowed by the war in Europe even before the first issue was printed.[2]

A book by Herbert Croly, who was a friend of Theodore Roosevelt, led directly to the establishment of the magazine. Willard Straight, an employee of J. P. Morgan and Company and a former State Department officer specializing in Far Eastern affairs, had read Croly's *The Promise of American Life* and was impressed by its theme: the subordination of the individual to a constructive national purpose. Straight arranged to meet Croly, and during their conversations plans for a new weekly journal began to take shape. Straight's wife, Dorothy, was a daughter of William C. Whitney, a wealthy Wall Street broker. Her money subsidized the publication.

Straight wrote to Learned Hand that the *New Republic* "will, I fear, set angel Dorothy back some hundreds of thousands of dollars . . . but she will get a little education for her money and so will I and so, I hope, will you and others."[3]

Within a year after the publication began, circulation reached 15,000 and during 1917–1918 averaged 25,000. The amount of subsidy from the Straights was not disclosed, but it was estimated in 1940 to have been seldom less than $75,000 a year. There is no record that the Straights violated the terms of their agreement with Croly that their money gave them no right to dictate editorial policy. Critics said that they did not need to because they and the editors shared the same shibboleths of middle-class liberalism.[4]

Though he might have disagreed with its phrasing, Lippmann probably would have admitted the gravamen of this charge. In an editorial in the *World* in 1929, commenting on an electric power company's acquiring a financial interest in newspapers, Lippmann said: "Although no evidence exists that the newspapers concerned trimmed their news and editorial policies to suit the interests of the power company, it is plain that the relationship is embarrassing . . . Yet it would be simple-minded to assume that a newspaper is independent simply because it is free from direct financial connection with such private interests." Financial independence provided only the foundation of freedom, he said. "There remains the vague but vast force of personal and social and official influences against which really independent newspapers have to be constantly on guard."[5]

Whatever the influences operating on the *New Republic,* they were not, in the beginning or later, considered to be conservative. *Time,* with its usual flair for cliché, paid tribute to its puny competitor in 1939 by saying: "Last week the pinko weekly *New Republic,* gave itself a 25th birthday party."[6]

At another birthday party, in 1964, Lippmann, who was the last of the original editors still at large, recalled what he and Croly, Walter Weyl, and the Straights were attempting to do fifty years earlier. "Our purpose was not partisan, factional, personal, or ideological; it was educational . . . And the attitude of this journal toward affairs was to be that of the scholar seeking the truth no matter whom it hurts or whom it helps . . . this is not the only kind of journalism by any means. There is need and there is room for advocacy and for causes and for parties and for ideologies. But this particular kind of journalism . . . is an interesting kind of journalism for the journalist, and one must hope, for the readers. So I've always been grateful to the Straights and to Herbert Croly and to the old board of editors . . . for having started me off headed in what I am confident was a good direction for a young journalist to take."[7]

When an anthology of selections from the magazine was published to help celebrate its fiftieth anniversary, reviewers marvelled at the excellence of the early volumes. "The 1914–1923 sample simply takes your breath away," said Norman Podhoretz, editor of *Commentary.* Naming Lippmann, Croly, Walter Weyl, Stark Young, and a half dozen others, Podhoretz added that "they speak as cultivated men of the world . . . never strident . . . never patronizing . . . never pretentious . . ."[8]

In addition to articles about the war in Europe and about politics, Lippmann wrote about the theater, about abstract art (Leo Stein, who was a member of the Dodge circle, said that Lippmann was on the side of the angels, but in insisting that art must be communicative he was "barking up the wrong tree"), about Freud, about the absence of utopias, about the dismal state of political writing, and about the deplorable taste for gossip exhibited by the masses.

"Every reporter is a receptacle of scandal," Lippmann wrote. "But the honest reporter has a moral code which says that the use of gossip for personal ends or to serve a personal grudge is as low an activity as that of a doctor who would talk about his patients at a dinner-table." There were reporters who were "Typhoid Marys," he said, spreading infection which was almost impossible to combat. For example, he said, it took Theodore Roosevelt years to disprove the rumor that he was a drunkard—by successfully suing an editor who was careless enough to make innuendo so explicit as to justify a libel action.[9]

During 1915 Lippmann articles also appeared in the *Metropolitan* under the headline "To-day and To-morrow," later the title of his syndicated column which began in 1931. The articles dealt with big business and the irresponsible rich.[10] Although he was busy with his third book, *The Stakes of Diplomacy,* he found time to write an article for *Harvard Illustrated* denouncing an editorial which urged the Harvard communtiy to "muzzle war utterances." The *Illustrated* editorial referred obliquely to the 1914 controversy about professors' pro-German speeches and demands by Harvard alumni that they be dismissed.

Preserving Harvard from entangling foreign alliances might seem laudable, Lippmann said sarcastically. "Yet somehow or other the spectacle of the undergraduate muzzling himself in the face of the greatest war in history, and then going on to lecture the faculty for its lack of discretion, is just too wildly absurd for belief."[11]

(Twenty years later when there was a hullabaloo about Harvard professors participating in the New Deal and teaching unorthodox economic theory, Lippmann was appointed chairman of an alumni committee to investigate. The report criticized professors who made their faculty positions "incidental to public careers." A New York *Times* headline said: "Inquiry Headed by Lippmann Finds No 'Propaganda' in Economics Classes—Oppose Outside Careers —Interest in Politics and Affairs Not Wrong but Overemphasis Is Frowned Upon.")[12]

Lippmann's own attitude toward the war in Europe, which was most fully revealed in signed articles and in editorials he wrote for the *New Republic,* has been thoroughly analyzed in Christine C. Cary's book, *The Influence of War on Walter Lippmann 1914–1944,* in Charles Forcey's*The Crossroads of Liberalism,* and in Christopher Lasch's *The New Radicalism in America.*

The month before the war began, Lippmann left New York for a tour of England and the continent, oblivious to the imminence of battle. The rush of events and the secrecy of diplomats were what most impressed him as he remembered the last days of peace. He spent the eve of the declaration of war at the National Liberal Club in London and found his friends there "sad and depressed" in contrast with the hysterically gay Bank Holiday crowds which jammed London.[13]

At least in the early stages of the war, Herbert Croly rather than Lippmann shaped the *New Republic's* views on foreign policy, partly because he was the senior editor, and partly because Lippmann had displayed almost no interest in foreign affairs until 1914. The goal for America, as the magazine saw it, should be neutrality without isolation. With this position, which events soon overwhelmed, Lippmann tacitly agreed.

His own contributions about international affairs were at first rather bland—how cheap life was in wartime, how dangerous

it was to subordinate social reform to armaments. Until he for-
mulated his own views in *The Stakes of Diplomacy,* he preferred
to write about domestic problems such as the importance of giving
women the right to vote.[14]

In the book, which he finished in September of 1915, Lippmann
seemed driven toward a pro-Allied position which in the *New
Republic* came first to be labeled "differential neutrality" and then
"aggressive pacifism." In the book Lippmann deplored the gravita-
tion of too much power to the President, saying that "on the
issue of our national existence we are not a self-governing people."
In the magazine he accused the President of offering the country
no leadership at all.

Patriotism was ready to flow wherever the President directed,
Lippmann said. "His decision as to what shall be published and
what concealed is one of the supreme attributes of his office.
He has no legal power of censoring the news. But often he alone
knows what the news is, he can publish when and how it seems
best to him." After the Lusitania sinking, Wilson could have
dramatized the issue and inflamed the press, Lippmann said.
Though the President chose the path of peace, the fact that the
decision was his alone to make proved, Lippmann said, that it
was only pretense to claim "that the people could control their
foreign relations in any possible way."[15]

In the *New Republic* of December 25, 1915, Lippmann blamed
the President for *not* exercising his overwhelming influence over
public opinion, saying that Wilson had failed to enunciate a great
national purpose. "We are roused by Belgium and forget it, we
are roused by the Lusitania and forget it, are roused and forget
again, a little like a man reeling down an alley, hitting one wall
and then the other . . . Ferment without issue, gestation without
birth is making us sullen and self-conscious and ashamed." The
fault was Wilson's, he concluded, because the President had never
said anything to rally the country. "Perhaps only a great genius
among statesmen could have risen to the opportunity. But for
lack of that genius America to-day is distraught."[16]

Rather wryly, considering his own apathy toward international
affairs until 1914, Lippmann lamented that people attended to
foreign problems only during a crisis. "Few people could even
locate on a map the places where most of the international friction
occurs." Part of the blame lay with the press, he said, because

it failed to give space to peaceable foreign developments. Newspapers generally, he concluded, were a maleficent influence,
increasing the tension in almost every crisis, not because publishers
wanted war, but because war was more interesting than peace.
"No one has discovered a way of making good will, harmony,
reasonableness, easily dramatic." Publications which believed that
"even good news is news" never were popular, he said, and presumably never would be.[17]

In the absence of an enlightened public opinion, well-informed
"insiders" must run the country, he said. From this premise it
follows that the basic function of the political journalist is to
influence the thought and action of the insiders and that the
best way to do this is from the inside, or at least close to the
entrance.[18]

During 1916 Lippmann and Herbert Croly began to meet frequently with Wilson's adviser, Colonel Edward M. House, and
Lippmann interviewed the President two or three times. The
delicate question of how much the *New Republic* influenced the
administration and how much the administration influenced the
policy of the magazine has often been explored. Many believed
in 1916 and 1917 that the opinions of the editors were official
or semi-official, and there is evidence that on one occasion the
stock market reacted to a *New Republic* editorial. Oswald Garrison
Villard, who edited the rival *Nation,* said that "it was considered
bad form in some official circles to be seen without it [the *New
Republic*] and its circulation climbed to about 45,000."[19]

When Herbert Croly died in 1930, Lippmann wrote a tribute
to him in which he categorically denied that the magazine served
as a mouthpiece for Wilson. "We never knew any secrets, we
never had a request to publish anything, and we were not in
a confidential relationship ... Occasionally the President and
Colonel House took an idea from the *New Republic* as they took
it from many other sources." The one overt attempt to influence
policy which Lippmann remembered came from an English publisher who was so pleased with a pro-British editorial that he
offered to buy 50,000 copies of the magazine every week if similar
articles were guaranteed to appear.[20]

The record seems to confirm Lippmann's statement and to
indicate that House was overly optimistic in thinking that his conferences with Lippmann and Croly, often held once a week, were

affecting the editors' opinions. "I gave them food for thought to keep them on the right road," House wrote, and he said after one of his "weekly quizzes" with Lippmann that he "outlined two or three articles for him . . ." But the one article that he mentioned, about conditions for joining a league of nations, did not appear in print after the "quiz." Though the magazine's policies and those of the President often coincided, it seems that Lippmann was correct when he said that this usually was the result either of coincidence or "a certain parallelism of reasoning."[21]

Generally the *New Republic's* position on Germany was more aggressive than Wilson's, though less bold than that of the daily press. On one occasion, early in 1917, the President borrowed from the magazine the phrase "Peace Without Victory" and used it in a speech to the Senate. The editors were "horrified," Lippmann said thirteen years later, because they used the phrase descriptively, not as a slogan for America. This incident, Lippmann said, helped establish "the legend of the *New Republic* as Wilson's personal organ." Yet at the time the speech was made, the editors seemed ecstatic about it. House recorded in his diary, "They [Lippmann and Croly] were pleased with the President's address to the Senate," and he reported to Wilson the night the speech was made that "Croly told me he felt it was the greatest event of his own life" and that Lippmann's praise of it was "in unmeasured terms." The President wrote to Croly two days later that in preparing the speech he was interested "to find an editorial in the *New Republic* which . . . served to clarify and strengthen my thought not a little."

This was not the first or the last time that a politician sought to flatter the intellectuals. Lyndon Johnson tried with only brief success in the early days of his Presidency to propitiate the Lippmann who had become the bellwether of the Washington press corps. Though in general "the impact of the editors on Wilson was slight," as Charles Forcey has said, nevertheless from the time of the Wilson speech "Croly's and Lippmann's reputation was made." That the reputation was probably undeserved was, at the time, of no consequence.[22] Wilson's own cynicism was expressed a year and a half later in a contemptuous reference to the "unorthodox" *New Republic.*

In March of 1917, after Germany resumed unrestricted warfare against neutral shipping, Lippmann wrote: "The only course of action is to assume that there will be war and to make it as evident as possible to Germany that it will be effective war." The day before his article appeared, House had met with Lippmann and Croly and recorded in his diary: "I am finding it difficult to keep them in line . . ."[23]

When the United States declared war in April, the *New Republic* boasted that it was the liberals and the intellectuals, among whom they included journalists, who, though they were "numerically insignificant," had exerted the successful pressure for American entry into the conflict. After the President's speech to Congress asking for the declaration, Lippmann wrote to House: "The President's address is magnificent . . . We are delighted with it here down to the last comma." The United States, Wilson had said, was "fighting not so much to beat an enemy as to make a world that is safe for democracy." This was the phrase which five decades later Lippmann was compelled to label "pernicious bombast."[24]

Lippmann wrote to Wilson April 3, 1917, outlining procedures he thought should be used to conscript a wartime army, and a few days later he sent Colonel House a blueprint for a bureau to publicize the war effort. The bureau should serve in general as a clearing house for information to the press, he suggested, and give specific attention to the importance of industrial warfare, to policy articles supporting the government, and to a surveillance of the foreign press, allied, neutral, and enemy. It should also keep a close watch over public opinion, and be vigilant to track down rumors and lies.

When a bureau was set up under the direction of George Creel, Lippmann grew increasingly dissatisfied with its operations, and his criticisms annoyed Wilson and House. One of the omissions in Lippmann's blueprint was any mention of safeguards to protect domestic dissent, in order to keep American democratic while it was waging war for democracy. This problem worried Wilson, who told Frank Cobb of the New York *World* that he feared "the spirit of ruthless brutality will enter into the very fibre of our national life," and "conformity would be the only virtue."[25] Suppression of dissent in time of war or grave emergency did not seem to trouble Lippmann greatly. Indeed, in World War II Thomas C. Clark, enemy alien control administrator, accused him of hysterical statements about the danger of "fifth columnist" activity among the Japanese Americans on the West Coast. This occurred shortly before the government itself succumbed to hys-teria and interned 117,000 Americans of Japanese ancestry.[26]

Soon after American entry into the First World War, the Post Office began a campaign to exclude non-conformist newspapers from the mail, and Lippmann was moved to object mildly. "I have no doctrinaire belief in free speech," he wrote Colonel House. "In the interest of the war it is necessary to sacrifice some of it. But the point is that the method now being pursued is breaking down the liberal support of the war and is tending to divide the country's articulate opinion into fanatical jingoism and fanatical pacifism."

Even men like John Dewey, who warmly supported the war and the President, were being alienated, he said, by the "brutally unreasonable" position of Postmaster General Albert S. Burleson. And in the labor movement, he warned, "The feeling on this issue is at white heat." If the New York *Call* and the *Jewish Daily Forward* were banned, he predicted, an increase in pacifist opposi-tion to the war and a rise in the Socialist vote would result.

The heresy hunting conducted by a large portion of the daily press also contributed to the problem, he said, by exerting pressure for the censorship of what he called "obscure and discredited" little publications. "Suppression of course gives these papers an importance that intrinsically they would never have. A great government ought to be contemptuously uninterested in such opinion . . ."[27]

In June of 1917, after discussions with Colonel House, Lipp-mann decided that it was more important to serve the government than the *New Republic.* Newton D. Baker, the Secretary of War, chose him as an assistant and he served with Franklin D. Roosevelt, who represented the Navy, on a new labor board to adjust disputes about wages in government plants.[28]

When Wilson requested House to organize a secret committee to gather and organize political, geographic and ethnic data to guide the American delegation at whatever peace conferences should follow the war, Lippmann was appointed executive secre-tary of the group. Almost 150 scholars and technical experts worked on the Inquiry, as it came to be called. Dr. James T. Shotwell, who subsequently wrote a history of the Inquiry, credited Lippmann with an important role in "interpreting and phrasing policy" and in furnishing general principles for the memoranda. Lippmann served as liaison with Colonel House, Shotwell said, and also, at times, directly with the President. Part of his work, for which he seemed especially gifted, was organizing the masses of data and writing lucid interpretive summaries of it. President Wilson relied on the Inquiry for information and advice long before the war ended, and some of Lippmann's ideas were said to have appeared in his speeches to Congress.[29]

Lippmann left the Inquiry in July of 1918, accepting a commission as captain in Military Intelligence to conduct political propaganda directed toward the German Army and the German people. Military Intelligence believed, Lippmann wrote to House, that the material gathered by the Inquiry was uniquely suited for propaganda across enemy lines and that Lippmann's journalistic training equipped him to conduct it. Furthermore, Lippmann said, he knew the President's aims and could promote them. "Unless the men who are writing and directing propaganda are in close touch with political [and diplomatic] developments," Lippmann said, "they cannot of course do anything effective."

The work of Creel's Committee on Public Information in London was very bad, Lippmann believed. He told House that the men in charge "do not know England, or English journalism, or European affairs, and the reputation of the committee among the English is very low." The European representatives on the Inter-Allied Board for propaganda, including Lord Northcliffe, were men of great prestige, Lippmann said, and their American counterpart, James Keeley, though "a very competent newspaper proprietor, feels completely lost . . ." Keeley should be replaced, he recommended, by a man who could speak French, who had a good presence and knew European personalities and problems. He suggested that Major Willard Straight, the *New Republic's* backer, be considered for the post. (Keeley had been managing editor of the Chicago *Tribune* and publisher of the Chicago *Herald*.)[30]

Lippmann's critical reports provoked a reprimand from House, who requested that the criticism cease. The colonel's letter upset Lippmann, because, he said, he had been erroneously led to believe that the Army rather than the Creel Committee was to supervise the propaganda. "You know, of course," he wrote House rather plaintively, "that I am a thousand times more interested in the Inquiry than in propaganda."[31]

The rebuke from House would have stung Lippmann even more sharply if he had known what prompted it. When Wilson learned of Lippmann's propaganda mission, he wrote House that he was "very much puzzled as to who sent Lippmann over to inquire into matters of propaganda . . . I have found his judgment most unsound and therefore entirely unserviceable in matters of that sort because he, in common with the men of the *New Republic,* has ideas about the war and its purpose which are highly unorthodox from my point of view."[32]

Lippmann's propaganda effort, as reported in American news-papers, was successful. "Germans Impressed by Our Propaganda," a New York *Times* headline said. "The Propaganda Department has a big printing establishment in Paris," the *Times* said, . . . "and the editorial work is under the direction of Walter Lippmann." Balloons and airplanes were used to drop leaflets inside German and Austrian lines. Speeches and diplomatic notes by Wilson, the kind treatment, and the good food and tobacco given to prisoners by the Americans were emphasized in the barrage of print from the sky. Search of prisoners disclosed that many of them had kept the leaflets hidden "in their sleeves and secret pockets against possible detection by German officers," the *Times* reported.[33]

Although he continued to help with propaganda, Lippmann joined Colonel House's staff in Paris as the war neared its end. House was busy with plans for an armistice and a German surren-der, which America sought to base on the famous Fourteen Points enunciated earlier in the year by Wilson. As secretary of the Inquiry, Lippmann had helped to draft some of them; and when the British and Italians requested a clarification of their meaning, House assigned Lippmann the task of preparing an interpretation. With the help of Frank Cobb he prepared fourteen memoranda, which were cabled to Wilson for his approval.[34]

Four days before the armistice, the Allied governments having agreed to the Fourteen Points, Lippmann wrote to House: "Frankly, I did not believe it was humanly feasible, under condi-tions as they seemed to be in Europe, to win so glorious a victory."[35] But two months later, disillusioned and dismayed, he left the Peace Conference and sailed for New York to begin working again

on the *New Republic*. His discouragement stemmed partly from
the conference proceedings and partly from a sense that men
closer to Wilson than he was were playing a role he should have
played. He opposed Wilson's decision to go to Paris and head
the American delegation while the terms of the peace treaty were
being drafted. Summit conferences, he believed, and said so
repeatedly in later years, were a mistake unless the heads of state
met to discuss and ratify agreements previously reached by their
expert advisers. And he opposed American and British attempts
to reverse the Bolshevik revolution. Discussing American intervention in Russia in an article in the *United Nations World* in 1947,
he said: "I tried in vain to remind Wilson of the incongruity
of the situation. I pointed out that by participating in this war
during the era of pacification we were bound to cancel out the
effectiveness of the peace treaty we were drafting."[36]

As early as December 1, 1918, Lippmann was fearful that the
peace would not be just or durable. Writing to Dorothy Straight
upon the death of her husband, who had been working with
the Peace Commission, he said that he and Straight had felt "a
fear that what we had meant, and what alone could justify it
all, was not the meaning and justification to those who would
decide."[37]

By June of 1919, Lippmann was accusing Wilson of breaking
almost all his promises. Writing to Newton D. Baker, he said
that the agreement on the Saar Valley was intolerable, and that
separatism for Austria and the cession of German territory to
other nations violated "solemn assurances." He denounced imposition of reparations on Germany and German exclusion from the
League of Nations. The League itself, he said, seemed designed
principally to preserve the status quo.[38] Writing to House, he
expressed the hope that Wilson would confess his failure. "The
world can endure honest disappointment, and no one can complain of a failure confessed . . . But I see nothing but pain and
disorder and confusion if this first act of honesty is not performed."[39]

The *New Republic's* decision to denounce the Versailles Treaty
as a "punic peace of annihilation" followed a period of agony
for the editors. In repudiating Wilson, Charles Forcey said, they
"also faced the humiliation of repudiating all they themselves had
stood for. It meant the final end of their closeness to men of
power."

"The decision to oppose ratification was Croly's," Lippmann said a decade later. "I followed him, though I was not then, and am not now, convinced that it was a wise thing to do." But Robert Morss Lovett, who dined with the editors the day they reached their decision, recalled "Lippmann's vigorous denunciation of the treaty as . . . a violation of moral obligations to the world."

The decision, right or wrong, was costly for the magazine. Ten thousand subscribers, disliking what they considered to be an endorsement of isolation, vanished, though the rival *Nation,* which also denounced the treaty, flourished. Herbert Croly wrote to Learned Hand that he feared "the loss of friendship of some of the people I most loved." Mrs. Straight loyally continued her subsidies, but a pall of moodiness seemed to descend on the magazine as the editors tried to probe for their readers the causes of what had gone wrong with America.[40]

An eight-page article by Lippmann entitled "Unrest," which appeared on November 12, 1919, was strewn with mournful sub-heads—"The Chief Hallucination," "The Bogus Revolution," "Grotesques," "The Higher Unrest," "Gamblers." The leaders of the nation "twittered and chattered" and saw "spooks," he said. They regarded the American liberal as pro-Hun, or pacifist, or Bolshevik. They were prone to fear, suspicion, and hysteria.

Americans could not understand their country and the world, he said, because for five years the truth had been kept from them. "Consider what we have been through: Period I. Be neutral in fact as well as in name. Period II. Fight like thunder to make the world safe for democracy. Period III. Stop before your anger is exhausted and spend the better part of a year standing around undecided while peace is made for you in secret . . . During that whole time of exhausting strain and still more exhausting idleness, most people were dealing with facts that they had to imagine because they did not see them."

First, he said, came censorship, which, because of fear of aiding the enemy or damaging morale, blacked out most of the news. Then came propaganda which was based on two false assumptions: that the citizens of the Allied countries were untrustworthy and that the enemy was capable of nothing but atrocity.

Even our leading citizens "were soaked in propaganda," he said, "And thus the nation finds itself in the face of aggravated problems without any source of information that it can really trust, and without leaders to interpret events." The only salvation lay, he said, in "trustworthy news, unadulterated data, fair reporting, disinterested fact."[41]

The coloration of news, the general absence of reliable information during World War I, seems indisputable. After the war, correspondents admitted that they had been duped and had duped their readers. In *Reporting the Wars,* an historian named Joseph J. Mathews says: "The news that emanated from World War I came to be so widely denounced, so severely censured, as to add up to a general and unusual indictment... World War II did not produce anything approaching its predecessor in the extent and severity of dissatisfaction..." Mathews suggests somewhat cynically that by 1941 we may have become so used to censorship, propaganda, and partisan news coverage that we regarded them as inevitable in wartime.[42]

Since Lippmann helped to conduct propaganda, it may seem hypocritical that he should have denounced it. His defense probably would be that his efforts were directed only at the enemy. But in the interpretation he wrote for the first of the famous Fourteen Points, which called for "open covenants openly arrived at, after which there shall be no private understandings of any kind, but diplomacy shall proceed always frankly and in the public view," Lippmann said that publicity should *not include* "confidential diplomatic negotiations involving delicate matters."

Throughout his career Lippmann struggled with this problem of reconciling the need for confidential negotiations with the public's need to know about the bargains and compromises made in its behalf. In November of 1919 he wrote: "What, for example, was the one most general criticism of the work of the Peace Conference? It was that the covenants were not openly arrived at... And in the last analysis lack of information about the conference *was* the origin of its difficulties... Publicity occurred when the covenants were arrived at, with all the emphasis on the *at.*" Unable to effect the negotiations and presented with a *fait accompli,* public opinion, he said, was confronted with a document "which it could not reject and did not wish altogether to accept."[43]

But late in 1945, recalling the days of the Fourteen Points, Lippmann defended secret negotiations then taking place in Moscow among Americans, British, and Russians. The "essential principle and the common sense," he said, is that "they shall publish their decisions, not that they shall publish the discussions by which they are seeking to reach decisions."

Perhaps his most lucid and persuasive defense of confidentiality was written by Lippmann in 1951 when Congress proposed to investigate the conduct of the Korean War and to publish secret papers of the Joint Chiefs of Staff. The proposal to publish, Lippmann said, though based on "the sacred right of the people to know all the facts," could result only in eventual concealment and falsification. Aware that letters they wrote, that memoranda and documents they signed might soon be publicized, officials would eventually utter only words which would look good in print, he said. "They will be phonies . . . a false front which does not reveal, which in fact is designed to conceal the truth."[44]

When he was asked in 1971, after publication of the Pentagon Papers, whether the press has a right to publish any secret documents it might obtain, Lippmann said that under the Constitution nobody has an absolute right to do anything—including the right to publish information or to classify it as secret. But he applauded publication of the Pentagon Papers, comparing the need to publish them to the American colonists' need to stage the Boston Tea Party. When you have an intolerable grievance like the secrecy and deception surrounding the Viet Nam war and cannot get redress, he said, "you have to do something to force information out in the open," even at the expense, if conscience dictates, of risking prosecution.[45]

As the years passed, Lippmann took a dimmer and dimmer view of the beneficent effects of public opinion on public affairs. As early as 1925, he was saying in *The Phantom Public* that voters are not "inherently competent to direct the course of affairs" and that "they are not making progress toward such an ideal."[46] And in 1955 he felt compelled to state explicitly in *The Public Philosophy* that "experience since 1917 indicates that . . . the prevailing public opinion has been destructively wrong at the critical junctures."[47] One of the questions arising from all this seeming inconsistency is, of course, whether a public not *inherently* competent could be educated into competence. To this question Lippmann addressed himself in his next two books, *Liberty and the News* (1920) and *Public Opinion* (1922).

Except for a short introduction, the text of *Liberty and the News* was published in the *Atlantic* in November and December of 1919. Soon afterward Lippmann collaborated with Charles Merz, who worked with him later on the *World,* in preparing a 42-page supplement to the *New Republic* entitled "A Test of the News," which documented newspaper weaknesses described in the book. The article was an exposé of the New York *Times'* coverage of the Russian Revolution from March 1917 to March 1920. Merz and Lippmann concluded that the *Times,* "as great as any newspaper in America, and far greater than the majority," had failed abysmally in the task of providing accurate information and that editorial policy had "profoundly and crassly influenced" the news columns.[48]

To Adolph Ochs of the *Times* and Lord Northcliffe of the London *Mail,* "edification is more important than veracity," Lippmann said in the book. "In so far as those who purvey the news make of their own beliefs a higher law than truth, they are attacking the foundations of our constitutional system."

In Lippmann's view, the root of the press problem lay not in corruption by advertisers or pressure groups, but rather in a false concept of the meaning of freedom. The notion of liberty which stressed the absence of restraints on the press no longer fitted the needs of nations in which public opinion was supposed to govern policies and programs, he said. The classic doctrine as expounded by Milton and Mill, emphasizing the importance of freeing ideas and opinions from repression, no longer served, Lippmann said, because, though Milton and Mill professed to be "absolutists," their principal concern was to define the difference between "liberty" and "license."

Attempts to make such distinctions might be important, Lippmann said, but the results were fundamentally negative and sterile. The important task, he said, was to make opinion responsible "to the facts," not to dogmas or to social and judicial customs.

Among the barriers to determination of the facts, Lippmann recited the increasing inability of news reporters to see or hear the events they were writing about. "Most people seem to believe," he said, "that when they meet a war correspondent or a special writer from the Peace Conference, they have seen a man who has seen the things he wrote about. Far from it." Other obstacles, he said, were limitations and expense of news transmission facilities, political and military censorship, government subsidy (in Europe) of news agencies, stereotyped definitions of news itself, official propaganda, and the propaganda of pressure groups.

In its theoretical analysis of press problems and specific suggestions for solutions, *Liberty and the News* was a pioneer work, though it was sparsely reviewed, and, unlike most of Lippmann's books, has long been out of print. There is no evidence that it had an appreciable impact on the press itself.

Safeguarding the news from contamination, keeping pure "the streams of fact which feed the rivers of opinion," was "the critical interest of a modern state," Lippmann said. Joseph Alsop, later Lippmann's admirer (though not on the issue of the Viet Nam war), analogized the reporter's work with that of a water commissioner who must keep his pipes open and clean.

Lippmann's specific proposals for helping to accomplish this included: publishing the names of all staff members of every journal; documenting every article; prominently retracting falsehood; establishing courts of honor in which publishers would be required to appear. "The regulation of the publishing business is a subtle and elusive matter," he said ... [but] if publishers and authors themselves do not face the facts and attempt to deal with them, some day Congress, in a fit of temper, egged on by an outraged public will operate on the press with an ax."

Some of the necessary reform, Lippmann said, required only an honest effort at self-improvement, but more was needed, particularly an effort to transform news reporting from a haphazard trade into a prestigious profession. It might be worthwhile, he suggested, to endow large numbers of journalism schools and require reporters to obtain diplomas from them. But having made the suggestion, Lippmann immediately recoiled from it, perhaps because he realized that his Harvard education would disqualify him. (Harvard has never offered courses in journalism.) It would be best, Lippmann said, "to avoid the deceptive short-cuts and make up our minds to send out into reporting a generation of men who will, by sheer superiority, drive the incompetents out of business." Training in inductive scientific method and "a rigorous discipline in the use of words" made up his basic prescription for journalism education.[49]

Through the years, the Lippmann proposals for reforming the press have fared both well and badly. The college graduate, though his degree need not be in journalism, was the rule rather than the exception in newsrooms in the 1960's. Whether this is desirable has been debated. Fears have been expressed quite seriously that "objectivity," which was Lippmann's goal in 1920, will be impaired if the ranks of reporters and editors are composed only of the "upper classes."

For example, James Russell Wiggins, executive editor of the

Washington *Post* and United States ambassador to the United Nations, complained in 1969 that "metropolitan newspapers of this day are hiring only college-educated personnel . . . many of them . . . from a relatively few colleges." There was a danger, he said, that the reportorial and editorial in-group would display "contempt for 'squares' " who lacked sophistication.[50]

Few newspapers, even the smallest, publish a complete staff roster, but a general increase in the number of signed stories and articles has served somewhat as a substitute. For the New York *Times* to publish a list of the thousand-plus men and women who write for it and edit it would be rather meaningless.

"Courts of honor" for publishers do not exist, but the libel laws of many states encourage publishers to correct mistakes and print retractions in order to escape punitive damages for defamation. This cuts two ways, however, for the person whose reputation has been damaged may be inadequately compensated for his loss. Furthermore, defamatory untruth constitutes only a small part of newspaper errors.[51]

Although not especially through his urging, another of Lippmann's suggestions has borne prodigious fruit—the establishment of research bureaus and institutes, in government, industry, universities, etc., to gather and process information which can be fed to the people through the press. Thousands of such organizations have been created throughout the world since 1920. But their efficacy in serving the press on a scale that Lippmann anticipated is open to question.

Summing up his suggestions, Lippmann stated he realized that change and reform within the press structure would not come automatically, because those "now in control . . . control the source of reform itself." So as his final proposal he urged the creation of a competing, non-commercial international news agency to be financed by benevolent foundations, militant liberals, and organized labor.

This heretical idea did not dismay reviewers of *Liberty and the News*, though similar suggestions, such as that of the Commission on Freedom of the Press in 1947 for the establishment of "yardstick" newspapers by foundations and universities, have caused the daily press to erupt with fury.

A long unsigned review in the New York *Times* dealt contemptuously with *Liberty and the News*. "Mr. Walter Lippmann is one of the editors of the *New Republic,*" the reviewer said, "and consequently may be presumed to know all about liberty; but he has never been a newspaper man and, while he knows a good deal about news, most of what he knows is not true."[52]

W. J. Ghent, a California Socialist who despised the *New Republic* and its editors ("Lippmann I have never had any use for and judged him capable of anything," Ghent told Morris Hillquit), wrote a surprisingly gentle review, calling Lippmann's press program a worthy one and expressing hope but doubt that it could be attained.

Lippmann's view that argument and debate about the boundaries of freedom of speech were a waste of time was incorrect, Ghent said. "No state, political party, church, guild, cooperative society, or trade-union can avoid the necessity." And Ghent disagreed that news juggling was confined to the commercial, capitalist press. In a jibe at the *New Republic,* he said that "the critical and pretentiously ethical journals" were equally at fault.[53]

Upton Sinclair's *The Brass Check,* an exposé of the press which held that newspaper dishonesty was deliberate and systematic, shared with Lippmann's book an essay-review in *The Bookman.* The author, Henry Litchfield West, was disturbed that neither Lippmann nor Sinclair attacked the basic problem, which, he said, was the need to suppress "papers which consistently denounce our form of government, attack our institutions, and advocate use of force." As an anarchic paper he singled out the New York *Call,* to which Lippmann and Sinclair had been contributors.[54]

In a speech in February 1920, Lippmann ridiculed the advocates of suppression. "There are some people in this country who believe they were chosen by God and the Union League Club to save the country from contamination," he said. Lippmann and Zechariah Chafee, Jr., of the Harvard Law School joined in denouncing a new anti-sedition law proposed for New York State. (Incidentally, with disregard for "rigorous discipline in the use of words," the New York *Times'* report misspelled the names of both speakers.)

"Blockaded news" and "propaganda fiction" had produced the Red hysteria in America, Lippmann said. To illustrate the blockading of news he cited a dispatch in the February 28 edition of the New York *Times* saying that the United States declined to make public a Soviet peace offer. To illustrate propaganda, he

cited a *Times* report the same day of a secret meeting addressed
by an important Russian Communist official. It was magic, he
said, that the *Times* was able to publish, in quotes, "what that
man said at a secret meeting."[55]

That kind of surreptitious reporting occupied the attention of
Lippmann and Charles Merz in "A Test of the News," published
in the *New Republic* on August 4, 1920. The standard they proposed
was deceptively simple—whether the reader of the news is given
a picture which survives the march of subsequent events or
whether he is led to believe that the outcome would be radically
different from what it turns out to be. This seems to install the
requirement that newspapers be prophets, each equipped with
its own Haruspex or crystal ball, but Lippmann and Merz pointed
out, in effect, that some events are susceptible of divination and
some are not. A definitive history of the Russian Revolution, they
said, would probably never be written, and it would be witless
to expect the *Times* to sift the "truth" from contradictory reports
of the virtues and defects of the Soviet system, or to expect it
to determine whether Red Terror or White Terror was more
beastly.

But there were, Lippmann and Merz argued, "a few definite
and decisive happenings about which there was no dispute." The
Russian army proved unable to stay in the war against Germany.
Times readers were led to believe it would continue to fight. The
Provisional Government of Russia did not survive. The *Times* was
foolishly optimistic about its prospects. The Soviet government
did make a separate peace with Germany. The Russian people
did not support Allied intervention. The campaigns of the White
Russian generals failed. Threats of Red Peril to India, Persia,
Mesapotamia, etc. did not materialize. The burden and the
emphasis of the *Times* reports of all this, of the headlines above
them, of the prominence given them, were generally misleading.

In summary, Lippmann and Merz said that the *Times* relied
too much on official information, on anonymous sources, on partisan news correspondents, and throughout permitted the wishful
thinking of the editorial page to influence the news columns. If
the *Times*, which they called "one of the great newspapers of the
world," could go so far astray, Lippmann and Merz said, then
the need for higher press standards, including a self-enforced
code of honor, was indisputable.[56]

The *New Republic* article and a brief sequel to it published August 11, 1920, named *Times* reporters who erred, including Harold Williams, Walter Duranty, and Edwin L. James (subsequently managing editor). The *Times* bore no grudge because of the blunt and severe criticism. Indeed it employed Merz in 1931 when the New York *World* was killed and named him editor of its editorial page in 1938. And after Lippmann began to write his syndicated column in 1931, the *Times* often found occasion to praise his work.[57]

Later Lippmann came to disapprove of press people criticizing each other publicly. In 1947, reviewing the report of the Commission on Freedom of the Press, Lippmann said it was true that there was no systematic criticism of press performance, no one who "watches the watchman," but he said that the Commission's proposal of "vigorous mutual criticism" by press people was not practicable.

"We are all tempted, and now and then we indulge, but on the whole we refrain . . . for there is a fellowship among newspaper men as there is in other crafts and professions . . . and life would become intolerable . . . if they practiced vigorous mutual criticism in public. I may say that I have tried it, and have had it tried on me, and my conclusion is that the hard feeling it causes are out of all proportion to the public benefits it causes."[58]

Many newspapers brushed off the 1920 criticism of the *Times* merely because it appeared in the *New Republic.* The Albany *Knickerbocker Press* said, "It is possible that the *Times* dispatches were incorrect, but it is not possible that the *New Republic's* opinion of them could amount to anything." The Richmond *News Leader* regarded the Lippmann-Merz articles as a *New Republic* promotion campaign: "If . . . the *Times* was a liar, the radical press was vindicated and the time to subscribe to the *New Republic* was at hand."

Predictably, much of the press comment dealt with the question of news as prophecy. "Prophesying is difficult and often unsatisfactory," the Mobile *Register* said lugubriously. No one could ever be quite certain about what news is, said the New York *Tribune,* but "there is general agreement as to what it is not. It is not prophecy." The *New Republic* responded to this by saying that it was not accusing the *Times* of employing bad prophets, only of employing reporters who presented false prophecy in the guise of news. "Take an illustration nearer home," the *New Republic* said. "Suppose that a Republican paper announces day after day

that Georgia is aflame with Harding enthusiasm, and then . . .
it turns out that Harding polled the usual insignificant Republican
vote. Would you call the Republican reporter in Georgia a bad
prophet or a bad reporter?" The fact that he obtained all his
information from respectable Georgia Republicans would not
excuse him, the *New Republic* said, implying that the *Times* men
got most of their information from respectable White Russians.
"A good reporter may venture a prophecy and go wrong. But
he will not muddle his own mind and the reader's by mixing
up what he sees with what he prophesies and both of them with
what he hopes." The core of its criticism, the *New Republic* insisted,
was that the *Times* permitted its anti-Bolshevik editorial-page policy
to dominate the news columns.

The effects of the Lippmann-Merz articles on the *Times* and
on the press in general cannot, of course, be measured. Louis
M. Lyons, curator of the Nieman Foundation at Harvard, has
said that it was "a strategic work that changed the pattern of
American reporting on the Soviets." The *New Republic* was confident that although it had elicited no comment from the *Times*
it had persuaded Charles Miller, the editorial page editor, to be
skeptical in evaluating the reports of his paper's correspondents
about Russia. "In the last few weeks," the *New Republic* said on
September 15, 1920, "the *Times* has begun to use its editorial
page for the excellent purpose of assessing its own news" and
warning its readers: "don't take our news too seriously."

The *Times* still opposed peace with the new Russian government,
the *New Republic* noted. "That is not what interests us. We have
discussed not the editorial policy of the *Times,* but the policy of
editor towards reporter. And here we note a change. On its editorial page the *Times* is increasingly wary. It points to sources of
news dispatches; it sometimes brands them as unreliable; it implies
that here and there is propaganda . . . It is, in other words, using
its editorial page to evaluate its news. That is the next best thing
to raising the standard of the news itself."[59]

But there remains the question of whether in the exposé of
the *Times* Lippmann and Merz were not placing on the press
a burden heavier than it can bear. Even when the portents are
plain, there are occasions when nearly all are blind to them. For
example, after failing to perceive that the stock market crash of
1929 was a symptom of the great depression soon to come, Lipp-

mann kept pleading for a balanced federal budget. He was not
alone.

In *The United States and World Affairs—1931,* which Lippmann
wrote in collaboration with W. O. Scroggs, later dean of the
Graduate School at Louisiana State University, the authors said:
"There was a very general assumption that the mood of depression
should be avoided . . ." and that "a failure to believe in [its] sound-
ness was the chief peril confronting the American economy." Mentioning some of their own optimistic editorials, the authors said
they did so "in humility."[60] And in *Public Opinion,* written soon
after the *Times* exposé, Lippmann reached the conclusion that
the press could report "news" but not "truth"—that keeping "the
court of public opinion open twenty-four hours a day" so that
readers could make infallible judgments was an impossible task.

By 1921 Herbert Croly was the only one of the original editors
still with the *New Republic.* Walter Weyl died in 1919, a year after
Straight's death, and in 1920 Lippmann resigned in order to finish
writing *Public Opinion.* Of all his books, this 1922 volume remains
most original and valuable.

No newspaperman can read it without unhappiness, for it dis-
parages the importance of the press unmercifully. Yet no newspaperman can afford not to read it, or to read later refinements
of its basic theme: the infinite complexity of the processes and
effects of mass communications. Reviewing it for the *New Republic,*
John Dewey said that the book provided "a more significant statement of the genuine 'problem of knowledge' than professional
epistemological philosophers have managed to give." [61]Reapprais-
ing the book in the *American Journal of Economics and Sociology,*
Heinz Eulau, who wrote a series of articles about Lippmann, said
that "after more than thirty years, [it] remains the remarkable
book that it was at the time of its appearance . . . one is struck,
above all, by Lippmann's uncanny ability to anticipate later
developments in the study of public opinion and mass communications."[62]

"The pattern of stereotypes at the center of our codes," Lippmann said in the book, "largely determines what group of facts
we shall see, and in what light we shall see them. That is why,
with the best will in the world, the news policy of a journal tends
to support its editorial policy." Using the analogy of maps vs.
territories, which later became a favorite comparison of the

General Semanticists, he said: "To traverse the world men must
have maps of the world. Their persistent difficulty is to secure
maps on which their own need, or someone else's need had not
sketched in the coast of Bohemia."[63]

The disparity between "the world outside and the pictures in
our heads" was due, he said, partly to censorship, to the urge
to simplify the complex, to an impoverished vocabulary for dealing
with public affairs, to the fear of facing facts which undermine
cherished beliefs. From his analysis of the barriers to effective
communication he was compelled to conclude that "there is no
prospect, in any time which we can conceive, that the whole invisi-
ble environment will be so clear to all men that they will spontane-
ously arrive at sound public opinions on the whole business of
government." The best hope, as he saw it, was that more and
more experts would educate themselves to keep, and help others
to keep, the pictures of the environment realistic.[64]

In his devotion to experts, his reliance on élites, his distrust
of the competence of mass opinion, Lippmann has been dogged
and at times defensive. In *The Public Philosophy* (1955) he wrote:
"Perhaps, before going any further, I should say that I am a
liberal democrat and have no wish to disfranchise my fellow citizens. My hope is that both liberty and democracy can be preserved
before the one destroys the other." But he remained convinced,
he said, that "where mass opinion dominates the government,
there is a morbid derangement of the true functions of power."[65]

Four chapters of *Public Opinion* deal most skeptically and pessimistically with the role of the press as educator. Though, as
the *Times* had pointed out, Lippmann had never been a newspaperman—and there are some who doubt in spite of his nearly fifty
years of contribution to daily newspapers that he ever was one—his
dissection of the press apparatus was more careful and complete
than any attempted until then. Present-day textbooks about news
editing quote it, and it is a rarity for any lengthy article or speech
about the press to omit reference to it.[66]

The assumption that the operations of a free press produce
truth about the environment is both blithe and false, Lippmann
said—truth does not flow spontaneous and pure as from a bubbling
spring. Indeed what one gets from newspapers usually, he said,
is not truth but fact, and fact in the narrow realm of what is
reportable. The realm is meager for many reasons: the economics

of publishing, scarcity and low pay of reporters, fear of libel, but, most of all, because in the ocean of possible truth nothing is reported unless it obtrudes on the surface. "Usually it is the stereotyped shape assumed by an event at an obvious place that uncovers the run of the news... the bulletins from the scene of action will note the trouble... [but not] the reasons which led to it. The reasons are intangible."[67]

Editors who evaluate news items and prepare them for publication, he said, usually have not observed the events the bulletins describe. The editor has deadlines to meet and competition to beat. So every item of news requires swift and complicated judgment—to fit it with other stories, to place it on page one or page twelve, to assign it a large or small headline. "Without standardization, without stereotypes, without routine judgment, without a fairly ruthless disregard of subtlety, the editor would soon die of excitement... the thing could not be managed at all without systemization."[68]

Within the system, Lippmann said, there are no objective standards. The editor intuits what will interest the reader and make him identify with the event, and the more deeply involved the reader becomes the more he resents later being told that his heroes have turned into villains and that foreign enemies have suddenly become friends. "That is why many a newspaper finds that, having honestly invoked the partisanship of its readers, it can not easily, supposing the editor believes the facts warrant it, change position."[69] (Perhaps the American experience with Russia serves to illustrate this. Having learned from the press the horrors of Communism and menaces of Red Peril, most readers found it disconcerting to accept the fact of Russia as an ally in World War II, and when the Cold War came they found quick comfort in being told that they and their newspapers had been right in the beginning. The ogre was still an ogre.)

The best way to explain the role of the press in the formation of public opinion, Lippmann said, is to recognize that news and truth are not the same, and that while the press can report the news well or badly, it can report the truth scarcely at all. "The function of news is to signalize an event, the function of truth is to bring to light the hidden facts, to set them into relation with each other, and make a picture of reality on which men can act." When the task of truth-finding is performed well by the institutions which the press watches—government, schools, churches—then the press as middleman can report the truth, but in and of itself, Lippmann said, the press is usually incapable of doing it.[70]

Though he retreated from this harsh judgment later, saying explicitly on his 70th birthday that "reporting is no longer what we thought of it in much simpler days" and that "fitting the unarranged pieces of raw news . . . together . . . is the inescapable job of a Washington correspondent," Lippmann persisted in the belief that without "truth" from institutions the press could not enlighten the public.[71] For example, writing about the steel strike in 1959, he asked, "How is the public to know, how is Congress to know, how are newspaper editors to know which of the facts are important and relevant? The task of finding the facts that matter and of judging how they matter . . . cannot be done without a specialized inquiry by trained minds."[72]

We are mistaken, the earlier Lippmann said, if we regard the press as the omniscient tribune of the people, rendering verdicts which settle all the troubled issues of the world. "The press is no substitute for institutions. It is like the beam of a searchlight that moves restlessly about, bringing one episode and then another out of the darkness into vision. Men cannot do the work of the world by this light alone."[73] For other, less refractory light, Lippmann suggested his favorite source of revelation—cadres of experts— proposing the establishment in each of the ten federal departments and elsewhere of intelligence services divorced from policy makers.

Recognizing that their work might produce mountains of fact and analysis, Lippmann said that the purpose would not be "to burden every citizen with expert opinions on all questions, but to push that burden away from him towards the responsible administrator . . . As a private citizen, as a sovereign voter, no one could attempt to digest these documents." Conceding in a most casual way that "there would be some study of this material by newspapermen," Lippmann said that the chief benefit to the citizen-outsider would be reassurance that the official-insider was making knowledgeable decisions based on sound procedures. The citizen could, Lippmann suggested, question procedure, but he should not expect to participate in it.[74]

Reviewing the book in the *Nation,* which he then served as managing editor, Ernest Gruening said that Lippmann seemed to be "aiming at a conflagration with a squirt gun," and John Dewey said in his *New Republic* review that the difficulty of democracy required a solution. more fundamental than "to side-track it to the task of enlightment of administrators and executives..." Gruening also disagreed that "news and truth are not the same thing." Often they seem not to be, he said, "but journalism affords numerous if isolated and temporary testimonies of serving most highly with truth... And again we differ from Mr. Lippmann's conclusion that public opinion must be organized for and not by the press."[75]

Considering that Lippmann was soon to become chief editorial writer for the New York *World,* which was during its lifetime as great a "mover and shaker" of public opinion as any newspaper in the country, it is striking that he neglected to emphasize the press as "a weapon of freedom, a sword in the hands of those fighting old or new tyrannies." The neglect, to be sure, seems deliberate, based on his persistent view that the extension of freedom is secondary to the capacity to use it. The most important role for the press, as for himself, Lippmann invariably conceived to be that of elucidator rather than thunderer.

In one of the finest histories of English journalism, *Dangerous Estate,* Francis Williams agrees with the Lippmann view that the issues of government are too subtle and complicated for the ordinary citizen to grasp. "They involve arguments on means and costs and the balance of advantage that require an expert knowledge and experience... beyond reach, or inclination of the majority." But one of the greatest functions of the press, Williams said, is to give the public "a voice that even the largest administrative monster will hear above the grinding of its own machinery..."[76]

In the next phase of his career, as editorial writer and editor of the *World,* it was Lippmann's task to help provide that voice. Many of his old friends and new colleagues who listened were sometimes disappointed. Though he was sensitive to their criticism, he was not moved by it. He had no intention, he said, of spending his life blowing a bugle.

Chapter III

THE WORLD,
AND A PREFACE TO MORALS

ON FEBRUARY 27, 1931, LIPPMANN WROTE THE OBITUARY OF THE *World*, but he did not attend the wake or take an active part in the post-mortems that sought to fix the cause of the death. In the general finding that it was malnutrition—a dearth of news and fact and a plethora of entertainment and opinion—he seemed to concur. The *World's* policy-making council, of which Lippmann became a member, often wrangled about the lack of news in the paper, and the editorial writers clipped and filed the *Times* rather than the *World* for background material.[1] Seven months before Roy Howard bought and killed the paper, Oswald Garrison Villard said that "the very feel of [it] seemed to suggest that it was an incomplete product."[2] Lippmann's own comments were oblique, perhaps because of sensitivity to the charge, by Villard, Heywood Broun, and others, that the editorial page which he directed had become somewhat namby-pamby. Writing about the press in general in March, 1931, Lippmann said, "If its owners lack foresight and energy and know only how to repeat the original formulae, the newspaper gradually fails." To succeed, he said, a paper should become "increasingly comprehensive" and "less Napoleonic at the top and less bohemian at the bottom."[3]

Lippmann began writing editorials for the *World* in 1921, became chief editorial writer in 1923, and assumed the title of editor in 1929 after Herbert Bayard Swope resigned as executive editor. Though he served on the policy council, Lippmann did not direct or control the newsgathering staff and showed no inclination to do so. In spite of his adulation of fact-finding, he seemed to regard the work of the reporter as a little grubby. James *(The Postman Always Rings Twice)* Cain, who wrote hundreds of editorials for the famous page, said that Lippmann was too remote, too detached even to be an editor. "Nobody who watched his boredom with his page, his impulse to wish all chores off on Merz ... could have supposed that he was an editor. He had no interest in editing ..."[4] Nearly forty years later, James Reston of the New York *Times* said of the 1967 Lippmann that "he has managed to avoid the tedious rubbish that occupies the time of so many reporters ..."[5]

Swope took credit for bringing Lippmann to the *World* and defended Lippmann's work against those who compared it unfavorably with the legendary Frank Cobb, whom Lippmann succeeded. Swope said that "it was a good editorial page that Lippmann put together, and it was quick to support the campaigns that were intended to serve the public purpose ..."[6] The notion that Lippmann was pusillanimous was also rejected by Cain, who said that "he will not trim, he will not back down, he will not compromise, whether his personal fortunes are involved or not."

Cain wrote about a conversation he had with Lippmann soon after Villard's criticism of the *World* and the tepidity of Lippmann's editorials.

" 'Well,' I said, 'if you ask me, the most that any newspaper can do is choose sides in a fight, and then fight as hard as it can, even when it secretly wishes the fight were going a little differently. But you are always trying to dredge up basic principles. In a newspaper it won't work. For example, turn to music. A piano has eight octaves, a violin three and a cornet two and a' —searching idly for an instrument of still smaller compass—'a bugle has only four notes. Now if what you've got to blow is a bugle, there isn't any sense in camping your self down in front of piano music.'

" 'You may be right,' he said, *'But God damn it, I'm not going to spend my life writing bugle calls.'*

"There," Cain said, "I think you have the explanation of Lippmann, his strength, his weakness, his pride, his general attitude toward his work."[7]

From 1924 to 1931, the years when a record was kept of who wrote what for the *World* editorial page, Lippmann produced at least 1,250 articles. Usually, when he was in residence, his editorial was the leader, and sometimes he wrote a second, shorter piece to accompany it. (On the *World's* last day he published, along with his valedictory editorial, a brief and acid commentary on the law's delay in dealing with Al Capone.)

An excursion through the brittle old pages, many of them in shards along the margins, is an awesome experience. The cartoonist almost always was Rollin Kirby, the Herblock of his day, whose bold quarter-page caricatures leapt at the reader. In the files, scrawled across the face of each editorial is the surname of its author—Allan Nevins, James Cain, Arthur Krock, Lawrence Stallings, W. O. Scroggs, Charles Merz, an occasional piece by James Barrett, the city editor who led the fight to save the *World,* by Franklin P. Adams, by Kirby, by the publisher, Ralph Pulitzer, and even by Felix Frankfurter. And there were veterans still writing under Lippmann's direction who had written for Joseph Pulitzer—L. R. E. Paulin and John L. Heaton. Heaton was expert on New York State and municipal government and Paulin on foreign affairs and Washington politics.[8] When Bruce Bliven of the *New Republic* wrote in 1927 that "Mr. Walter Lippmann guides what is on the whole the best editorial page in any American newspaper," it is improbable that many newspapermen would have disagreed.[9] In depth and exuberance of talent the page was unsurpassed.

Arthur Krock did not concur in this judgment, even though he helped produce the page. Krock believed that, in addition to providing better coverage of the news, the New York *Times* published sounder and more timely editorial comment. During his three years of service as assistant to Ralph Pulitzer, one of Krock's tasks was to write a daily critique of the paper. Both Swope and Lippmann, Krock says in his *Memoirs,* resented him and helped to make his job untenable.

Swope's disapproval was more frequent and forceful than Lippmann's. Krock says that Swope "telephoned me every once in a while to say, 'Keep your goddam hands off my [news] department.'" And Lippmann contributed directly to his demotion from his job and his office under the golden dome, Krock says he believes. His office was next to Lippmann's, and on one occasion, Krock says, Lippmann overheard a telephone conversation from which he concluded that Krock was attempting to sabotage the editorial page. Although he was able to convince Lippmann that he was mistaken, Krock says, the incident helped to damage his standing with Pulitzer.[10]

Nevins has said that the salary cost of the page was less than $100,000 a year, but this is deceptively small.[11] Total annual expenses of the morning and Sunday *Worlds* of 1930 were about $10,000,000.[12] Total expenses of the New York *Times* in the 1960's were more than $100,000,000, so equivalently the salary cost of the *Times* page would be more than $1,000,000 to pay John B. Oakes and the ten others who produced it. In spite of inflation, it is doubtful they were paid so well.

Lippmann's contribution usually was on the paramount issue of the day, and this precluded him from specializing. About one third of his editorials were on foreign affairs, and the rest spanned the range of local and national interest—Prohibition, Al Smith, Tammany Hall, William Jennings Bryan and the Scopes trial, Coolidge and Hoover, Daddy and Peaches Browning, the Lindbergh flight, the Leopold-Loeb case, Teapot Dome, the Klan, Houdini. (In 1925 Lippmann presided over a Houdini thought-transference experiment in which Houdini was supposed to think that Lippmann was "thinking of Lord Curzon in the Foreign Office last January." Houdini's telepathic capacity was not equal to the task, but later in the experiment, while Ralph Pulitzer, Arthur Train, Bernard Baruch, and others concentrated on a portrait painted by Mrs. John Barrymore, Houdini, stripped naked and shut in a cabinet in another room under Lippmann's and Swope's surveillance, was said to have managed to squeeze out the name Barrymore.)[13]

Except for an occasional lapse, the *World* was usually a Democratic paper, and many of Lippmann's friends, especially Herbert Croly, feared that his flexibility would be inhibited by rigid editorial policy. The fears seem to have been groundless, for as Lippmann pointed out: "The thing which the *World* cared about most, deeper than any of its political convictions, was the restoration of tolerance after the phobias and hatreds of war" and the exposure of the corruption, hypocrisy, provincialism, and materialism of the postwar decade.[14] So apparently with the same full conviction that Rollin Kirby expressed—"During my entire 19 years on the *World* I was never once called off an issue or ordered to go light"[15]—Lippmann wrote dozens of editorials against Coolidge, Andrew Mellon,

Hoover, and for Alfred E. Smith, Mayor James Walker, and Franklin Roosevelt.

He saw Coolidge as fatuous and apathetic and treated him with satire almost as wicked and vivid as the treatment in the Kirby cartoons. (At least once, though, Coolidge invited him to the White House for lunch.) The President's relationships with the press and the conduct of presidential press conferences were, during the *World* years and later, a matter of concern to Lippmann.

"There is a name for the kind of press Mr. Coolidge seems to desire," Lippmann wrote in 1927. "It is called a reptile press . . . It prints what those in power wish to have printed . . . It takes what is handed to it and does what it is told to do."[16]

And later the same year Lippmann wrote: "In his address to the United Press Mr. Coolidge disclosed in a most interesting fashion the way his mind works. He believes firmly and sincerely in all the broad principles which no civilized man can dispute. On Monday night he declared for peace, good-will, understanding moderation; disapproved of conquest, aggression, exploitation; pleaded for a patriotic press, for a free press; denounced a narrow and bigoted nationalism, and announced that he stood for law, order, protection of life, property, respect for sovereignty and principle of international law. Mr. Coolidge's catalog of the virtues was complete except for one virtue. That is humility. That is the humble realization that God has not endowed Calvin Coolidge with an infallible power to determine in each concrete case exactly what is right, what is just, what is patriotic . . . Did he recognize this possibility he would not continue to lecture the press in such a way as to make it appear that when newspapers oppose him they are unpatriotic, and that when they support him they do so not because they think his case is good but because they blindly support him. Mr. Coolidge's notion . . . would if it were accepted by the American press reduce it to utter triviality . . ."[17]

From early in 1913, when Woodrow Wilson inaugurated the regular press conference, until the present (David Lawrence and Arthur Krock attended his first conference), Presidents have altered the format of the discussions in many ways, and the increase in size of the Washington press corps and the coming of radio and television have also produced changes. Wilson held his conferences in his office, and this custom continued through Franklin Roosevelt's tenure. Under Wilson and at first under Harding, correspondents were permitted to quote the President directly and were not required to submit questions in advance. Some of Harding's blundering answers led to the regulation that questions had to be presented in writing before the conferences, and under Coolidge the rule of no attribution except to "a White House spokesman" was invoked.

Although Lippmann came to favor reinstating the written-question regulation after it had been abandoned, the Coolidge strictures amused and irritated him. On May 19, 1927, he wrote about "a new rule to be obeyed by those White House correspondents who twice a week are graciously admitted to his presence."

Summarizing the old rules, Lippmann said: "The correspondents may not say they saw the President. They may not quote what the President said . . . The information given out by Mr. Coolidge is supposed to be presented to the public as if it had dropped from heaven . . ."

"And now, as a climax, Mr. Coolidge has forbidden the correspondents to mention that they asked him a question which he declined to answer . . . these conferences are now little more than the personal publicity machine of Calvin Coolidge . . .

"Mr. Coolidge's idea of a righteous state is one in which there is no Congress to call him to account, no press to call him to account, but only a daily publication of news which Mr. Coolidge thinks is fit to print.

"For a modest and a timid man Mr. Coolidge has a quite extraordinary fondness for the privileges of an autocrat."[18]

In the summer of 1930, when Coolidge began to write a short syndicated column for the *Herald Tribune* (the fable was that Mr. Coolidge made it precisely 100 words: if he had written 97, he added 3, and if it came to be 104, he deleted 4), Lippmann said: "In spite of the cordial welcome extended to Mr. Coolidge by the columnists' guild of the city, it is plain from his first article in the *Herald Tribune* that Mr. Coolidge is still just another public man. The distinguishing marks of the public man in this relation are that he does not write about what he is interested in or about what his readers are interested in but about what he thinks it would be good for his readers to be interested in. Mr. Coolidge is emphatically no columnist. For the charm of the best columnists is that they manage with great art and an amiable deception to make public characters out of selected aspects of their private selves. Mr. Coolidge is an incurably public personage and, as Disraeli said of Gladstone's dealings with Queen Victoria, he treats his readers like a public meeting."[19]

From the soon-to-be syndicated columnist of the *Herald Tribune* these remarks are doubly interesting, for it might be argued that the formula which failed for Coolidge—writing about what he thought would be good for his readers—succeeded for Lippmann, and it is unarguable that Lippmann never made public capital out of his private life. And, too, there may have been a jibe here at Broun, F. P. A., and Alexander Woollcott, whose private lives filled considerable space on the famous *World* "page-opposite" Lippmann's editorial page.

Although he was critical of some of Hoover's policies, particularly his adherence to the Volstead Act and the protective tariff, Lippmann never criticized his press conferences, perhaps because he realized that Hoover's depression problems were not amenable to solutions that might derive from answers to press conference questions. Lippmann respected Hoover, though he weighed his qualifications short as opposed to Alfred E. Smith's and later, grudgingly, to Franklin Roosevelt's. Hoover quarreled with the *World's* treatment of him in the news columns, but he found the editorial page required reading, because of its reasonableness.[20]

First Amendment problems occupied Lippmann's attention in more than fifty *World* editorials. He agreed with Holmes and Brandeis, a minority of two, in the Gitlow case in 1925. "The minority believes," Lippmann said, "that it is more consistent with American traditions to let dissentients have their say, even when they say it flamboyantly and outrageously, as Gitlow did, provided there is no clear danger that speech will be an incentive to action . . . Two judges have adhered to the older, and, it seems to us, sounder doctrine that the speech of a wind-bag like Gitlow which creates no 'clear and present danger,' should however much we dislike it, be tolerated."

(The "clear and present danger" test for free speech and press was first proposed in 1919 by Justice Oliver Wendell Holmes to replace a doctrine, carried over from English law, that utterance with a "reasonable tendency" to undermine government was punishable. In the Gitlow case, as in others arising from criticism of government, Holmes and Justice Louis Brandeis sought to refine and apply the new test so that even speech conducive to violence should not automatically be suppressed. In the 1940's and 1950's the Supreme Court applied the Holmes doctrine in many cases, sometimes concurring in the punishment prescribed in the lower courts and sometimes overruling it. Justice Hugo L. Black and William Douglas led the fight within the court to give the widest possible latitude to thought and speech—"to punish men for what they do, not what they say and think." Lippmann's old friend Felix Frankfurter often disagreed with their view, arguing that the guarantees of the First Amendment should be balanced against considerations of public order.)[21]

The power of judges to punish editors for contempt of court incurred the wrath of Lippmann and the *World* in 1926. "If the editor of a newspaper criticizes the President of the United States," Lippmann said, "the President can sue him, but the President cannot summon him, try him, and, if he chooses, sentence him to prison. But if the editor of a newspaper criticizes the most obscure judge of a court of record in New York, that same judge can summon him, can try him, and . . . can sentence him to prison . . . our New York law . . . is unjust and barbarous." (The power of judges to punish editors for criticism of their acts was not limited to New York state. But again, in latter-day decisions, the Supreme Court has given the press almost unlimited freedom to criticize the courts. Judges must be "men of fortitude, able to thrive in a hardy climate," the court said in a 1947 majority decision.)[22]

The use by the press of its right to print salacious testimony given in the courts troubled Lippmann, who seemed to see a clear line between what was obscene and what was not. "All indecency now purveyed by books, magazines, the stage and the radio combined is an insignificant trifle compared with what is produced by the courts of law in conjunction with the new tabloid journalism," he said in a 1927 editorial on the Peaches and Daddy Browning case.

"The combination between the courts and the tabloids has produced a situation for which there is really no precedent: If you take the succession of cases—Arbuckle, Rhinelander, Hall-Mills, Browning and Chaplin—and consider how they are worked up by officers of the law, by lawyers and journalists . . . how they are exploited for profit, it is evident that what we have here is a series of national spectacles put on for the amusement of the crowd . . . the whole atmosphere of them is fraudulent. They are produced by swindlers for suckers . . ."

Then, attempting to make clear the way he distinguished between pornography and art, Lippmann said, "This is a wholly different kind of thing from the frank animalism which in the Bible and Homer, through Chaucer and Shakespeare to the great modern novelists, has been a permanent strain in human nature. These modern spectacles are not ribald. They are not gay. They are not searching. They are not profound . . .

"The theory of the purging power of frankness does not fit these spectacles. It may be said that when the tabloids have squeezed the last bit of sensations out of the Rhinelander case, for example, their public would then be bored with another spectacle dealing with miscegenation; that after the Browning case their public will be immunized against further interest in the psychopathology of an old lecher . . . then the publishers of the tabloids have to look around for a new case which has some hitherto unexplored variations of the sexual theme."

Then Lippmann, who was soon to publish his tenth book, *A Preface to Morals,* tried to probe for the causes of what he called a progressive disease, concluded that its roots were "deep in our modern urban civilization" and that "those who think they can cure it with another law are almost certainly deceiving themselves."

Roscoe (Fatty) Arbuckle, one of the most famous comedians of the silent screen, was tried for the murder of a woman named Virginia Rappe in a case which produced an orgy of salacious testimony. After his acquittal, he was banished from the film industry by Will Hays, administrator of the "decency" code, then reinstated, and finally forced into retirement by groups of crusading clergymen and other reformers.

The Rhinelander case involved a divorce action brought by socialite Leonard Kip Rhinelander against his dark skinned young wife who, he claimed, had falsely represented herself to be a Caucasian. The case reached its climax when Mrs. Rhinelander, who said that her husband should have known from the first that she was not white, stripped before the judge.

The Hall-Mills murder trial in New Jersey produced 160 news stories and editorials in the New York *Times,* filling twice as much space as the tabloid *Daily News* devoted to it. The Rev. Edward

W. Hall and his choir leader, Mrs. Eleanor Mills, were murdered, and Mrs. Hall and three others were tried for the crime and acquitted. Millions of newspaper readers were enthralled by the case for five months in 1926, especially by the testimony of Jane Gibson, a witness whom the tabloids called "The Pig Woman." When the *Times* was criticized for joining the tabloids in lavish reporting of big crime stories, Publisher Adolph S. Ochs, said facetiously, "The yellows see such stories only as opportunities for sensationalism. When the *Times* gives a great amount of space to such stories it turns out authentic sociological documents."

The Browning affair was so pornographic that several news-papers proclaimed they would not print the testimony, and others announced their intention to "sanitize" it. Injunctions were sought to stop the sale of the New York *Graphic,* which had no inhibitions. The case began when Frances (Peaches) Browning, 16-year-old bride of Edward W. (Daddy) Browning, left him in October, 1926. His suit for separation and her countersuit continued in the courts until the following July. The New York *Times* followed the proceedings carefully and published an epilogue to them on August 5, 1927, in which it was reported that Browning advocated "raw food and exercise for rejuvenation."

Charles Chaplin was sued for divorce by Lita Grey, the second of his four wives, in 1926. Charges and counter-charges of mental cruelty and fitness to take custody of their children filled dozens of columns of Page One space.[23]

Efforts of the police to clean up the newsstands and the stage won the approval of Lippmann and the *World.* After a police raid on Earl Carroll's "Vanities," Lippmann wrote: "Mr. Carroll sells spectacles aimed to provide the maximum erotic excitement the law will permit... His obscenity is deliberate and commercial... At some point in a career of this sort it is inevitable and necessary for the public authorities to accept his challenge... The punishment of Carroll, preferably in his pocket book nerve, will serve just one useful purpose. It will for a time discourage the too-rapid advance of competitive smut."[24] The problem of eroticism on the stage was complicated, Lippmann admitted, because by gesture, innuendo, inflection, performers could make a clean script dirty, but he believed that pornography on the newsstands was simple to deal with. Salacious magazines, he said, "should be driven off the newsstands and put out of sight...

There is no more reason why these things should be displayed on the streets than that the garbage should be dumped in City Hall Park."[25]

If this view of literary and artistic recititude appears a little austere, it should be remembered that even as a young man Lippmann seemed to be "a Puritan in Babylon." John Reed wrote of him as "one who builds a world and leaves out all the fun" and Margaret Marshall said "he was born fifty years too late in the wrong country . . . He would have enjoyed an earldom and a British country seat." If he had had a castle, one could be sure that all the high jinks there would have been as ingenuous as those at P. G. Wodehouse's "Blandings."[26]

Although he was too sophisticated to credit it, Lippmann gave the appearance of believing that censorship meant prior restraint only, and that punishment after publication or performance was legitimate if due process intervened. Writing about the customs censorship provision of the Smoot-Hawley tariff bill, which Ogden Nash immortalized in verse ("Smut if smitten/ Is front-page stuff"), Lippmann argued, "It cannot properly be called censorship, for the essence of censorship is prohibition by administrative act. Prosecution and trial by jury is a wholly different kind of procedure." There were those, Lippmann conceded, who "would prefer to have no law dealing with obscene publication . . . [but] it will be impossible today to persuade the overwhelming mass of Americans that there should be no law to deal with commercialized pornography."[27]

In another editorial—on censorship of the drama—Lippmann argued the same point: that subsequent punishment of plays alleged to be obscene did not constitute censorship, because it gave the accused his day in court before a jury and was "consistent with the spirit of American law."[28] (It is interesting to note that in the historic decision freeing *Ulysses* from customs censorship both the government and the defendant agreed to waive trial by jury because, as Judge Woolsey said, "a jury trial would have been an entirely unsatisfactory . . . method.")[29]

Administrative self-censorship of the movies, in Lippmann's view, meant hypocrisy "practiced as a fine art in Hollywood." When Will Hays promulgated a censorship code in 1930, Lippmann said, "That the code will actually be applied in any sincere and thorough way we have not the slightest belief . . . [for] many things outlawed in the Hays code are enormously profitable. The best brains of the industry will therefore, have to consider how to merge the appearance of virtue with the attractions of sin . . ." His *World* editorial berated the movies for "a vicious falsification of human values," for a "constant celebration of acquisitive and competitive instincts," and for "doing more to undermine taste and custom and popular integrity than schools, universities and churches can hope to restore."[30] Twenty years later in "Today and Tomorrow" columns, Lippmann found a similar lack of virtue in television and engaged Frank Stanton of CBS in public controversy.

Inhibition of another First Amendment guarantee—the right of assembly the *World* regarded with extreme disfavor during the era of Red hysteria. After a Communist demonstration in Union Square in 1930, during which police were accused of clubbing some of the demonstrators, Lippmann wrote: "One set of people argues that since the Communists wish to overthrow law and order by force . . . they can be suppressed by any and every means available . . .

"There are other Americans, however, who . . . hold that while there may be occasions in time of war when the very existence of the Republic is at stake which would justify suspending the civil laws, there is no reason for doing it and no justification for doing it in the presence of a few rioters and a few agitators. They hold that the American system is built to withstand shocks . . .

"As between those who believe in maintaining the rules and those who are ready to abandon them in the face of the Communists, this newspaper is unhesitatingly in favor of maintaining them."[31]

(The controlling word here is "few." In 1935, writing about Huey Long and Louisiana, Lippmann said: "A free nation can tolerate much, and ordinarily toleration is its best defense. It can tolerate feeble communist parties and feeble fascist parties as long as it is certain that they have no hope of success. But once they cease to be debating societies . . . they present a challenge which it is suicidal to ignore . . . It is a betrayal of liberty not to defend it with all the power that free men possess."[32] (If this notion that agitators and subversives are to be tolerated as long as they are few and feeble seems to be gross and superficial, it is nevertheless a logical deduction from the "clear and present danger" doctrine.)

The protection of minorities from what he called the tyranny of majority rule was a problem that troubled Lippmann frequently, and though later he came to believe that only minorities which embrace democracy are entitled to civil liberties, in 1927 he said: "It is the minority which needs protection even though that minority may consist of persons who if they had the power would destroy the liberty which as a minority they invoke." This was written in one of two editorials defending the right of Ku Klux Klansmen to take part in holiday parades in New York City. "We believe in freedom of speech and have often fought for the right of others to say things we thought wrong and detestable ... We are prepared to defend the legal right of any one to say anything he chooses short of actual incitement to a breach of the law. That means Klansmen as well as anybody else."[33]

The *World* was a righteous newspaper under Pulitzer, Cobb and Lippmann, and when the occasion arose it preached public sermons to other papers which it found deficient in virtue or intelligence. When the *Daily News* rebuked Colonel Lindbergh for marrying in private and embarking on a secret wedding trip, Lippmann wrote: "Disappeared on his honeymoon, mind you. The ungrateful wretch disappeared! Without an interview! Without a careful analysis by the sob sisters and Bernarr Macfadden of the exact state of his mind and feelings before, during and after the ceremony."[34]

When the *Herald Tribune* confessed its confusion about why the *World* opposed Judge John J. Parker's appointment to the Supreme Court and approved Owen J. Roberts', Lippmann wrote, "It does sound a little complicated as the *Herald Tribune* puts it in its not wholly unprejudiced way, but we do not despair of explaining the matter even to the *Herald Tribune*." The test of a liberal judge, Lippmann said, "turns upon such things as his capacity to distinguish between his own convictions as to what legislatures ought to do and his conclusions as to what under the Constitution they have the right to do." Lippmann then admonished the *Herald Tribune* to study conscientiously for a while Justice Holmes' views on the role of judges.[35]

When the *World* deplored the whispering campaign against Al Smith in 1928 and suggested that Hoover was "uncomfortable at being the beneficiary of these slanders," the *Herald Tribune* resented on Hoover's behalf the poor taste, the "innuendo" and

"absurd exaggeration," the "tubthumping," of the *World.* Lippmann replied that "if there is any bad taste in this whole affair
it is in the way in which the *Herald Tribune* itself refrains from
attacking and denouncing . . . these disgraceful manifestations of
bigotry and intolerance."[36]

In a prelude to the *World's* involvement in the Sacco-Vanzetti
case, Lippmann said that, if the states are incapable of administering justice in their own courts, popular government is a farce;
but, he added, "There are occasions, however, when local public
opinion fails, and having failed can be revived only by outside
appeal to general opinion." The occasion for the comment was
criticism by the Charleston *News and Courier* of the *World's* med-
dling in the investigation of an Aiken, South Carolina, lynching.
The *World* took up the case, Lippmann said, because "after the
official inquiry accomplished nothing, the press of South Carolina
did nothing." The need to appeal to the national conscience was
deplorable, he said, but, "Massachusetts has such a case in the
Sacco-Vanzetti affair. South Carolina has one in the Aiken lynching. New York may have one tomorrow. If it does have one,
and if our press is silent . . . we hope and trust the press of Massachusetts and South Carolina will intervene to save us from the
disgrace."[37]

(Three Negroes on trial in a murder case were shot to death
by a mob which broke into jail. A South Carolina sheriff was
accused of taking part in their lynching. A coroner's jury returned
a verdict of "death at the hands of unknown parties.")

It is anomalous that Lippmann's reputation as a crusading liberal
began to go into eclipse because of his Sacco-Vanzetti editorials;
for beginning on April 12, 1927, he wrote a total of 12 articles,
carefully reasoned yet forceful, against imposition of the death
sentence. But his pen was not dipped in the vitriol that Heywood
Broun used; and after the *World* stopped publishing Broun's Sacco-
Vanzetti columns and eventually fired him, Lippmann was defense-
less against Broun's criticism. (Broun's remark that "W. L. could
score a field goal for Harvard and a touchdown for Yale on the
same play" is the one most frequently quoted.)[38]

Lippmann's friend, Allan Nevins, concedes that "he was perhaps
too intellectually cool when he came to the Sacco-Vanzetti case,
and showed too much judicial aloofness until Felix Frankfurter
awakened him . . ." But the *World's* voice during Sacco's and Van-

zetti's last summer was the loudest and most widely heard. The
Boston newspapers took no firm position, except for the *Transcript*,
which believed the two men should die.[39]

The first of Lippmann's editorials, April 12, 1927, urged Governor Fuller to intervene against the execution. Next Lippmann
pointed out that of the eleven surviving jurors five had expressed
doubt that the two men had a fair trial. (They had been tried
six years earlier.) From May to August Lippmann wrote ten editorials, including one in collaboration with Merz and Cain which
occupied a full page. He described Wesley Thayer, the trial judge,
as "an agitated little man looking for publicity." He appealed to
Governor Alvan T. Fuller to moderate the sentence... out of
respect for a very important part of the opinion of mankind."[40]
The opinions included those of John Galsworthy, Alfred Dreyfus,
H. G. Wells, Eve Curie, Ramsay MacDonald, Anatole France. The
author of *The Revolt of the Angels* said, "Listen to the appeal of
an old man of the old world who is not a foreigner, for he is
the fellow citizen of all mankind... The death of Sacco and Vanzetti will make martyrs of them and cover you with shame. Save
them for your honor..."[41]

(Nicola Sacco and Bartolomeo Vanzetti, Italian immigrants,
were put on trial in 1921 on charges of murdering the paymaster
of a South Braintree shoe factory and a guard who accompanied
him. When they were found guilty and sentenced to death, the
verdict was disputed on the grounds that their radical affiliations
had prejudiced the judge and jury. Motions for a new trial and
appeals to higher courts failed. On April 9, 1927, their execution
date was set and on August 23, 1927, they were electrocuted.)

The exploitation of the case by agitators in America and abroad
worried the *World* and its editor. American embassies in Europe
were stoned. There were demonstrations frequently in New York
and daily in Boston. (Though the *Transcript* disapproved, many
well-bred ladies of Boston and Cambridge joined the morning
demonstrations, dressed for lunch or tea and confident that after
spending an hour or two in jail as disturbers of the peace they
would be free to attend to their social duties.) A package of
dynamite was discovered in Governor Fuller's mail. This prompted
Lippmann to write that "the activities of the Communists and
anarchists are the greatest of all obstacles now in the way of a
calm reconsideration of the Sacco-Vanzetti case... They have

irritated that great body of moderate opinion which, whether they like it or not, is nevertheless the body of opinion which in a public crisis decides the question . . ."[42]

Meanwhile on the page opposite the editorial page, Broun was writing in his column: "The men in Charleston prison are shining spirits, and Vanzetti has spoken with an eloquence not known elsewhere within our time. They are too bright, we shield our eyes and kill them." Abbot Lawrence Lowell, president of Harvard, was chairman of a committee appointed by Governor Fuller to review the case, because for technical reasons the defense found it impossible to obtain judicial review by the Massachusetts appellate courts or by the United States Supreme Court. Paying his respects to Lowell, Broun wrote: "It is not every prisoner who has a President of Harvard University throw the switch for him . . . If this is a lynching, at least the fish peddler and his friend the factory hand may take unction to their souls that they will die at the hands of men in dinner coats or academic gowns, according to the conventionalities required by the hour of execution."[43]

The next day Broun wrote another savage column which ended: "From now on, I want to know, will the institution in Cambridge which once we called Harvard be known as Hangman's House?"[44] Ralph Pulitzer was a Harvard man, but the column was allowed to run. Broun's next piece arrived too late for publication. (Like Lippmann he frequently did his work at home or elsewhere and sent it to the office.) Before his fourth column about the case reached the *World,* the editorial board met and decided that Broun should write about something else. An editorial in the *Times* may have had something to do with the decision. Expressing what it called national concern over explosive radicals, the *Times* said that "if we are to measure out condemnation for cowardly bomb throwers, we should not overlook men like Mr. Heywood Broun, who asks in the *World* whether . . . 'Harvard will be known as Hangman's House.' Such an educated sneer . . . shows better than an explosion the wild and irresponsible spirit which is abroad . . ."

Refusing to write about anything else, Broun went on strike, and the *World* was obliged to explain why the column had disappeared. The explanation, signed by Ralph Pulitzer, told readers of the page opposite the editorial page that the *World* believed in "the fullest possible expression of individual opinion" and that "straining the interpretation of this privilege, the *World* allowed

Mr. Broun to write two articles... in which he expressed his personal opinion with the utmost extravagance.

"The *World* then instructed him... to select other subjects... Mr. Broun, however, continued to write on the Sacco-Vanzetti case. The *World*, thereupon... has omitted all articles submitted by Mr. Broun."

His contract had three years to run, and it stipulated that Broun could not write for another newspaper, but he found an audience, first in the letters-to-the editor column of the *World*, then in Villard's *Nation*. In his letter Broun said that he had been given only a casual hint that his Sacco-Vanzetti columns were intolerable but that even if "my instructions had been definite I would still have been unable at that time to write about anything else," and he added, "I am willing to admit that I am too violent, too ill-disciplined, too indiscreet to fit pleasantly into the *World's* philosophy of daily journalism."

This sally produced a graceful but firm rejoinder signed by Pulitzer, which said, "The *World* still considers Mr. Broun a brilliant member of its staff, albeit taking a witch's Sabbatical. It will regard it as a pleasure to print future contributions from him. But it will never abdicate the right to edit them."[45]

The *World's* final comments on the Sacco-Vanzetti case appeared in two Lippmann editorials after the executions. In the first he expressed "understanding of the ordeal" of the Lowell committee and said that "whether they were right or wrong, well-advised or ill-advised is a matter which long will be in dispute. But that as individuals they faced a disagreeable duty bravely is something that cannot be disputed."

It was proper also, Lippmann said, "to recognize the services of those citizens of Massachusetts who defended the two dead men"; and he named Felix Frankfurter, Arthur D. Hill, and William J. Thompson. "Those who are prepared to generalize glibly about the conservative classes in Boston and about Harvard might remember these three names. For they stand very high and very honorably in the roster of patriots."[46]

People like Broun regarded the commendation of the committee as outrageous and others less partisan found it mealy-mouthed. James Cain said later that Lippmann shunned combat, and when required to take part, preferred racquets to swords. He had, Cain said, an "invariable desire to shake hands afterwards. He published a piece praising the good intentions of the Lowell Committee after Sacco and Vanzetti were burned, he had a kind word for Mr. Hoover after the election of 1928, he 'saluted' the new owners when they finally took possession of the *World.* What he never seemed able to see was that the handshake after a tennis match is public proclamation of the fact that it didn't really matter. But the sole excuse for a newspaper's activity is that it *does* matter. For my part, I esteem a certain churlishness in a newspaper. But Lippmann is, always has been, and always will be, a gentleman. You have to admire it, but at the same time you have to query it as a qualification for an editor."[47]

Perhaps sensing the revulsion or distaste for his sympathy toward the Lowell committee, Lippmann wrote a final editorial entitled "Aftermath." Governor Fuller, he said, had courage and honesty but he lacked profundity. "And he was confronted with a profound issue. And so, one way or another, he allowed himself to be backed into a dilemma where he had to choose between seeming to yield solely because of public clamor, or of subjecting social confidence throughout the world to a serious strain. It was not a situation where a plain, blunt, honest but shallow and short-sighted man was good enough."[48]

In one of a series of articles which Lippmann felt were the fairest of those written about him, John Mason Brown said: "Lippmann was as disturbed by Broun's violence as Broun was amazed by Lippmann's calm. Lippmann felt that such unrestrained invective was more an individual indulgence than a public service, since it was bound to anger Governor Fuller and stiffen his resolve not to stay the execution."[49] The relationship between Broun and Lippmann, never cordial, turned to ashes, and until his death in 1939 Broun jibed again and again at his Harvard classmate.

The extraneous uses of the newspaper—to wrap the garbage, line the pantry shelves, etc.—have been a favorite theme. In 1937 when Broun was writing for the *World-Telegram* and Lippmann for the *Herald Tribune,* Broun wrote: "I want to pay a tribute to the New York *Herald Tribune.* Of all the newspapers I have tried it is far the best for starting a fire . . . It will do the trick even when there is little kindling and the logs are wet and green." The *Tribune,* Broun added, "burns much like a driftwood log. Your eye detects blue and purple flames, and even a hint of red upon occasions. Then will come a loud pop like the sound of a bandit's gun. This I explain upon the theory that one of the paper's many gifted columnists is exploding under fire ... Visitors who sit about the open fireplace are inclined to say when some part of the kindling merely smoulders, 'You've either struck a knothole or Walter Lippmann.' That's not fair, and in my house I demand cricket on the hearth."[50]

An experiment in 1965 would have amused Broun considerably. Two biochemists, one at Harvard, discovered that putting insects in contact with ground-up newspapers reduced the bugs' pro-creativity. *Time* reported that the chemists started with a Lippmann column and went on to the New York *Times* and the *Wall Street Journal*.[51]

Like Herbert Swope, executive editor of the *World*, Broun was fond of the race tracks, and an early morning visit at the barns in Saratoga in 1934 inspired an "It Seems Me" column about Lippmann. After watching Max Hirsch try to teach a two-year-old to stand in the starting gate, Broun said: "I had an uneasy feeling that I was watching black magic and that if Hirsch had said: 'Go over to my cottage and chew Walter Lippmann's column out of the paper; the horse would have done it. To be sure, I'll admit that Hirsch would have to tell the horse what Lippmann was talking about." And this, Broun said, Hirsch could easily do because he and the horse were as one, just as Lippmann after several years of serving as "a sort of mild medical missionary to the Men of Wall Street ... has begun to look like a banker and broker."[52]

When a general strike occurred in San Francisco in 1934, Lippmann viewed it as "a conflict between organized labor on the one hand and, on the other, the general public, the city, the state, and perhaps ultimately the federal government." Broun said: "Mr. Lippmann, I think, is far too cynical. America is not yet ready to let a small and pernickety group of employers identify themselves as embodying the state, the city and the federal government."[53]

In his novel, *The Sun Field*, Broun created the character of an editor who is supposed to represent Lippmann. "We were in college together and even then it seemed to me he was all finished. There wasn't room to put any more education on him."[54]

Broun's witch's sabbatical from the *World* lasted four months. Swope, who spent every August at the Saratoga races, began to patch up the break when he returned to the city; and Broun, penitent but unregenerate, resumed the column. His articles for the *Nation*, begun during the hiatus, continued; and when in one of them, apparently in total insouciance, he took the *World* apart, Ralph Pulitzer promptly and publicly fired him. "You could have knocked me over with a feather," Broun said later.[55]

"There ought to be a place in New York City for a liberal newspaper," Broun said expansively in his *Nation* column of May 9, 1928. Then he went on to document why he believed the *World* did not qualify: "It does not seem to me that the paper possesses either the courage or tenacity. Of the honest intentions of all its executives I have not the slightest doubt." But, he continued, they were squeamish and prudish and afraid of offending anybody, and especially the Irish, who, Broun said, "are the cry-babies of the Western world." For example, he said, there was a squabble over a proposed birth-control exhibition in Grand Central Palace. About this a *World* editorial commented: "Now it is quite obvious that a building swarming with children is no place for a birth-control exhibit."

"I should think," Broun said with deadly plausibility, "that a building swarming with children ought to be a very logical place for a birth-control exhibit. The fact of the matter is that in the mind of the *World* there is something dirty about birth control." Margaret Sanger, Lippmann's old acquaintance of Mabel Dodge days, was to be in charge of the exhibit, and, Broun said, she "intended nothing more dreadful than an exhibit of charts showing population curves . . ."[56] Lippmann, as Broun probably knew, wrote the birth control editorial.

On May 5 readers looking for Broun's column in the *World* found instead an unsigned notice in bold-face type which said: "The *World* has decided to dispense with the service of Heywood Broun. His disloyalty to this paper makes any further association impossible." Less than three years later when the *World* expired, there were many who thought that of all the mistakes which contributed to its failure the dismissal of Broun was the worst. F.P.A. said so, James Barrett, city editor, said so, even Harpo Marx said so. Broun went to work for Roy Howard on the *Telegram*, where he was promised complete freedom to write what he pleased provided "it is not libelous and as long as it is interesting." The *Telegram,* by then the *World-Telegram,* fired Rollin Kirby in the

Spring of 1939 and fired Broun in November. Long before that, some of Kirby's cartoons had been mutilated and Broun's columns censored.[57]

Lippmann, who never was fired, apparently never was censored either. In 1932 there was a rumor that the *Herald Tribune* abridged a column accusing Hoover of playing politics with federal loans. Lippmann promptly denied it, saying that, though the article had been revised, he had ordered the changes, because "I felt on reflection that the language was too strong . . ."[58]

During his nine years with the *World* Lippmann wrote four books—*The Phantom Public, Men of Destiny, American Inquisitors,* and *A Preface to Morals,* which was a Book of the Month selection and his first big best-seller. Besides this and the editorials for the paper, he contributed profusely to the magazines—*Vanity Fair, Century, New Republic, Yale Review, Harper's, Atlantic, Saturday Review of Literature, Forum, Golden Book, Woman's Home Companion.* As his fame increased so did the number of his detractors and admirers. The sheer volume of his work then and later tended to overwhelm and dismay his critics. In 1963 the editors of the anthology called *The Essential Lippmann* said they had culled about 200,000 words from a total production of more than 10,000,000.[59]

Anyone who works so hard must, simply in self-protection, be somewhat insular, and most *World* reporters regarded Lippmann as a man apart—"lord of the tower." The editor and the editorial writers had circular offices just under the great gilded dome of the 16-story building that Joseph Pulitzer built on Park Row. Allan Nevins recalled "the quick step of Walter Lippmann as he handed his secretary the script of the leader that he had written at home and nodded to his associates to file in [for a conference]."

The "tower boys," as reporters called them, had nothing to do with news coverage, and Lippmann seldom visited the newsroom on the 11th floor. Nevins said that though Lippmann "did his best to see that news policy and editorial policy were coordinated . . . Lippmann's concern with the news was limited to pleas for coverage of special subjects . . . and an effort to see that gifted young men like Laurence Stallings and William Bolitho were given the opportunities they coveted." Accustomed to polishing his own editorials, Lippmann expected his colleagues to do likewise, once rebuking Nevins for using "farther" rather than "further." He admired Cain's style especially, but reproached him too whenever he deviated from "the King's English" as taught by the brothers Fowler and Copey of Harvard.[60]

James Barrett, the morning *World's* city editor, who regarded Lippmann as the spokesman for "socially minded intellectuals of America (whoever in hell they are)," said that Lippmann "really got mad in print for once" over the radium poisoning of five young women who worked in a New Jersey factory painting luminous dials on clocks and watches. Lippmann's campaign on behalf of the victims, Barrett said, was his "most effective work in the Joseph Pulitzer tradition" and prodded the city staff into intensive reporting of the case.[61]

In Lippmann's own opinion, his greatest contribution was a series of editorials designed to help keep the United States from invading Mexico after the Mexicans expropriated American property. In 1926 and 1927 he wrote more than 30 pacifying editorials (including two denouncing William Randolph Hearst), and he felt that the appointment of his friend Dwight Morrow as ambassador crowned his success.[62]

The Hearst editorials concerned the famous documents, never authenticated, presumed to be forgeries, and obtained through bribery, which disclosed sinister Mexican plots—to organize all of Central America for war against the United States, to import hordes of Japanese to aid in the war, to expand Communism, to bribe American senators. (Mexican President Calles had confiscated part of a Hearst ranch and had given the land to peasants.)[63] Lippmann said that "Mr. Hearst's behavior in publishing these documents without adequate investigation was both unfair and cowardly. His own testimony convicts him as totally lacking in the scruples which are elementary in honest and patriotic journalism." After Hearst commented that there was no proof the documents were forgeries, Lippmann said, "There in a nutshell is the morality of yellow journalism. The accused must prove their innocence; the accuser does not have to prove his charges."[64]

The annotated pages of the *World* covering the seven years between March 24, 1924, and February 27, 1931, indicate that Lippmann contributed on the average an editorial, usually the leader, every other day. Some days he wrote two and, very rarely, three. Almost always when he was absent for a long time—weeks and sometimes nearly two months—the pages bear the notation "C.M. [Charles Merz] in charge." So it is not surprising, since he wrote only about four days a week and preferred to write at home, that his was not a familiar presence to most members of the *World* staff.

On the last night that the paper functioned, he appeared in the city room where everyone waited for the inevitable decision, which came about midnight, that the Surrogate's Court refused to suspend the sale. His "valedictory" editorial was already in type, and he had the galley proof in his hand. It paid tribute to the *World's* loyal readers, to the staff, and "saluted" (the salute that Cain deplored) the new owners. It was reprinted in *The End of the World,* the book of post-mortems by staff members. The warmest tribute to Lippmann came from the *World's* famous columnist F.P.A., who wrote of his "lasting friendship for Walter Lippmann, who, I imagine, fought harder for more justice for more people on the *World* than anybody else; and for more of them than most of them knew, or ever will know."[65]

Even if the *World* had lived, Lippmann would not have stayed with it. The day the sale was announced he told the New York *Times* that he had already planned to leave as soon as he could "to travel and then to settle down to do some writing." He said he had informed Herbert Pulitzer of this in the summer of 1930, because he felt that "after seven years of continuous responsibility for the editorial page of the *World,* an intermission seemed to be in order."[66]

A month after the paper expired, at a dinner in his honor given by the Academy of Political Science, Lippmann spoke appreciatively about the *World* as an institution and about his colleagues. He said that there had been no way to keep the paper both alive and independent. "Therefore, I had rather have the *World* dead and be able to tell you that no hidden hand ever controlled its opinion than to have it alive and the organ of a faction or the instrument of an ambition." Ralph Pulitzer, he said, never let "his editorial page be used except to express the honest convictions of its editors" and after naming them—Merz, Heaton, Kirby, Scroggs, Cain, Paulin and Nevins—he said: "I cannot tell you what each of them contributed, for it would be impossible to tell where one man's contributions left off and the other's began." Here he was speaking, of course, of the fact that though the authorship of individual editorials could be identified, the substance of the whole page was communal.[67]

For his address at the Academy dinner Lippmann chose "The Press and Public Opinion" as his title. His theme was the increasing complexity of events and the dissolution of standards to judge them by. The naive era of reform and crusade was over, he said, and none but the most gullible could any longer believe "that our problems can be dealt with by rallying the people to some crusade that can be expressed in a symbol, a phrase, a set of principles or a program."

The best and in fact the only hope, he said, was that by nourishing the spirit of skeptical inquiry men might grope, relatively unscathed, into an uncertain future. The testament of liberalism, he said, "is fixed upon the importance of remaining free in mind and in action before changing circumstances . . . This concern with human freedom is not only a matter of resisting encroachment upon civil liberties. It is a matter of personal honor . . . to confront the facts with a mind and heart that have no hidden entanglements."[68]

A month before the end of the *World,* Lippmann made a speech at Yale encompassing his views about the evolution of the press —from government monopoly under kings and colonial governors, to partisan control by political parties, and finally to commercial independence. Beginning with James Gordon Bennett's *Herald* in 1836, the American press, Lippmann said, grew to become "freer from hidden control than any in the world . . . the first politically independent press which the world has known." But this freedom, he lamented, had an inevitable price tag, for the press, "escaped from the tutelage of government, fell under the tutelage of the masses," developing first into yellow and then into tabloid journalism.

'This type of journalism," Lippmann said, "is not, I believe enduring . . . It selects from the events of the day those aspects which most immediately engage attention, and in place of the effort to see life steadily and whole it sees life dramatically, episodically, and from what is called, in the jargon of the craft, the angle of human interest. This is highly effective—for a while. But the method soon exhausts itself. When everything is dramatic, nothing after a while is dramatic; when everything is highly spiced, nothing after a while has much flavor . . ."

Though the failure of the *World* and the *Sun* and eventually of the *Herald Tribune* and the *World-Telegram* seem to belie it,

Lippmann said that as readers of the press mature they seek newspapers "more and more sober, less and less sensational, increasingly reliable and comprehensive."[69] There is evidence, in spite of the disappearance of scores of "sober" papers—the Boston *Transcript* included—that Lippmann's general thesis was correct. In a study of newspapers in twelve big American cities from 1940 to 1960, Jenkin Lloyd Jones of the Tulsa *Tribune* found evidence to warrant the conclusion that "fact" newspapers tend to survive and "entertainment" newspapers tend to die.[70] And Lippmann was accurate in his statement about tabloid journalism in New York when he spoke of the "growing respectability" of the *News* and the steady degeneration of the disreputable *Graphic*. The *News* has become the biggest newspaper in America. The *Graphic* vanished in 1932, and Hearst's tabloid the *Mirror*, begun in 1924, succumbed in 1963 to the pressures exerted by the *News*.

In one of his infrequent references to journalism schools, admitting he knew little about them, Lippmann said, "I cannot say, therefore, whether they are vocational courses designed to teach the unteachable art of the old romantic journalism or professional schools aiming somehow to prepare men for the new objective journalism." By 1959 he had reached a decision about this, for in his 70th birthday address he said, "After all, there is nothing to teach at a school of journalism; what a journalist needs is an education."

Actually what troubled Lippmann was not that there was nothing to teach in a journalism school but that there was everything to teach, because "the field of journalism is the field of omniscience." In a speech in the 1920's to the faculty of the school which Pulitzer founded at Columbia, Lippmann said that "while we who practice journalism seem to have no trouble being omniscient, all who teach journalism must often wonder how you can teach omniscience. No other academic work aims so high."

Knowledge of the entire realm of human affairs was impossible to possess, synthesize, and impart to students, he said, and once the triviality of learning the formula for writing a news story and the symbols for editing copy and the technique of making up pages was disposed of, where then was the attention of the students to be directed? Since the journalist could not himself be expert in all areas, what he needed most to learn, Lippmann said, was how to recognize "the stigmata of expertness, so that he can tell the man who knows what he is talking about from the man who doesn't know what he is talking about. He needs to know, almost with a kind of animal scent, who is a charlatan and who is not." Although he did not say so explicitly, it is clear that he believed that, although the necessity of learning how to detect expertness should be emphasized, the ability to do it could not be taught.

Students should be encouraged to believe that in practicing journalism they might find the opportunity to lead an interesting, intellectual life, Lippmann said, but they also should be warned that this opportunity would be hard to grasp. The journalist's contacts with an enormous variety of events are so ephemeral, Lippmann said, that he lives "under a kind of barrage of jazzed impressions and jazzed information" which is likely to produce an eclectic state of mind to which all facts are value-free. Against what he called this "assault on his sensibilities," the journalist, Lippmann said, is tempted to take refuge behind a cover of indifference or cynicism. "The remedy for all this seems," Lippmann said, "is to make the novice in journalism realize that for his own salvation he needs perhaps to carry on in addition to his day's work some serious and consistent intellectual labor . . . to preserve some sort of unity in his inner life."

The essence of the frustration of intellectual life for the journalist, Lippmann continued, derived from the fact that "the interests of the people are not necessarily interesting to the people" and the need to give the public what it wants rather than what it should have posed a moral dilemma which should be confronted rather than rationalized. One of the objectives of journalism and journalism teaching, Lippmann said, was to realize that in providing for readers "the raw meat" of crime, vice, sex, and sin the reporter need not regard himself as a panderer. The objective, he said, "should not be to suppress and ignore such matters, but to reveal them with far more understanding and penetration than they are ordinarily reported today."

Finally, Lippmann said, the neophyte journalist should be made aware that he might encounter menaces to his freedom. The time might come, he said, when journalism would rise to such stature as a profession that the pressures to compromise with conscience would disappear. "But as things stand today if I had to advise any young man who wanted to go into newspapers, I would say

to him: Go in, but before you go in, train yourself, train your
wants, organize your standard of living in such a way that you
could quit without wrecking your life. A journalist who can do
something else, if only drive a taxicab or make shoes, is a free
man if he wants to be." Regretfully, he concluded that "no man
ought to go seriously into journalism who is absolutely and solely
dependent upon what he can earn by it."[71]

For Lippmann the central problem of education continued to
be the creation of informed public opinion. He despaired of it,
but he kept emphasizing its importance. "The constructive task
of liberalism today," he told a national student convention at Harvard, "is to find out the means of supplying modern democracies
with the information they need."[72]

Though civility was the way of life for him, Lippmann scorned
what he called the Enormously Civilized Minority which regarded
public affairs as contemptible. When George Jean Nathan wrote,
"I have no interest in politics. I have too humorous a disesteem
for the democratic form of government to be guilty of any such
low concern," Lippmann said, "Mr. Nathan is free, white and
twenty-one, and if he chooses to live in an ivory tower or at a
Broadway hotel, as blandly unconcerned as my dog with the historical process of which he is a part, I salute him and pass on. But
when he has the brass to make a virtue out of his unconscious-
ness . . . I suggest to him that this is nothing but Philistinism mas-
querading as high disdain."[73]

Since H. L. Mencken ran in tandem with Nathan amongst the
Smart Set, Lippmann paid his respects to him as well. "There
are a number of Menckens of varying excellence," he said, "there
is Mencken the philologist for whom I have the greatest admiration. There is Mencken the literary critic whom I respect as I
would a somewhat discriminating one-eyed bull in a china shop.
But there is another and more pretentious Mencken . . . the
prophet of a new aristocracy." Then referring to Mencken as
the Holy Terror and as Henry Louis Zarathustra, Lippmann said,
"Mr. Mencken has a dream. He would like as an expert in words
to recreate the world by words in the image of that dream. What
does he see in that dream? He sees himself as the companion
of a small masterful minority who rule the world and who, because
it is so simple to rule the world, have ample leisure for talk. In
that circle Mencken is the gayest spirit of the lot, the literary

pope, of course, but with a strong flavor of Rabelais and Voltaire about him. The hard work of the world is left to the subject masses, who are uneducable and are therefore destined to feed him, clothe him, keep him warm and print books for him."[74]

Scarcely the man to lie low and say nothing, Mencken wrote that Lippmann "started out in life with high hopes for democracy and an almost mystical belief in the congenital wisdom of the masses," but, Mencken said, he now concludes "that the masses are ignorant and unteachable. Government must be carried on by small minorities, partly made up of intelligent and altruistic men, but mainly made up of Hylans and Coolidges ... Mr. Lippmann, of late, has begun to discover the virtues of Tammany; he praises it eloquently in the New York *World.* I go with him gladly. Tammany, perhaps, is not perfect, but compared to the gang of thieves that you will find in any American country-town it almost seems like a mob of saints."[75]

Mencken's comments appeared in a review of *The Phantom Public,* the first of the four books Lippmann wrote while he was editor of the *World.* It is, as Mencken said, "extremely distressing stuff." "The private citizen today," Lippmann said in the book, "has come to feel rather like a deaf spectator in the back row, who ought to keep his mind on the mystery off there, but cannot quite manage to keep awake ... He lives in a world which he cannot see, does not understand and is unable to direct." Any intelligent theory of public opinion, he continued, "must assume that a public is inexpert in its curiosity, intermittent, that it discerns only gross distinctions, is slow to be aroused and quickly diverted; that ... it personalizes whatever it considers, and is interested only when events have been melodramatized as a conflict."

The most that public opinion can effectively do, he said "is to align men during the crisis of a problem in such a way as to favor the action of those individuals who may be able to compose the crisis ... with the substance of the problem it [public opinion] can do nothing usually but meddle ignorantly or tyranically."[76] (If this is true, one wonders about the purpose of an editorial page during a Sacco-Vanzetti case or a crisis over Mexico—to chill the ardor of the Brouns and Hearsts and to exert direct influence on judges, governors, presidents who read the page? The true aim of the page, Mencken has said, is to appeal, not the the masses, but to the intelligent reader in his most intelligent

mood. With this, Lippmann, who has been read by every president
from Theodore Roosevelt through Richard Nixon, presumably
would agree.)

Arthur M. Schlesinger, Jr., has called *The Phantom Public* "a
brilliant and unrelenting exercise in skepticism." Lippmann
found, he said, that "every universal pattern, every central perspective, seemed to have washed out from under him: first: Socialism;
then majority rule . . . ; then the common method of science; then
the common area of valid fact; then the provision of expert reports
to insiders by disinterested social scientists. He had supposed that
a fully informed people could govern modern society, but he
had discovered, first, that the people were not fully informed,
and second, even if the facts were fully available, only a small
minority were capable of absorbing them."[77]

So, as Lippmann saw it, the role of the citizen-outsider in the
great game of politics and democracy was to insist that the rules
of the contest be enforced, to eject the officials who failed to
enforce them, to urge that impedimentary rules be changed—and,
for the rest, hope for "the piecemeal resolution of pressing problems through the wisdom of statesmen and the knowledge of
experts."

Part of the rules of the game are the limits that public opinion
and the law set on the communication of ideas. In his next book,
Men of Destiny (1927), Lippmann devoted a chapter to the problem
of censorship. (The book consisted chiefly of reprints of magazine
articles which Lippmann published while he was editor of the
World—about Coolidge, Smith, Bryan, Borah, Mencken, Sinclair
Lewis.) In the censorship chapter, Lippmann developed the theory
that suppression varies according to the size of the audience: the
more massive the medium, the more it courts censorship. So the
motion picture is restricted the most, the stage next, then newspapers and magazines, then the novel. Finally, Lippmann said:
"And in the jargon of a learned treatise a man may if he likes
discuss with equanimity the advantages and disadvantages of incest
among the Egyptian Pharaohs, or assassination as a method of
social reform."

"The essence of censorship has always been," Lippmann said,
"not to suppress subversive ideas as such, but to withhold them
from those who are young, or underprivileged or otherwise unde-
pendable." The battles about liberty, he added, are visceral, not

rational. "The rebel feels his rebellion not as a plea for this or that reform but as an unbearable tension . . . The true conservative has the same sort of organic need: the threat to destroy [his institution] fills him with anxiety and fury." And returning to one of the themes of *Liberty and the News,* he said that Milton and Mill were wrong in assuming "that almost all men have the ability to weigh evidence and choose reasonably. Whether almost all men have the ability or not, they certainly do not use it."[78]

The struggle over censorship of teaching in Tennessee and Illinois was the central subject of Lippmann's next book, *American Inquisitors* (1928). In a prelude to a discussion of the Scopes trial and of Mayor William Thompson's crusade against history text-books used in Chicago schools, Lippmann said that newspaper writers "have never been so thoroughly convinced as they are today that the measure of events is not their importance but their value as entertainment. This is the mood of the people. When my friend Mencken says, 'I enjoy democracy immensely. It is incomparably idiotic, and hence incomparably amusing,' the democracy replies, or would if it could express itself, 'You said it, old man . . .' For the booboisie and the civilized minority are as one in their conviction that the whole world is a vaudeville stage . . . It is a new and marvelous profession, this business of entertaining a whole nation at breakfast. It is a profession which the older and more sedate editors look upon much as if they were deacons and had been asked to dance the Black Bottom."

Although he was sure, Lippmann said, that "the intelligence and wit of the community" were opposed to inquisitions of the Dayton-Chicago variety, he had been unable to discover a consistent theory of liberty with which to resist them. Then in a series of dialogues on Olympus, with Socrates, Jefferson, William Jennings Bryan, a Fundamentalist, a Modernist, an American, and a Scholar participating, he proceeded to explore the conflict between rule by majorities and freedom of thought and expression—the question whether censorship by the taxpayer is less inhibiting than censorship by kings and cardinals.

The dialogues between Jefferson and Socrates are the most interesting, as they should be. (The book derived from lectures by Lippmann at the University of Virginia; and Jefferson's Bill for Establishing Religious Freedom, passed by the Virginia Assembly in 1786, provides the basis for beginning the discussion.) The intent of the Virginia law and the Tennessee statute prohibiting the teaching of the evolution theory, Lippmann pointed out, were the same—to free men from the requirement of furnishing tax money to be used to help propagate opinions which they disbelieve. If it is constitutional to prohibit the teaching of Calvinism in the public schools, Lippmann said, then why is it unconstitutional to prohibit the teaching of agnosticism in the guise of science?

Inevitably, in the dialogues, Socrates, Jefferson, and the others all sound as if they are quoting Lippmann. (This tendency is difficult for anyone who reads Lippmann to overcome. When Eisenhower was trying to make up his mind about running for the Presidency, he began to read "Today and Tomorrow" columns and, as David Schoenbrun has pointed out, began to sound like them.) Aware of the hazard, Lippmann disarms criticism by saying:

> *Socrates* (to Jefferson): You rather enjoy quoting yourself.
> *Jefferson:* No, these speeches are being put into my mouth.
> *Bryan:* Newspapermen like to put words into people's mouths.
> *Socrates:* I do not complain. I am going to make a speech.

The burden of the speech and of the other speeches was that the "common people" hate reason, that it is unreasonable to expect them to welcome attacks on their cherished beliefs, and that it is equally unreasonable to expect that many men will risk the loss of life, liberty, and property in pursuit of truth wherever it may lead.

> *Socrates:* Have you ever stopped to think what it means when a man acquires the scientific spirit? It means that he is ready to let things be what they may be, whether or not he wants them to be that way. It means that he has conquered his desire to have the world justify his prejudices. It means that he has learned to live without the support of any creed... There are not many men of this sort in any age.

In summation, Lippmann said that "just prudence" should be the philosophy of the teacher and the editor. "I do not think," he said, "it is in very good taste to advise other men whether or not they ought to be martyrs. It would surely be very bad taste in a newspaperman, for no newspaper of large circulation can possibly represent the full, candid, unhesitating mind of its editors. They are compelled almost every day to weigh the advantages and disadvantages of candor, and to strike a prudent balance on which they act... Though timidity often makes it excessive, wherever men are bent upon persuading and influencing other men, some prudence in respect to their prejudices is necessary to success."

So for the teacher caught up in a struggle with his "sovereign, the reigning majority of the voters," Lippmann said, "the question then is not how prudently the teacher ought to act in the presence of the will of the majority, but what weight he should inwardly give to it." "Once this is clear," he said, the teacher, and presumably the editor, too, need have no haggard doubts about whether cowardice masquerades as prudence. But what a sea of troubles is becalmed by that phrase—"once this is clear."[79]

One would assume that the time of transition from fundamentalism to modernism, which was the way Lippmann described the 1920's, is time past, and that the prudent and the imprudent together have prevailed at least to the extent that the teaching of biology is unfettered by Biblical lore. But it was not until 1967 that Tennessee repealed the law under which John T. Scopes was convicted. A similar statute in Arkansas was declared unconstitutional by the Supreme Court in 1968, leaving only Mississippi with an anti-evolution law. One of the principals in the 1925 Dayton trial survived to comment on the 1968 decision. "It's what I have been working for all along," John T. Scopes, then aged 67, told the Associated Press.[80]

The acids of modernity, as he called them, had eroded the lives not merely of the educated minority, but the lives of almost everyone, Lippmann said in *A Preface to Morals* (1929). There were no longer, he said, "recognized leaders." "No one is recognized as the interpreter of morals and arbiter of taste. There is . . . no social hierarchy, there is no acknowledged ruling class, no well known system of rights and duties, no code of manners."

All books are, in a sense, autobiographical, and *A Preface to Morals* is an especially personal book. "It is common," Lippmann said regretfully, "for young men and women to rebel, but that they should feel sadly and without faith in their own rebellion, that they should distrust the new freedom no less than the old certainties—that is something of a novelty."[81]

In a diagnosis which sounds like the report of an autopsy, Heinz Elau, Stanford political scientist, saw Lippmann as beset by bogeys and fears, uncomfortable and insecure, who when "the fervor of [his] early years had evaporated, when he had established himself [became] a rather empty intellectual shell—without much life, without human beings, still grandiose and often brilliant..."[82]

The search for a positive though not fervid commitment to life proceeds throughout *A Preface to Morals*. Rebellion, Lippmann said, was no answer, except for the young and perhaps no longer for them. Speaking of the rebel, he said: "He goes forth to destroy Caesar, Mammon, George F. Babbitt, and Mrs. Grundy. As he wrestles with these demons, he leans upon them ... They provide him with an objective which enables him to know exactly what he wants to do ... he has an aim in life which absorbs all his passions ... [but] when he has slain the dragon and rescued the beautiful maiden, there is usually nothing left for him to do but to write his memoirs and dream of a time when the world was young."

For inner guidance, Lippmann said, modern man has "only a conscience which consists ... of the confused echoes of earlier tunes" and the world of which he tries to make sense seems to grow more complicated and senseless with each passing day. "The machinery of intelligence, the press, the radio, the moving picture, have enormously multiplied the number of unseen events and strange people, and queer doings with which he has to be concerned ... These experiences come to him having no beginning, no middle, and no end, mere flashes of publicity playing fitfully upon a dark tangle of circumstances."[83]

And the task of adjusting to the modern world is further complicated, Lippmann said, because "each man finds himself the center of a complex of loyalties"—to his government, his state, village, neighborhood, to his family, his wife's family, his church, his wife's church, his corporation or his trade union or professional society, his political party, his clubs, his social set. "It is impossible for him to give his whole allegiance to any person or to any institution ... It may be ... that in each of these associations he follows a leader. In any considerable number of people it is certain that they will group themselves in hierarchical form ... but these allegiances are partial ... sanctioned by expediency."

This diffusion of loyalties, Lippmann said, has the advantage of blunting partisanship, of stimulating a disposition to live and let live. "In complex communities life quickly becomes intolerable if men are intolerant ... But in a simple community a kind of pastoral intolerance for everything alien adds a quaint flavor to living."[84] But the cool intellectual comfort flowing from non-partisanship does not warm the lives of most people, and the ideal of "disinterestedness," admirable in the professional life of a reporter or a columnist, is not universally enticing, as Lippmann knew.

A Preface to Morals was translated into four languages, including Arabic, and was reviewed at least a thousand times. Santayana was one of the reviewers. In the *Saturday Review of Literature,* describing his former student as "not only a brave philosopher, but also the editor of the New York *World,*" he said: "It would be interesting to hear what he foresees will be the ruling passions, favorite pleasures, and dominant beliefs of mankind, when the hitherto adventurous human animal has become thoroughly socialized, mechanized, hygienic and irreligious. In this book we learn little of this, save that love and marriage may still, sometimes, remain associated."

(The book contains a chapter on "Love in the Great Society," which discusses the consequences for "modern women" of being freed from effective chaperonage "by the very general knowledge of contraceptive methods." Irving Babbitt, who resented the fact that Lippmann styled himself as a humanist, churlishly suggested that the Macmillan Company exploited the sex chapter in order to sell the book. Readers who bought it for this were disappointed. It would not have shocked any grandmother capable of reading it.)

Lippmann, Santayana continued, "rises at once from the ruins of Christianity into the empyrean, and what he sketches for us is . . . an ultimate and ancient attitude of the spirit which he calls 'high religion' and which he identifies, somewhat surprisingly, with domestication or incorporation of the individual's life in the world's work, which demands and fosters in the good workman 'maturity, detachment, and disinterestedness.' "

This, Santayana indicated, left out too much of life. "Far from guiding human morality, these ultimate insights of a high religion are in danger of subverting it." The disinterested scientist, artist, workman, he said, "in all the residue of his mind, may be irritable, lecherous, and half-idiotic." And, considering the great depression soon to come, he might have added another adjective—"unemployed."[85]

Chapter IV

THE NEW DEAL,
AND
THE GOOD SOCIETY

A MONTH AFTER THE *World* CEASED PUBLISHING, THE *Herald Tribune* announced that Lippmann would join its editorial staff, contributing three or four articles a week with "the greatest freedom in writing on all subjects in which he is interested." (The day the announcement was made, Lippmann and his wife sailed for Europe, together with Mr. and Mrs. Thomas W. Lamont, for five months of rest and recreation.) The New York *Times* said: "It is handsome of the *Herald Tribune* to offer its columns to a writer who will have a free hand to express his own views, even when they go sharply contrary... Each is free to differ openly with the other. That must seem to Mr. Lippmann to be in accord with his own favorite doctrine of the liberal mind."[1] This emphasis on freedom of the press amused Broun and everybody else who remembered his summary dismissal from the *World.*

The first "Today and Tomorrow" column was published on September 8, 1931. Renewing its promise of a "perfectly unfettered pen," the *Herald Tribune* welcomed Lippmann in an editorial which said: "A scrupulously fair presentation of news and a wide-open door for the expression of every variety of opinion are the standards by which a reader is entitled to test the greatness of his newspaper."[2]

Decrying the front page prophets "who predicted a magical return to prosperity," Lippmann's first column said: "It is a marvel, looking back upon it now, that we could ever have so complacently thought that a boom under such treacherous conditions was permanent. It is more marvelous that many should still think so ..."[3]

Although he should not be blamed for it, Lippmann failed to see the dimensions of the central problem of the depression—relief for the unemployed. In one of his first columns on the subject, he said that federal aid should be the last resort, because it would lead to "the corruption of the electorate itself ... Therefore, the demand on those who have money to give is doubly urgent. They must give to help their neighbors."[4] In 1932 Lippmann urged that unemployment insurance be collected in good times to be distributed in bad times, but in 1935, his opposition to the New Deal having hardened, he said that "the case for it is dubious."[5] Addressing the Conference for Mobilization of Human Needs in 1935, Lippmann said: "We do not regard it as the function of the Federal Government to take care of the young, the dependent, the disabled or the handicapped. A very sure instinct for liberty ... tells us that the central government in Washington cannot and must not reach into the cities and villages in order to manage such intimate affairs." And he added, "The system of Federal relief, however necessary it may have been, is in its very nature, demoralizing, wasteful and repugnant to the sentiments of this country. We shall fail completely to have understood the temper of the people if we do not realize that they are determined to end it."[6]

Equally certain and prophetic about what needed to be done generally to promote recovery from the depression, he said, in 1935, "I believe that if next winter it appears that recovery is not proceeding satisfactorily, there is only one safe course, and that is to put above every other consideration the balancing of the Federal budget by retrenchment on the one hand and by increased taxes on the other."[7] (Lippmann was a friend of John Maynard Keynes, and as a footnote in the "It's a Small World Department," the girl Heywood Broun first sought to marry, Lydia Lopokva, a Russian ballet dancer, later became Lady Keynes.[8] The precise point of Lippmann's conversion to Keynsian economic theory is uncertain, but by 1962 he was saying that Kennedy's premature balancing of the budget was stifling economic development. And in 1965 he spoke admiringly of the "new art" by which "we have learned how to control, regulate, and promote the production of wealth in an advanced industrial society. We are able to produce more wealth by putting on taxes, interest rates, and all the budgetary arrangements that we use, and make the thing grow . . . and nobody is any poorer, everybody's richer.")[9]

"Today and Tomorrow" quickly became a best-seller. Within a year nearly 100 papers with a combined circulation of nearly 10,000,000 were buying it. The *World* had tried to syndicate Lippmann's editorials but without much success. Allan Nevins said that "the belligerent tone upon which the *World* prided itself" was out of place in a column designed for both liberal and conservative newspapers North, West and South, and that though Lippmann "made no essential compromise with his convictions, here and there he has naturally softened his utterances" since he began to write the column. Lippmann's popularity, as Nevins saw it, was due at least in part to the definite philosophy and fundamental doctrines which lay beneath the surface of topical commentary on day-to-day events. Nevins did not spell out the doctrines.[10]

Nevins' intimation that Lippmann had more freedom for vigorous expression as an anonymous editorial writer for the *World* than he allowed himself in a column under his own signature contradicts the conventional view of editorial writing. The relationship between a newspaper's chief editorial writer and the rest of the paper's hierarchy — especially the principal proprietor—defies definition, because it depends on the temperament of those in the hierarchy and the temperament and prestige of the editorial writer.

Joseph, the original Pulitzer, who made the *World* a great newspaper, told his editorial writers that though they should never write what they disbelieved they should be silent when their views were sharply contrary to his. Except for lackeys who will write whatever they are told to write and rebels who insist (for a while) on writing precisely what they please, most editorial writers appear to conform to Pulitzer's stipulation, and, if required to be silent too often, they seek employment elsewhere.

Speaking of Lippmann's relationship with Ralph Pulitzer, Joseph's son for whom Lippmann worked, George Cornish, managing and executive editor of the New York *Herald Tribune,* has said: "Obviously Lippmann did not write, and would not have written, editorials advocating positions with which he himself did not agree. On the other hand, he could not—at least for long—have advocated causes against which Pulitzer felt strongly . . . I feel certain that Pulitzer and Lippmann agreed on major policies and that Lippmann for this reason had almost complete freedom. Whatever Lippmann wrote he must have written with the realization that he was in a sense putting words in someone else's mouth. The circumstances were different when he wrote editorials under his own name as a columnist."

Yet even columnists, as Nevins said, sometimes modify their own opinions to conform to public opinion, or discover that they can be censored or silenced, as Ralph Pulitzer silenced Heywood Broun.

The political column has become such a permanent fixture in the press that it is hard to realize that Lippmann and the Ogden Reids originated it.

Cornish, who was on the staff of the *Herald Tribune* when Lippmann first wrote the column, says: "I remember in the 1950's, at a time when Lippmann was beginning to get a bit wearied, he said that Ogden and Helen Reid had invented the political column and perhaps the time had come to invent something else . . . Of course there were columns long before Lippmann but most were intended to be light comment.

"Broun, for example, did not often discuss political or economic matters until the depression. There was also some political comment in the form of Washington dispatches which appeared under news heads on a more or less regular basis. Mark Sullivan wrote such articles several times a week for the *Herald Tribune*. But I don't think there was a columnist anywhere who openly expressed his own opinions on political matters—and certainly not opinions which frequently differed with his paper's editorials. Lippmann is the journalistic father of every columnist in this field, from Max Lerner to Bill Buckley."[11]

Lippmann's new fame was exemplified in a *New Yorker* cartoon showing two ladies in a dining car, one peering over her newspaper at the other and saying: "Of course, I only take a cup of coffee in the morning. A cup of coffee and Walter Lippmann is all I need."[12] His views, especially about Franklin Roosevelt and the New Deal, provoked praise and abuse, parody and caricature.

Old friends—Edmund Wilson, Corliss Lamont, Amos Pinchot —accused him of betraying the liberal cause, and new admirers—William Allen White, James Truslow Adams—acclaimed him as a "new American phenomenon" with a unique position in journalism. The controversy over the merits of the

column involved both content and style. Those who liked it found
perspective and clarity, those who disliked it saw distortion and
obfuscation.[13]

Through the years, Lippmann's disinclination to take an inflexi-
ble position on either issues or men attracted praise for his disinterestedness and obloquy for his vacillation. His attitude toward
Franklin Roosevelt, in whom he failed to find the quality of greatness that he discovered in Churchill and de Gaulle, typifies Lippmann's flexibility.

Early in 1932 Lippmann wrote: "For Franklin Roosevelt is no
crusader. He is no tribune of the people. He is a pleasant man
who, without any important qualifications for the office, would
very much like to be President." As Governor of New York, Lippmann added, Roosevelt had mastered the "art of carrying water
on both shoulders," of perfecting the "balanced antithesis."[14] It
was an art, Lippmann's critics quickly retorted, that Lippmann
himself had brought close to perfection. ("Emblem of his period,
he [Lippmann] has been the very incarnation of Heraclitean flux,"
Ernest Sutherland Bates said.)[15]

Other journalists of what were considered liberal inclinations
—Villard, Broun, and Elmer Davis—shared Lippmann's disdain
for Roosevelt's qualifications, but it was the Lippmann stricture
that stung Roosevelt to reply. "In spite of his brilliance," Roosevelt
said, "it is very clear that he [Lippmann] has never let his mind
travel west of the Hudson or north of the Harlem!" Three years
later, from the vantage of the White House, Roosevelt was able
to speak of Lippmann more charitably. "He writes so lucidly and
charmingly," Roosevelt said, "that we are apt to overlook the fact
that he is, to say the least, not always consistent. I wish sometime
that he could come more into contact with the little fellow all
over the country and see less of the big rich brother!"[16]

When the Democrats nominated Roosevelt to run as Vice-
President in 1920, Lippmann sent him a telegram which said:
"When cynics ask what is the use we can answer that when parties
can pick a man like Frank Roosevelt there is a decent future
in politics." Roosevelt's "Happy Warrior" speech nominating Al
Smith at the 1924 Democratic convention was "perfect in temper
and manner and most eloquent in it effect," Lippmann said in
a letter, and in a *World* editorial he said that Roosevelt was entitled
to any public office the electorate could bestow.[17]

Early in 1932, urging the nomination of Newton D. Baker, Lippmann said of Roosevelt that he was a man "who might make a good Cabinet officer, but who simply does not measure up to the tremendous demands of the office of President."[18] After Roosevelt's nomination in July of 1932, Lippmann said: "Those who can find in any one of these men [Hoover, Roosevelt, Norman Thomas] the ideal of their hearts' desire are fortunate indeed. The rest of us will, I imagine, spend the next few months realizing that John Morley was right when he said that politics was the science of the second best."[19]

But a month before the election, Lippmann announced in his column: "I shall vote cheerfully for Governor Roosevelt." Roosevelt, he said, had either been underrated or had matured during the campaign, and there was no prospect of restoring national unity should Hoover be reelected.[20]

In the early days of the New Deal, Lippmann defended Roosevelt against charges that he was seeking to establish a dictatorship, condoned the hasty passage of emergency legislation, and the assumption by the President of temporary emergency powers. Roosevelt's performance of his task, to revive the industrial system from the depression and to reform it by instituting new control, Lippmann at first found superb.[21]

"From the day he took office," Lippmann wrote, "he began to govern. In a series of sharp and decisive acts he convinced the whole people that the government was master in its own house as against all lobbies, minorities, factions, and vested interests."[22]

Within two years, however, convinced that the emergency was over, Lippmann said: "All the reasons which called for the grant of undefined powers and the handing over the blank checks have ceased to exist . . . The people have the right to feel sure that their government is that of a democratic republic, and that is not a government concentrated in the personality of one man."[23]

When Roosevelt chose to broadcast his annual message to Congress in July of 1936, Lippmann was horrified by the "propagandist procedure," which, he said, was calculated to establish one man's domination of public opinion, and to frustrate debate. Considering the uses politicans now make of radio and particularly of television, Lippmann's objections seem singularly naive, but in 1936 newspapers were the primary source of fact and opinion, and it was as a newspaperman that Lippmann demurred.

"By selecting 9 o'clock Eastern time and a Friday evening for this direct appeal to the people," Lippmann wrote, "the President has not merely obtained the largest possible audience. He has shut off effective discussion of what he has to say for nearly three days ... For it should be understood that considered comment by Congress or by the editors cannot be made late on a Friday evening ... There can be some comment in the Saturday afternoon papers, but it will have to be comment based on hurried judgments unaided by the opinions of competent authorities. The Sunday newspapers are normally, as editorial writers well know, unsuited for effective comment on immediate events. Thus not until Monday will the country begin to hear any real debate on the message." And by then, Lippmann added, the emotional effect of the message, unchecked by critical opposition, would have solidified. He concluded by calling for some "hard thinking" on the problem of the personal broadcast before "the vital essence of representation government" was lost.[24]

After announcing his support for Governor Alfred M. Landon of Kansas, the Republican candidate in 1936, Lippmann said that "the time has come to put an end to personal government through rubber stamps by blanket powers and blank checks."[25] By refusing to collaborate with the leaders of American business and finance, he added, Roosevelt had divided the people "frivolously, unnecessarily and perhaps dangerously."[26]

More than 20 years later, in a television interview, Lippmann reappraised Roosevelt in a rather slapdash way. After calling him one of the three great Presidents of the 20th Century, Lippmann said: "Well, I have long had mixed and confused feelings about him, having known him, as a very young man—years before he had his polio—in the First World War, when I thought he was extremely attractive. He was one of the most handsome, attractive young men—quite superficial, rather uneducated, but so charming that everybody liked him, though nobody ever conceived of him as President of the United States. Then came his illness and during that period he grew up. Even then, he had really not become the Roosevelt that the world knows. Even when he was nominated—even during the campaign of 1932, none of the New Deal was visible. Then, I had an in-and-out feeling about the New Deal. The first part of it I thought was very bad—the part that terminated in the attempt to pack the Supreme Court. And the second part of it, which had to do with the compensated economy, you know, the economy of balancing the business, I thought was very good. Then be became a war President, and on the whole, he was a great war President."[27]

A rereading of the "Today and Tomorrow" columns of the 1930's scarcely produces the impression that Lippmann favored Roosevelt's brand of a "compensated economy." In one of his pro-Landon columns in 1936, when about seven million were still unemployed, he wrote of "a budget which is tending to crystalize at a scale of expenditures which is colossal."[28] In two of the books which he published during the New Deal, *The Method of Freedom* and *The New Imperative*, Lippmann frequently proclaimed that laissez-faire was dead and must be superseded by Free Collectivism or a Compensated Economy in which the state would "redress the balance of private actions by compensating public actions" and "repress a too rampant individualism in the use of property."[29]

But when the government sought to put this theory into practice, Lippmann often inveighed against it. He deplored "the dangerous tendency of the New Deal to centralize power in Washington by the use of money and by administrative law" and described the National Recovery Act, the Agricultural Adjustment Act, the Public Works Administration, and the Works Progress Administration as "unworkable except through highly centralized executive control." To the National Labor Relations Act and federal wage-hour laws, Lippmann was implacably opposed; toward the Social Security program, he was tepid, in favor of old age pensions but against unemployment insurance.[30]

Yet Lippmann's view that the government could effectively regulate the economy through general fiscal policy alone rather than by detailed intervention in industry—"The power to fix the wages paid for killing chickens is negligible," he said in a comment about the Supreme Court decision which killed the NRA—was a forecast of the direction the New Deal later would take. And Lippmann's position, as Arthur Schlesinger has pointed out, was the position of Keynes, in advocating central rather than piecemeal controls.[31]

Several press and censorship problems occupied Lippmann's attention in the 1930's—the code for newspapers under the NRA, freedom of radio, the establishment of the American Newspaper Guild, the performance of the press in the Lindbergh kidnapping and the Hauptmann trial, and in the abdication of Edward VIII.

Lippmann urged the nation's publishers to refuse to submit to regulation under the NRA, arguing that better wages and hours and collective bargaining would force the weaker newspapers, which he said were more often than not the liberal and progressive ones, out of business. "In order to have a press able to say what it thinks, there must be," he said, "many newspapers of all shades of opinion, not merely a few industrially sound institutions." The tendency toward mergers and combinations of newspapers, he said, had already gone too far. Answering the argument that what the powerful, conservative publishers really objected to in the code was not the possibility of loss of freedom but rather a threat to profits, Lippmann said: "For myself, I do not care what their motives are." But he urged those who could afford it to put the labor provisions of the code into effect voluntarily.[32]

After an agreement on a code was reached, Lippmann said that the publishers should have resisted and carried their challenge to the Supreme Court. Heywood Broun, who was in the midst of his attempt to form the American Newspaper Guild, reacted to this with his usual fervor. Referring to Lippmann as "journalism's slightly less famous Walter (the other was Winchell), and remarking that "one keeps his eye to the keyhole, and the other buries his head in the sand," Broun said that Lippmann was one of the liberal gentlemen who are "vigorously progressive as to any change which happened in the past and as to salutary reformation in the not too distant future. But it is always impossible to pin them down as to readjustments which may be achieved today."[33]

Before the Supreme Court invalidated the NRA and the codes, Lippmann appealed to the publishers to reject any renewal of economic regulation, charging that it could lead to censorship. His appeal, early in 1935, came at a time when the American Newspaper Publishers Association was fighting ratification of the proposed Child Labor Amendment. In an editorial entitled "Newspaper Blood Money" the *Christian Century* magazine accused Lippmann of "firing the first gun" in the campaign to permit a renewal of the exploitation of children as newsboys and news carriers.[34] And Broun recalled that Lippmann had written eloquent editorials in the *World* contending that a Child Labor Amendment would infringe States' Rights.

In his assessment that economic strangulation would continue to drive newspapers out of business or into mergers Lippmann was correct. In the period between 1933 and 1935, when he was attacking the NRA, there were nine daily newspapers of general circulation in New York City. In 1968 there were three. Throughout the country, morning and afternoon papers diminished from a total of 1,950 in 1935 to 1,750 in 1968. Yet it is doubtful that continuing to hire children 12 years old to deliver newspapers for $3.40 a week, which is what publishers told the NRA they paid, or employing beginning reporters at wages ranging from $8.40 to $17.50 a week, which were the publishers' recommendations for their code, would have kept many of the marginal newspapers alive.[35]

The publishers' association consistently opposed, both under the code and in the provisions of the Wagner Act, which was passed in May of 1935, the right of news and editorial department employees to organize for collective bargaining. Allegiance to a union, they said, would sully reporters' objectivity and interfere with publishers' rights to employ whomever they chose. Lippmann agreed with the latter contention, saying that government could never compel employers to bargain collectively in good faith. Lippmann also aligned with the publishers in opposing the wage and hour act, which provided for minimum wages of from 25 to 40 cents an hour and a maximum work week of 40 hours for all industry in interstate commerce. This proposal, he said, was part of Roosevelt's intention "to gather an irresistible power of the economic life of this country."[36]

Though they were not obliged to do so, Lippmann, together with other famous columnists, including Dorothy Thompson and Westbrook Pegler, joined the American Newspaper Guild, which Heywood Broun organized in December of 1933. Though Broun's intention to emphasize wages and hours and collective bargaining was clear from the start, some of the members regarded the Guild as a professional organization like the American Bar Association rather than as a labor union. When the Guild voted to affiliate with the American Federation of Labor in 1936, many members were unhappy and were made unhappier still by the passing of political resolutions at Guild conventions and by the decision, in 1937, to join John L. Lewis' CIO.

In a letter to the secretary of the New York Guild, after a

convention in which the Guild had endorsed the cause of the Loyalists in Spain and Roosevelt's plan to enlarge the Supreme Court, Lippmann announced that he was refusing to pay his membership dues, and offered to resign. After receiving assurance that members of the Guild were not committed to its political resolutions and were free to express their own opinion, Lippmann replied rather hotly that the higher officers of the Guild were "exploiting an organization founded to protect and promote the professional interests of newspapermen" and said that, though the assurances of his continued personal freedom of expression were undoubtedly well intentioned, they "do not interest me."[37]

In the "It Seems to Me" column in which he announced his plan to organize newspaper writers, Broun said, "I think I could die happy on the opening day of the general strike if I had the privilege of watching Walter Lippmann heave half a brick through a *Tribune* window at a non-union operative . . ."[38] Broun's eventual reward for founding the Guild was loss of his job on the *World-Telegram*. First the notice accompanying the column which assured readers that Broun wrote as he pleased disappeared, then the column was mercilessly edited, and finally, in 1939, he was fired.[39]

Lippmann's column, never censored, continued to flourish. In 1939 it was available to more than seven million daily newspapers subscribers. The problems of the press which troubled him were ethical and philosophical, not economic. Newspaper incursions against the rights of individuals, including those accused of crime, Lippmann found deplorable. Many of his comments dealt with the Lindbergh case, which occupied national attention for more than four years. When Colonel Lindbergh was trying to establish contact with his son's kidnapper and appealed to the press to give him freedom from surveillance, Lippmann said that it was "cruel curiosity which forces him to devote so much energy to evading publicity"[40]; and when the Lindberghs fled to England in December of 1935, Lippmann said that they were "refugees from the tyranny of yellow journalism . . . They have been denied their human, their inalienable right to privacy. And in their protest they speak for the conscience of all civilized men."

The problem of accommodating the liberties of the press to the liberties of the individual could not be solved, Lippmann said, by passing new laws or by protestations of outrage in newspaper editorials. The only remedy, he added, was "a change in the public philosophy" which would "make it dangerously unprofitable to prostitute the liberties of the press" by pandering to "an infantile curiosity to learn the inside story of the inside story . . ."[41]

After the case was over and Bruno Hauptmann was executed for the kidnapping, Lippmann reviewed it in a column and in a speech to the American Society of Newspaper Editors, making specific suggestions for the reform of press conduct and the conduct of trials. Describing the case, from the first news of the kidnapping to the accounts of the electrocution, as a "criminal circus," Lippmann said the time had come to "make things hot for the clowns, the daredevils and the barkers," "to set new precedents by having a lot of persons up for contempt of court," and to brand as incompetent "judges and lawyers who make the show or permit it."

Although he did not exculpate the press, Lippmann said that "without the connivance of the regular officers of the law"—among whom he included police, lawyers for the defense and prosecution, the trial judge, and the Governor of New Jersey—"the intolerable abuses of publicity would have been reduced to manageable proportions."

"I suggest," he told the convention of editors, "that we challenge the police, the judges, the lawyer . . . that we declare that they are subverting the processes of law, that they are acting corruptly, and center public attention on them rather than on the criminal in the dock."[42]

Lippmann's suggestion that we emulate the English system, which prohibits the reporting of anything except the details of an arrest before a case comes to a hearing and a trial and all comment about it while it is being tried, has never been popular with American editors. When, after a three-year study, the American Bar Association in 1968 approved new ethical guides for lawyers and judges designed to regulate the release of crime news, the American Newspaper Publishers Association, the American Society of Newspaper Editors, and the broadcasting networks all objected. They contended that the new procedures would interfere with responsible press coverage of crime and the courts.[43]

In commenting on the reticence of the British press about the divorce of Mrs. Wallace Warfield Simpson, Lippmann again indicated his preference for English procedures. "It is interesting to ask ourselves whether the British practice or our own makes for the greater freedom in human society," Lippmann wrote. In America the individual who gets into court, he said, is almost entirely without protection against publicity.

"Though liberty is cherished in this country," he said, "our liberty is defective in that the rights of the individual are not sufficiently protected. Mr. Hearst, for example, is properly outraged when a Senate Committee ransacks his files and publishes his communications to his editors. But Mr. Hearst will gladly publish any bit of gossip about Mrs. Simpson that he can lay his hands on. Mr. Hearst as a publisher can subject Mrs. Simpson or a college professor or anyone else to any kind of torture and indignity, and they have no recourse." (Actions for libel were of little use, Lippmann said, because they were "cumbersome, expensive and embarrassing.") But a publisher like Hearst, he said, proclaiming the "principles of freedom of the press, claims an immunity which his papers concede to no individual who comes under the harrow . . .

"In fact, the American public has become curiously insensitive to private rights . . . Congress continually abuses most gravely its own prerogatives. Individuals are attacked in debates, they are charged, tried and condemned in legislative hearings without any of the ordinary legal protection that every man is supposed to enjoy."

Writing rather regretfully of the requirement that Edward VIII abdicate or give up Mrs. Simpson, Lippmann said that "the press and the camera have destroyed the privacy which his ancestors enjoyed." Democracy, he noted, requires that everyone, including kings, conform "to its desires and its morals, and, if you like, its prejudices."[44]

Although in the 1930's Lippmann was a celebrity whose views about public affairs were continually damned and defended, his private life was seldom exposed to publicity. *Time* reported in a 1937 issue whose cover pictured Lippmann that his income was $54,329, that he maintained three residences, in Manhattan, Florida, and Wading River, Long Island. He was a good tennis player and a fair golfer, liked to fish and ride horses, and preferred the social company of J. P. Morgan partners to labor union leaders.[45]

When Lippmann's first wife, the former Faye Albertson, sued him for a divorce in Bradenton, Florida, on October 19, 1937, the case received little publicity. An Associated Press story of six brief paragraphs reported that Mrs. Lippmann charged that her husband "treated her with absolute coldness" and that "the defendant is shrewd and quick in his mental processes, commands a vocabulary virtually unlimited, is a facile veteran in the use of invective and development of criticism, a phase of his equipment that he constantly uses in administering verbal punishment..."

And in March of 1938, when Lippmann married Helen Byrne Armstrong, who had recently divorced her husband, Hamilton Fish Armstrong, editor of *Foreign Affairs,* the *Herald Tribune* devoted 150 words to the private ceremony. "They will shortly take up their permanent residence in Washington," the report concluded.[46]

(Except for summers in Maine, the Lippmanns lived in Washington for nearly 30 years, until the summer of 1967, when he announced that he was ending his regularly scheduled column and establishing permanent residence in New York again. He had become tired, he said "of the necessity of knowing, day in and day out, what the blood pressure is at the White House and who said what and who saw whom and who is listened to and who is not listened to." President Lyndon Johnson, he added, had made Washington political commentary difficult to do because "he rules like an absolute monarch ... and has frightened his subordinates from talking to journalists.")[47]

Lippmann's intimacy with bankers and the leaders of society irritated some of his old friends. Corliss Lamont, son of the Morgan partner Thomas and a contributor to leftwing publications like the *New Masses,* wrote in 1937 that Lippmann "ended up by giving over his exceptional gifts to the service of reaction smirkingly posing as liberalism. And by some strange coincidence he has at the same time attained an eminent position in New York and Long Island society."[48]

Defending Lippmann half seriously, half in jest, one of his classmates at Harvard, Harrison Reeves, who had been on the staff of the *World* and the *New Republic,* said, "I think Mr. Lamont gives his change of heart too grave an importance ... Old Uncle George—that is what we theme writers and theme readers used to call Santayana—used to quote a Greek proverb, from Solon, I think: 'A youth who is not an anarchist is a knave; an old man who is not a conservative is a fool' ... one should not, I think,

get too excited about such things . . . I think Mr. Lamont should
bear this in mind when he writes about the changes in men's
economic or political views. The whole business needs humaniz-
ing."

What was so surprising, Reeves asked, about Lippmann as social
lion and referee of polo matches at Westbury? "I have interviewed
several thousand polo players who rode along as an avocation
the profession of investment banking. These gentlemen have vo-
cabularies of eight hundred words . . . their women folk speak
four hundred units . . . Lippmann is just the lion to amaze these
insular folk . . . What would Old Westbury and Sands Point not
give to be in the presence of a vocabulary, practically unlimited?"[49]

Unworried about the effect that the enticements of social prestige might have on a journalist, the Hearst newspapers and the
Philadelphia *Inquirer* expressed great concern for Lippmann when
the French government sought to make him a chevalier of the
Legion of Honor. "No American writer should accept one of these
colored ribbons, which are like the little red flags on which unwary
frogs are caught," the New York *Journal* said. "Why does the
French Government pick out Lippmann?" the *Inquirer* asked. "Is
it because of his broad education and his keen logical mind? Or
is it the color of his eyes, or the way he wears his clothes or
parts his hair?" These honors were appropriate for soldiers, the
Inquirer said, but not for newspapermen. "Propaganda has its
legitimate uses," the editorial said. "But any person regularly connected with this newspaper [the *Inquirer* published the "Today
and Tomorrow" columns] who lends himself to its dissemination
must do so as a propagandist first, last and all the time . . . for
the United States of America."[50] Lippmann declined the French
ribbon, though later he accepted decorations from the governments of Belgium, Norway, and the Netherlands.

The threat to detachment which Lippmann feared the most
for journalists arose from their intimacy with persons of power
in government. The way to avoid it troubled him. The conflict
that stems from the ties of loyalty and friendship on the one
hand and the duty to criticize on the other he said he regarded
as the most unpleasant aspect of newspaper work. "Newspapermen cannot be the cronies of great men," he said. More
than once the need to tell what he believed to be the truth about
friends who rose to positions of authority cooled the friendship.

He said that Coolidge was the only high public official who seemed impervious to criticism. "He achieved this miracle," Lippmann observed, "by conveying the general impression that he had never heard of the newspaper with which his guest was connected, and had never had anything printed in it called to his attention . . . But Mr. Coolidge was an imperturbable man living in an interlude of quiet times, and it was perhaps rather easier for him to be a philosopher than it had been for his successors."[51]

None of his adversaries—and during the days of the New Deal they were numerous and often shrill—accused Lippmann of currying favor with officials. Indeed it was his status as a leading member of Roosevelt's loyal opposition that disturbed them. When the President decided that his overwhelming victory over Landon in 1936 gave him a mandate to reform the Supreme Court by enlarging it, Lippmann charged that if Roosevelt succeeded in "packing" the court he would next attempt to muzzle the press. He accused the President of regarding himself "not as a constitutional chief magistrate but as a specially selected leader enjoying some special and almost mystic inspiration from the subconscious wisdom of the crowd." Absolving the President of being motivated by "sinister ambition" or seeking to perpetuate his own personal power beyond a second term, Lippmann said that the court plan was "a bloodless, deviously legalized *coup d état.*"[52]

Reviewing six Lippmann columns about the court plan, Max Lerner said in the *Nation:* "Something in his subject had clicked with him as never before. I found spread out before me the entire anatomy of his mind—his easy expository tone, his dialectical skill, his genius for clarity to the point of bareness, his rhetoric which is always just on the point of becoming eloquence, his magisterial air, his talent for opening his mind to no more of his subject than for the moment he cares to admit, his tone of fairness . . . the smugness about his own motives and the attribution of dishonesty to others which I can only describe as a moral megalomania. . . . And I found in addition what one finds when the usually cold Mr. Lippmann gets really excited—a sort of glacial hysteria . . ."[53]

Other leading columnists of the day were equally perturbed about the court plan and the potential excesses of majority rule. Paying his respects to four of them, George Sokolsky, Dorothy Thompson, Westbrook Pegler, and Lippmann, Heywood Broun wrote: "For several seasons the mind of Walter Lippmann has been open to visitors every day except Sunday, when a small admission fee is charged . . . He will find the excursion listed in the guide book under the heading 'Cave of the Winds.' "[54]

The court enlargement plan failed to pass Congress, partly because of the fury engendered against it in an almost unanimous daily press, and Lippmann and his fellow opinion makers were vindicated. But three of the recalcitrant judges retired or died, and Roosevelt soon had an opportunity to appoint successors, the first being Hugo L. Black from Alabama.

Lippmann did not admire Black as senator and once said of him that "in the realm of justice he is an obvious illiterate." His reference was to the activities of a Senate Committee investigating lobbying, of which Black was chairman. The committee, with the help of the Federal Communications Commission, obtained a private telegram from William Randolph Hearst to one of his editors. Investigating committees, Lippmann said, were becoming "an engine of tyranny in which men are denied the elementary legal protection that confirmed criminals caught redhanded in the act can count on." In Black's conduct of the hearings, Lippmann said that there was "never one word, never one hint, that anyone ever has been, ever could be, unjustly accused, unfairly inconvenienced, unnecessarily embarrassed, carelessly injured, that those who are investigated have any rights of any kind . . . From first to last, without a quiver of doubt to restrain him, he glorifies himself as a sleuth out to get his man, as a prosecutor out to hang him."[55]

In his investigation of the public utilities industry, Black was tough to the point of brutality, Arthur Schlesinger says, but he adds that Black inquired only into people's actions. "He did not slander reputations, drag in innocent persons or indulge in promiscuous character assassination . . ."[56]

Lippmann's position on Congressional investigations was nearly always consistent. The procedures of the House Committee on Un-American Activities and the Senate Internal Security Subcommittee horrified him, though he did concede that the House Committee in its earliest days served a useful purpose. In the 1950's he denounced Senator Joseph McCarthy repeatedly and rebuked President Eisenhower for failing to restrain him. In the instance of the seizure of the Hearst telegrams, Lippmann said that the publishers' association, in charging violation of freedom of the press, invoked the wrong principle. It was an outrage, he said. "But the outrage did not lie in the fact that Mr. Hearst is a publisher ... the outrage was not against the freedom of the press but against the freedom of all individuals ..." Mr. Hearst had no special rights in this field because he was a publisher, Lippmann said, nor did he have special privileges or immunities. The First Amendment, specifically protecting the press, is vital to the preservation of liberty, he argued, but "freedom of the press in America is protected ... in a much more substantial degree by all the constitutional guarantees given to all persons.

"It follows from this that the press can never defend its own liberties alone. The defense ... must be given to the whole system of liberties—to the rights of all individuals, the limitation under the law of all organs of government, and the capacity of all men to defend their rights before independent tribunals." The "outrage" by the Black Committee, he concluded, violated not the First Amendment but the Fourth, which prohibits unreasonable search and seizure.[57]

The defense of the Bill of Rights Lippmann sometimes found paltry. Most of the orators about liberty, he said, "are comfortably blind about those liberties which happen to be the birthright of the disagreeable people they do not like." Thus, he said, Mayor Frank Hague of Jersey City suspended all known constitutional guarantees in order to combat communism, Secretary Harold Ickes regarded critics of the New Deal as conspirators against the rights of man, the Civil Liberties Union was blind to Senator Black's encroachment on the rights of Hearst, the National Association of Manufacturers took no notice of Mayor Hague's persecution of labor organizers. The requirement that lovers of liberty should cherish the rights of their enemies, he said, was "more than a piece of abstract idealism too high and too rarefied for this rough world ... It is sound policy in a democracy to be the first to see the mote in one's own eye."

It was no longer intellectually respectable, he said, to affirm, as the authors of the Bill of Rights affirmed, "that any principle is self-evident, inalienable, eternal and universal," immune against all arguments of expediency. But men need to remember, he said, that though the constitutional system in general is based on the rule of majorities and is subject to change, the Bill of Rights is not subject to change.[58]

To the specific charge that one of the basic freedoms—that of the press—was being subverted by wealthy newspaper proprietors, advertisers, and corporate interests who conspired against the New Deal, Lippmann responded with two arguments. First, he said that propaganda against many New Deal measures flourished because of general ignorance about them rather than because of organized hostility to them. Almost never, he said, had the New Dealers taken the trouble to provide to the press information that responsible interpreters needed in order to explain the complicated reforms which were proposed. Even he "had to go back to school and do the freshman year all over again," he said.[59] Second, Lippmann said, there had been no crusade against Roosevelt or the New Deal. "Any idea that there was a general concerted effort made by newspapers to defeat Mr. Roosevelt is, in my opinion, absolute poppycock." And there had occurred even within a few years, he said, a decided improvement in the standards of newspapers. "Impartiality in news presentation is incredibly higher today than it used to be."[60]

(*Editor & Publisher,* which keeps score on newspaper support for presidential candidates, reported that in 1936 more than 70 per cent of the daily newspapers which expressed a preference supported Landon. But there is no conclusive evidence that editorial page support for candidates, in that or subsequent elections, generally influenced the presentation of the news; and it should be remembered that although most newspaper publishers were against the New Deal, most reporters and news editors were in favor of it.)[61]

Although he was convinced that the press was neither subservient to the New Deal nor hostile to it, Lippmann had doubts about radio—about its freedom to be non-partisan and its ability to share equally with the press the task of informing the people. Licenses to broadcast, necessary because channels were limited and because wave lengths needed to be assigned in order to keep stations from interfering with each other, were issued in the early days of the New Deal by the Federal Radio Commission. In 1933 one of the commissioners warned stations that their licenses might be forfeited if they permitted "greed or lack of patriotism" to produce broadcasts which were not in the public interest.

"This threat," Lippmann said, "was tantamount to suppression of criticism of the NRA." Further, Lippmann pointed out, the

secretary of the commission was in charge of obtaining broadcast
time for the Democrats in the campaign of 1932. To remedy
this impropriety, Lippmann said, would be easy, but removing
a partisan secretary would not solve radio's fundamental problem
of subtle dependence on whatever administration happened to
be in power. The only solution, Lippmann said, was to appoint
disinterested commissioners—"men of the kind qualified to be
head of a popular university or editor of an independent newspaper." To make stations completely independent of government,
he said, "would mean that the air was pre-empted for those who
could pay the highest price for it. That would be intolerable."
And government ownership of stations, he added, "though it
seems to work reasonably well in England, would be obnoxious
to American sentiment."[62]

The way the news was broadcast disturbed Lippmann. He
believed that, once radio discovered that its unique capacity was
to broadcast an eyewitness account of an event, there came a compulsion to make every report seem instantaneous. Praising H. V.
Kaltenborn and Raymond Gram Swing as exceptions, he deplored
the broadcasters "who threaten the listener in a hot, moist, and
fervent voice, conveying a mood of breathless alarm and mounting
danger." He also regarded radio's instantaneous ability to broadcast the news as inherently dangerous because of "the constant
temptation to announce news before it has been properly checked
and edited. The newspapers have to act quickly enough, but at
least they have some time between editions to think of what they
are doing . . ." He suggested that, except for news of transcendent
importance, there be only two news reports a day and that they
be recorded for delayed broadcasting so as to minimize the danger
of error.

Lippmann marveled at how well some of the commentators
who were on the air several times a day, talking about everything,
performed their tasks, but he said that radio must recognize that
"a sound product cannot be improvised." Sensitive, as he was
frequently, to the criticism that he and his fellow columnists wrote
too much about too many things, Lippmann said: "The radio
has perhaps been misled by the crew to which I now belong . . .
we write too much, and even when we have the good sense to
say nothing on a subject because we have nothing to say, we say
something about some other subject because it would be too much

trouble to explain to our readers that we are not dead, sick, assassinated, in jail or suppressed by the censor, if we omit an article when our minds are a blank."[63]

Despite the rather Olympian slope of most of his columns, Lippmann was capable of depreciating his work and its importance to the world. On departing for Europe in the summer of 1937, he said, "I have not the same confidence I once had in my capacity, or in that of most other men, to learn much that can be depended on in a few weeks of travel and interviews about the situation in Europe . . . I once heard Count Keyserling, who wrote *The Travel Diary of a Philosopher,* say that he needed only twenty-four hours in any civilization to perceive its ethos, [but] the Count not only was but knew that he was an exceptional man." Yet he himself, he added satirically, would be perfectly prepared to explain "the Situation in America" to his friends in Europe. After four of five days on the ship, "I shall have forgotten," he said, "all the differences of view among the people at home and there will have crystallized in my mind a description of the American Situation that will seem to me most illuminating when I expound it to foreigners." Columnists, he said, naming himself, Broun, Arthur Krock, Westbrook Pegler, Dorothy Thompson, Mark Sullivan, David Lawrence, and Eleanor Roosevelt, "have the reticence of magpies and the weight of the world on our shoulders."[64]

Lippmann's big book of the 1930's—he published five—was *An Inquiry into the Principles of the Good Society* (1937), which represented, he said, 20 years of thought devoted to the problem of reconciling capitalism with the extension of freedom. Since the beginning of World War I, he wrote, "the scheme of the future has been less clear to me. For more than twenty years I have found myself writing about critical events with no better guide to their meaning than the hastily improvised generalizations of a rather bewildered man . . . I was not able to find in any of the schools a working philosophy in which I could confidently come to rest . . . But gradually it became clearer to me why I could not make up my mind. It was that my personal confusion reflected the fact that in the modern world . . . those who seek to improve the lot of mankind believe they must undo the work of their predecessors . . . the programmes of reform are everywhere at odds with liberal tradition. Men are asked to choose between security and liberty . . ."

Security for most men could be achieved, Lippmann argued, without tainting the economic system with the arbitrary controls of collectivist planning. The collectivist in a democratic society, he said, was caught up in an insoluble contradiction, for a planned society required a design to which people will thereafter conform, and a democratic society requires that the plan shall change whenever a majority wills it. This is equivalent to saying, he contended, that in so far as democratic people "desire a planned economy they must suspend responsible government."[65]

The either-or-ishness of Lippmann's point of view—the insistence that planning precludes change, that the choice must be clear-cut between liberalism or government by "administrative demands from a ruling officialdom"—troubled some reviewers, including John Dewey. "For a writer who at times shows a wide acquaintance with the history of social thought," Dewey wrote, "he strangely identifies every form of socialism with state or governmental socialism, and hence with overhead control of the activities of groups and individuals by a bureaucratic officialdom."

Lippmann's liberalism, Dewey said, was social philosophy in a vacuum, calculated to give encouragement to reactionaries. It is all very well, Dewey said, to define the good society as one governed by law which regulates the equal and reciprocal rights and duties of individuals, but it is not very helpful, when the legal system fails to do this, to appeal to "higher law," "intuition," and "spiritual essence." "Anything that can justly be termed 'spiritual' in any intelligible sense of that word," Dewey said, "is the fruit, not the source, of the continual bettering of culture and civilization." And this improvement, Dewey added, is possible only when economic, political, and legal institutions foster civilized human relationships.[66]

Other writers disagreed with Dewey and praised Lippmann for his rejection of humanism and his affirmation that man's "immortal soul, which only God can judge," was the rock on which all freedom rested. Lippmann had come to recognize, Louis J. A. Mercier said, that "the foundation of true liberalism lies in God and religion; and bravely he issues a call to reconstruct on that rock a democratic philosophy to oppose the aggressive forces of atheistic naturalism."[67]

(When a magazine called *Humanist* conducted a questionnaire asking a score of writers whether they considered themselves nat-

uralistic humanists—Albert Schweitzer, Max Lerner, Sinclair
Lewis said "yes"; Bertrand Russell, Thomas Mann, Santayana,
and Lippmann equivocated. Professor Mercier's statement that
Lippmann had given up his naturalistic humanism in favor of
theistic humanism, Lippmann said, was based entirely on Mercier's
interpretation of *The Good Society*. "I should like to add," Lippmann
said, "that if there is any implication ... that I have recently
changed my views profoundly, that is not the case ...")[68]

Though it was true, Dewey said, that Lippmann suggested a
number of needed reforms—"reforms suspiciously similar to the
theory, if not the practice of the New Deal which he criticizes
as gradual collectivism"—he ignored the central problem. "I would
not have supposed," Dewey said, "that anyone, much less a person
as widely read as Mr. Lippmann, could have written a social and
economic analysis without reference to the main feature of the
present economic system, namely, that it is a profit system. Yet
Mr. Lippmann must be given credit for accomplishing this impossibility."

Other reviewers were equally unkind. Corliss Lamont said that
The Good Society represented "the definitive debacle of a mind
that was once most promising" and Max Lerner said that "the
intellectual world in which this book moves is arid, mechanical,
and in a final sense reactionary." But said Lerner: "The author
pleads his case with integrity ... Lippmann has not had to sell
out. He has been able to adhere to the ideals of his liberalism
and the idols of the market place at the same time, for the two
are good companions ... Mr. Lippmann is a rich man; his friends
are the possessors of the earth; he is their prophet and they find
in him, as possessors of the earth have for centuries found in
the liberalism of the right, a rationalization of their economic
claims and their political fears." Others than the rich took comfort
from Lippmann, too, Lerner concluded—"The professors and
editors and lawyers who want at the same time to preserve the
status quo and their self-respect."[69]

Lippmann's four other books of this decade included *Interpretations 1931–1932* and *Interpretations 1933–1935*, which were reprints
of selections of "Today and Tomorrow" columns edited by Allan
Nevins, his former associate on the *World*. Reviewing the first
of them, James Truslow Adams attempted to explain the "Lippmann phemomenon" — why he had "the largest public daily

[audience] of any publicist in the world." Lippmann's success, Adams said, stemmed from the fact that he did not amuse or soothe or write down to his readers, but in an unemotional, unbiased, intellectual fashion gave them the kind of explanation of the terrible complications of the day that relieved their bewilderment. Adams regarded Lippmann's work as an "asset of major importance" and saw in his popularity the possibility that "the scientific attitude of mind toward all our problems had permeated a larger section of the public mind than we had hitherto believed."

To William Allen White the Lippmann columns revealed a man who "writes with crystalline clarity because he thinks straight and thinks things through . . . His most characteristic quality is his intellectual integrity." Lippmann's following, White said, was not among "the smart and sophisticated, who love snappy phrases, wisecracks, sparkle and exhibition of literary jiujitsu. His following is among the leaders of America—business men, editorial writers, the rulers of cities and states, the 'satraps' of higher education and the literary world."[70]

Lippmann's other books of the 1930's were *The Method of Freedom* (1934) and *The New Imperative* (1935). The first consisted of the E. L. Godkin lectures which Lippmann delivered at Harvard and the second of a Phi Beta Kappa oration at Harvard and an article in the *Yale Review*.

For the Godkin lectures Lippmann used the ideas that he was developing for *The Good Society* and presented them in skeletal form. When the lectures were published they received the same sort of skeptical reviews which *The Good Society* later evoked. Clifton Fadiman regarded the book as the prescription for a classless society in which the plutocrats would mute their acquisitive instincts and the proletariat would derive ampler rewards for their labors. There was nothing wrong with this picture, Fadiman said. "The prollies are pleased because they get compensated right into the bourgeoisie. The plutes are pleased because Mr. Lippmann arranges for them to be bothered only *after* the prollies have been promoted, which may take a little time."[71]

Part of Lippmann's prescription was to add to man's basic rights the right of access to remunerative work, to be guaranteed if need be, by employment on public works projects. But, he was careful to add, "The operating principle should clearly be to pay wages which represent an adequate minimum . . . for a bare but

self-respecting existence ..." To provide more than this, Lippmann said, would discourage the citizen "to look for private
employment, or to go pioneering on his own initiative for a higher
standard of life."[72]

Lippmann was confident that the acquisitive psychology of the
19th Century was no longer rampant. "When they attain a middle-
class standard of life," he said, "the wants of most men are sated;
they do not have the tastes for spending a lot more money. To
earn it is not worth the trouble; to spend it is more trouble than
it seems ..." So the Good Society would be the Good Satiety,
in which neither the very rich nor the very poor would combine
in pressure groups to frustrate responsible government.[73]

Proletarianism or plutocracy, Lippmann said in *The New Imperative,* produced "the fatal diseases of concentrated power
and concentrated wealth." The alternative to being swallowed "by
an imperious state socialism," he said, was "to govern successfully
this capitalist democracy." And the way to do this, he concluded,
was to begin by recognizing that the ideal of laissez-faire was
dead.[74]

But the trouble with Lippmann, many of his critics said—and
in the 1930's he was subjected to more criticism, some of it brutal,
than during any other period in his career—was that he could
not bear to see practiced the doctrines that he preached, or, worse
yet, that having abandoned socialism he had forsaken liberalism
too.

Edmund Wilson, who was still starry-eyed about Russia, chided
Lippmann for talking "as if there were no important difference
between capitalist America and Communist Russia ... You must
take newspaper readers for very innocent persons—you must
assume that all your old audience of educated people has deserted
you—when you compare one of the foulest episodes of human
exploitation with the unprecedented opening of a regime which
is designed to make exploitation impossible." (Lippmann's folly
had been to say, in 1931, that it was too early to tell whether
the Russians had found a "magic device" for solving economic
problems that America had already solved.)

Lippmann had already exposed the orthodox God of the
churches, Wilson said, presumably referring to *A Preface to Morals.*
"But God was already old—he was a pushover. Today there are
more dangerous myths to be discredited. Modern capitalism, with

all the bogus ideals and intoxicating illusions with which it has bemused Americans, is a far more formidable fraud. Why not tell your countrymen about it . . . ?"[75]

Henrik Willem van Loon responded to this by saying that Lippmann was a pioneer who was trying to instruct American economic illiterates in their ABC's. "And I think," he said, "that if Mr. Wilson will study the articles written by the late Carl Marx of Dean Street, London, England, when he was correspondent of the New York *Tribune,* he will discover that the Great White Father himself somewhat tempered his style to the exigencies of the day." Wilson seemed to have forgotten, van Loon said, that "the illiterates of Park Avenue still regard a socialist . . . as a creature hiding a long spiked tail in his trousers' pocket and ready to blow the White House to pieces (Heaven forbid!) at the bidding of some mysterious black-bearded Monster, hidden in a dark cellar of a Moscow slum."[76]

In a series of four articles which he later told Lippmann he wished that he had not written, Amos Pinchot delivered the bitterest attack. Lippmann had been described by Beverly Smith in *American* magazine as "A man with a flashlight mind, the Great Elucidator." Pinchot chose "The Great Elucidator" for the title of the first of his articles in the *Nation,* and headed the third one "Obfuscator de Luxe."

Pinchot said that "once a votary in the House of Marx, our Elucidator now worships in the house of Morgan" serving as "a salesman of plutocracy." Lippmann's work, he said, conveyed only "the illusion of intellectuality," produced "largely by references to irrelevant authorities but partly by a good journalistic technique [which] causes him to be regarded by unthinking people as a seer whose lips are wet with water from the well of truth." Posing as a liberal, Pinchot said, Lippmann was neither liberal nor democratic, and the effect of his writings was "to counteract the efforts of the men and women of good-will who . . . are trying to check plutocracy's advance and bring into American life a saner division of power and a more decent distribution of wealth and opportunity."[77]

It was unjust, Pinchot said, "to criticize Lippmann for what his former associates refer to as his swing to the right . . . On the contrary, whatever his youthful opinions may have been in the remote days when he founded the Harvard Socialist Club in company with John Reed, his writings show that, despite his employment of the vocabulary and certain cliches of liberalism, he has been a conservative on major questions for the last twenty years. It is true that now and then, on moonlight nights, and especially during general elections, his conservatism may philander a little with liberalism . . . But it violates few of the proprieties, and invariably returns to its own chaste bed by midnight."

Pinchot conceded that Lippmann's style was smooth, but complained that it either served to camouflage banality of content or produced a residue of meaning which concealed the real intent. "While he does not tell us in so many words," Pinchot said, "that democracy should be abandoned . . . that is the unspoken conclusion. As usual [the reference here was to *Public Opinion* and *The Phantom Public*], Mr. Lippmann airs his talent for not saying the thing he implies . . . Thus, though Mr. Lippmann refuses to slay his democracy outright, his assault upon it is like the Chinese torture of a thousand cuts. While no single gash inflicted by our writer is fatal in itself, the sum total leaves democracy little more than a bleeding stump."

Summing up, Pinchot said: "Mr. Lippmann has, I think, done an immense amount of harm. He has confused the thinking of his readers. He has confirmed them in unconscious Bourbonism. He has written persuasively against democracy, and persuasively for plutocracy, which, however, he has not described . . . He has told his readers what they want to be told, offering complacency instead of truth. And it is regrettable. For Walter Lippmann with his active mind, his great talent, his industry, and his brilliant style, might have been a rain that would have helped freshen the streams of American thought."[78]

Others took Lippmann to task for what they considered to be sins of commission or omission. Ernest Sutherland Bates wrote of him: "Whatever he says today, one may be sure that he will say the opposite tomorrow. Whenever he prophesies a certain result, one may confidently expect the contrary." Bates said that though Lippmann's admirers argued that he changed only as events changed, they neglected to add that he never confessed to being wrong except on minor matters. Bates said that Broun told him, "When Walter wants to change his mind he goes into his study and pulls down all the shades so that no one can see in."[79] Although the critics used different epithets—Humpty

Dumpty, Tight-wire Artist, Juggler, Self-Deceiver, Purveyor of Pablum, Jingoist, Snob—the theme was the same: that a slick style permeated with fake erudition concealed a superficial content, and the residue, however meager, invariably turned out to be reactionary. Attempting to explain the lack of originality or profundity in the columns and in the later books, Silas Bent, a former New York *Times* writer, wrote that it might be because Lippmann had said as a young man all that he had to say, and "had got to the top of the egg and naturally slid down the other side."[80]

Publicized as no other journalist was, Lippmann imperturbably continued to produce at least four columns a week, make commencement speeches and receive honorary degrees, write for magazines, and work always on the new book that was invariably in preparation. In the New York days, before he moved to Washington in 1938, he worked in a penthouse studio on the roof of his house at 245 East 61st Street. The room was sound proofed (his aversion to noise was almost as strenuous as the great Pulitzer's), and the windows were far above his head so that he could not be distracted by the view.

Work on the column began about 8:30 a.m., and the 1,200 words were written in about two hours. The text, composed in longhand in a ragged, miniscule scrawl, was delivered by messenger for his secretary in her office on the 11th floor of the *Herald Tribune* building to type. Rarely did the unconventional handwriting lead to mistakes in transcription, but once a headline which should have read "Mr. Nelson's Future" appeared in print from coast to coast as "Mr. Nelson's Failure."[81]

By the end of the decade, "Today and Tomorrow" was appearing in 184 newspapers with an aggregate of 7,147,000 subscribers. In a *Fortune* survey of the popularity of columnists, Lippmann ranked fourth. Winchell, Dorothy Thompson, and Boake Carter, who was widely known as a broadcaster, had larger followings. Winchell recruited his readers from the lower middle-class and the poor. Lippmann was admired most by the prosperous. Poor people liked him least, perhaps because they recognized him as a scotch rather than a beer type and because they could not afford the luxury, as Kenneth Fearing phrased it in a poem, of being "soothed by Walter Lippmann and sustained by Haig & Haig."[82]

Chapter V

U.S. FOREIGN POLICY,
AND THE
PERILS OF PROPAGANDA

IN THE 1940 PRESIDENTIAL CAMPAIGN LIPPMANN DID NOT ANNOUNCE a preference for Wendell Willkie or for Roosevelt. He felt at the time, he said later, that much more important issues were impending than the choice between two men to be President of the United States.[1] Lippmann's views about the war in Europe, like the views of millions of Americans, had vacillated during the rearming of Germany, the agreement at Munich, and the conquest of France. In a remarkable article in 1933, speaking of the danger that the Nazis might go to war, he wrote: "How great this danger is no one can be certain, for no one can be quite certain as to just how far the hysteria will run. The hope that it will not run to the point of an explosion on the frontiers would seem to rest on two things: the strength of the French army and the persecution of the Jews . . . the persecution of the Jews, by satisfying the lust of the Nazis . . . is a kind of lightning rod which protects Europe . . . It may serve as a temporary substitute for the glorious victories . . . that Herr Hitler has promised his followers." Lippmann's use of the word "temporary" may have been egregious, but it was prophetic.[2]

In 1935 he wrote that "our best course is to stand apart from European policies . . . By proceeding with our own social reconstruction we can, by its example, hearten the supporters of freedom and peace throughout the world."[3] The belief that if war could be postponed for a few years it might be prevented altogether consoled him, but he advocated American rearmament, particularly a big increase in the size of the navy. When the war came in 1939 he drew comfort from the hope that it might be localized in Europe and that the United States might preserve its neutrality. But, he emphasized, it should be armed neutrality and should not prevent the sale of United States armaments to France and Britain. This loophole, he insisted, was necessary, because if France and Britain fell and aggressors reached out into the two oceans, America would then be vulnerable as never before.[4]

Yet his belief that America could be spared involvement was faltering. In the spring of 1939 he wrote: "If there is another world war . . . it will be fought on every continent and in every ocean." The longing to be isolated, the fear that it was impossible, the reliance on rearmament, Lippmann shared with a majority of Americans and with members of the Congress. The Gallup and *Fortune* polls, he pointed out, "have shown a rapidly growing belief that if war broke out, the United States would be unable to remain securely isolated." And the polls were confirmed, he added, by overwhelming votes in Congress to expand armaments.[5]

After Munich, Lippmann said, American sentiment had changed dramatically. First there was a revulsion against the appeasers and a rebirth of the post-World War I conviction that all European powers were immoral, and then, when France and Britain displayed a determination to resist Hitler, a new conviction that morality was on their side. "Where the issue between nations is not a moral issue the Americans are . . . very pacifist," Lippmann said. "But they are not at all pacifist when they feel that something morally vital is at stake in a specific war. The frontier spirit remains, and Americans are, once they are exasperated, very quick on the trigger."[6]

By the time that Roosevelt made his position clear, curiously enough by saying that an editorial in the anti-New Deal Washington *Post* exactly expressed his views, support for his foreign policy was coming from newspapers which had opposed the New Deal and opposition from those which had endorsed it. In addition to the *Post*, the *Herald Tribune* and the New York *Sun* were interventionist, and the New York *News* and *Evening Post* were strongly opposed to aid to Britain and France. The big name columnists, whose opinions were supposedly more influential that those of editorial writers, were divided. Eleanor Roosevelt, whose column

"My Day" was available to nearly five million readers, opposed neutrality, and so did Mark Sullivan and Dorothy Thompson. Broun, Raymond Clapper, and David Lawrence were more cautious. Westbrook Pegler, saying that he was speaking "for the people, who had not been consulted," wrote that if France and Britain had to fight another war that would be "just their hard luck." Boake Carter, Winchell, and General Hugh Johnson, who had administered the NRA and then had become an anti-New Deal columnist, were with Pegler. The Washington *Post* editorial which the President said expressed his position asserted that America must if need be help crush Germany and Italy on the battlefield.[7]

In March and April of 1940, while the war in Europe was being described as "phony," Lippmann visited England and the continent and became convinced of the possibility of an Axis victory. On his return to Washington he began to plead insistently for the reorganization of industry, for the building of new shipyards, airplane factories, and munitions plants. "What those facilities can produce immediately we should sell to the Allies. With those weapons they may be able to withstand the attack."[8] Oswald Garrison Villard, never a warm admirer of Lippmann, wrote that "Walter Lippmann has got the jitters again." In advocating a totally militarized state, Villard said, Lippmann would "destroy democracy in order to defend it." When the war came, Villard said, Lippmann and others cried for rearmament at any cost. "They forgot all their horror over Franklin Roosevelt's unbalanced budget, their bitter indignation..." Lippmann, he concluded, had nothing to "contribute to the defense problem of the United States except mere emotion and an incredible ignorance of military affairs..."[9] Dorothy Thompson and Lippmann visited Bernard Berenson in Florence in the winter of 1939–40. Nicky Mariano, Berenson's secretary, said that Miss Thompson's information about the war turned out to be "amazingly exact," but Lippmann, she added, "was still a firm believer in the solidity of the Maginot Line."[10]

Two of Lippmann's criticisms of the national defense program evoked official replies. When Lippmann charged in August of 1940 that "politicians and bureaucrats have not yet seriously begun to put national defense above all other considerations," Frank Knox, the Secretary of the Navy, said, "There is some truth in the charges made by Mr. Lippmann. But this does not mean that progress has not been made. Knox promised "to leave no stone unturned to speed up wherever it is possible to do so."[11]

The second Lippmann criticism, to which the government responded after it was repeated in a column by Westbrook Pegler, produced a counter-charge of "gross exaggeration." Pegler reported that Lippmann had said, after a trip to San Francisco in February of 1942, that "the Pacific Coast was in imminent danger of attack and that communication was taking place between the shoreline and enemy agents at sea." Thomas C. Clark, enemy alien control coordinator for the West Coast, labeled the reports of signalling as rumors and suggested that Lippmann give the source of his information. He denied that there was danger of invasion, and said, "If Mr. Lippmann wants to make California a ghost state he can keep on writing stories like that ..."

But Clark conceded that under the circumstances—Japanese submarines had attacked coastal shipping and the F.B.I. had seized signalling devices from Japanese aliens—no chances would be taken. Consequently he recommended to the Attorney General that Japanese citizens as well as aliens be relocated in the interior of the state.[12]

After the "phony war" was over, and France fell, Lippmann wrote what was for him an unusually savage column attacking the isolationists for waking up too late and for failing to see that the Lippmann view of the world since 1917 was the correct one. Singling out Ernest Lindley, the *Newsweek* columnist, and the current editors of the *New Republic*, who, he said had been trying to prove that its founders [Croly, Weyl, Lippmann] were misguided fools, Lippmann said that the generation between the two World Wars had been "duped by a falsification of American history."

That generation, Lippmann said, was supposed to be "too realistic and too sophisticated to be bamboozled by any idea which is not directly concerned with the physical security and economic well-being of the American people. For twenty years they have specialized in making themselves hard-boiled, buncombeproof, antiseptic to flag waving, deaf to the bugles ... They have been miseducated by a swarm of innocent but ignorant historians, by reckless demagogues and by foreign interests, into believing that America entered the other war because of British propaganda, the loans of bankers, the machinations of President Wilson's advisers, and a drummed up patriotic ecstasy. They have been taught to believe that anyone who challenges this explanation of 1917 and insists that America was defending vital American interests is himself a victim or an agent of British propaganda."

America got into the first World War for the same reason that it must prepare for the second—to protect its own vital interests, Lippmann said. As one of the editors of the *New Republic* in 1917, he said, he knew "at first hand what was in President Wilson's mind," and paramount was the threat to the safety of the Atlantic highway and the danger of "a German-Russian-Japanese coalition against the Atlantic world." To the charge that in regarding the maintenance of British sea power as a vital American interest Wilson himself was a victim of British propaganda, Lippmann replied that "those who say this are merely betraying their abysmal ignorance of American history." Was Thomas Jefferson, who supported two American wars against England, also a victim of British propaganda when he supported the negotiations with England that led to the Monroe Doctrine? Lippmann asked. Lindley and other isolationists who had just become converts to the idea that British sea power was vital to American interests were not the victims of propaganda either, Lippmann said. They were merely beginning to see "what Wilson saw twenty-five years ago and what Jefferson and Madison and Monroe saw more than a hundred years ago . . ."[13]

When the presidential campaign of 1940 began, Lippmann urged the nomination of Wendell Willkie so that the Republicans might repudiate their "appalling record of indifference, complacency, unpreparedness and of unconscionable appeal to laziness and ignorance." Governor Dewey and Senator Taft, he said, were tied to the indefensible record and must try to defend it. "Mr. Dewey . . . is always more concerned with taking the popular position than he is in dealing with the real issue," Lippmann said. Taft, he regarded as "so sunk in complacency that in the days after the Nazi breakthrough at Sedan, he expressed his regrets publicly that the American people were more interested in the war news on the first three pages than in his criticism of the W.P.A. on page nine."

Equating Dewey with Premier Edouard Daladier and Taft with Prime Minister Neville Chamberlain but saying that the

Frenchman and the Englishman were "far abler men," Lippmann said, "With politicians of this sort to lead them democracy could not survive in Europe. Nor will it here." (Dewey, it will be remembered, later developed, according to Lippmann's view, such capabilities that he was the columnist's choice over Truman in 1948. Taft, of course, was no match for Eisenhower in 1952.)[14]

When the Republicans convened in Philadelphia in June of 1940, Lippmann derided the efforts of the "word manipulators" who were drafting the platform. He said that "the tide of events is so strong and swift that in ten days there will not be five hundred persons in the world who will still be able to remember the formulae that are being painfully contrived in the hotel rooms of Philadelphia." Instead of giving thought to foreign affairs, he said, they were thinking only "of how a *plank* on foreign affairs could be used to defeat Willkie."[15]

After Willkie was nominated, Lippmann continued to berate the "old guard" and the "old manipulators." In a savage paraphrase of the platform, stripping it of "the rhetoric in which it was swaddled," Lippmann said: "This was their platform . . . The Republican party promises to end unemployment, to make the farmers prosperous, and to increase the productivity of the nation by not doing many of the undesirable things that the New Deal has done. It will also arm the country in a world where, so far as the party is concerned, the total victory of the totalitarian states is to be accepted as an accomplished fact . . . By refraining from making the mistakes of the New Deal, the party will enable the nation to have its cake and eat it too. The party will provide both guns and butter, a great fleet and a great air force and a big army along with high wages, high prices, good profits, and no such nonsense as universal service."

Then, after mentioning the protection afforded by the Atlantic Ocean, the need not to say "too many unpleasant things about Hitler," "to exclude the imports produced by the regimented serfs of Europe," "to continue, nevertheless to do business with totalitarian Europe," Lippmann concluded his paraphrase of the platform: "Finally, we are idealists, not starry-eyed idealists but nevertheless idealists. Therefore, though we regard ourselves as too weak to help the Allies, and are even afraid to mention them by name, when they are safely defeated we shall, as Mr. Hoover pointed out, invite ourselves to Hitler's peace conference and there we shall persuade him to be kind, there we shall use our enormous and uncontaminated moral influence, to save free men from destruction."[16]

Willkie, Lippmann said, was under no political obligation to adhere to this nonsense of the old guard. Furthermore, he added, by nominating Willkie the Republicans ensured for the nation a bipartisan policy on foreign affairs and national defense and hence removed the only reason for Roosevelt to break with tradition and seek a third term. "Now it is no longer necessary for Mr. Roosevelt to accept the nomination . . . no one can now pretend that Mr. Roosevelt is the only presidential candidate who understands the national interest and is determined to organize the country to protect its national interests." Lippmann tried to appeal to Roosevelt's patriotism. The Republicans had been patriotic, he said, in rejecting Taft and Dewey, who would have made foreign policy a partisan issue. "The shoe is now on the other foot . . . it would now be unpatriotic for the Democrats to disrupt the country by a useless and destructive conflict over a third term." The logic of this argument would be clear to Roosevelt, Lippmann predicted, and "as a matter of principle and of personal inclination he will choose not to run again."[17]

After Roosevelt was renominated at the Chicago convention, Lippmann explained the situation to his readers by saying that the rush of events in the outside world had forced the Republicans to choose a candidate who had just joined the party and had forced the Democrats to scrap the no-third-term tradition. "Both Mr. Willkie and Mr. Roosevelt were nominated because they were the men who most obviously and clearly represented the profound sense of the American people that they are facing one of the very greatest crises in their history . . . and that is why both conventions did such inconceivable and impossible things."[18]

Lippmann's enthusiasm for Willkie ebbed as the campaign progressed. The Republicans in the Senate, led by Willkie's running mate, Charles T. McNary, and the Republicans in the House, led by Joseph Martin, continued, both by speaking and by voting, to oppose legislation designed to strengthen national defense. This led Lippmann to the conclusion that Willkie was floundering. "For if he is unable to lead his own party and has quarreled with the other one as well, just how is he going to translate into reality all his excellent personal pledges, hopes, and ideals?" Lippmann asked. The Gallup polls, he said, confirmed the impression that the campaign had faltered, and it was impossible not to conclude that the first two months of the effort "have not been worse than wasted." Willkie, he complained, had been "remote from the scene of action, reserved on the great controversial issues, and personally isolated from the critical decisions which are shaping the destiny of the country."

To Lippmann, whose very life was the production of words, Willkie's mistake was that he thought he could win by words alone. Lippmann said that "this is not a talking contest and words have no credit unless they are issued against a reserve of acts. Mr. Willkie has not yet done anything."[19]

The two big calumnies of the campaign—the Democratic effort to label Willkie "appeaser," and the Republican attempt to tag Roosevelt as "warmonger"—Lippmann found frightful, and he deplored especially Willkie's joining in the charge that Roosevelt's pledge to work for peace was not to be trusted.

On November 5, 1940, just before the election, Lippmann publicly chided two of his fellow columnists—he rarely engaged in debate in print with anyone—for what he considered the excesses of their zeal and their failure to remember the enduring strength of democracy. Mark Sullivan had been contending that the re-election of Roosevelt would destroy democracy and Dorothy Thompson had been writing that only Roosevelt could save it. Sullivan was especially irritated with Miss Thompson, who had been an anti-New Dealer, for changing her mind, and he quoted her own words against her.

Nowhere in the world, Lippmann told them, had a democracy ever voted itself into totalitarianism; always it had been imposed by force. Both of his journalistic neighbors, Lippmann said, had forgotten this, and had assumed that mere "ideological tendencies" which Sullivan discerned in the Democratic party and Thompson in the Republican party would lead to dictatorship. Reminding Sullivan that a free press had prevented Roosevelt from "packing" the Supreme Court, and telling Thompson that she was helping to create an atmosphere of "debilitating nervous anxiety," Lippmann said that no matter which candidate won, the nation, as always, would rally to him and would "deal with all the tendencies and ideologies that present themselves."[20]

Immediately after the election Lippmann wrote that a great

opportunity seldom comes twice for the same man to grasp, but it had come again to Roosevelt—the opportunity to unite the diverse people of a powerful democracy. In 1936 Roosevelt had had a chance to do this, Lippmann said, but tossed it away and instead produced dangerous disunity by his attack on the Supreme Court. The President must not again, Lippmann warned, regard his re-election as a mandate given to a party leader, but rather must make unification for national defense the test of all his actions.

Lippmann was unperturbed about the breaking of the two-term tradition, pointing out that the people had never been willing to accept any of the innumerable proposals to write a no-third-term prohibition into the Constitution. "They have decided," he said, "that the living generation . . . in the situation which it faces and in the situation which no previous generation may be able freely to anticipate must remain free to decide for itself whether it wishes to make an exception . . ."[21] (The rule having once been broken, the people decided by favoring ratification of the 22nd Amendment that it should not be broken again.)

The unity which Lippmann seemed to believe that Roosevelt could have for the asking did not ensue, because the charge of warmongering continued to be made against the President and his cabinet, and made by important people: Landon, Hoover, Colonel Lindbergh, Senator Burton Wheeler. Lippmann urged that debate on the issue of whether the warmongers were the leaders in Washington or the leaders in Berlin and Tokyo be conducted more responsibly.

"If free speech is not to degenerate into mere shouting and name-calling, we shall have to define this issue and debate it," Lippmann said. "For the right of every one to say anything he pleases is only the beginning, and it is not the end of freedom of speech. The end and purpose of free speech is to arrive at the truth by a meeting of minds in open debate."

What America and the world were listening to, he said, was not debate but "a collision of vehemently uttered opinions." Deploring "mere loud speaking, mere public uttering, mere broadcasting and declaiming," he said the rival contentions must be "brought down to truth and reality by cross-examination and debate."[22] As the controversy persisted, Lippmann desperately suggested that Roosevelt end it by declaring a full state of national emergency to put a stop to the futile debate and to partisan politics.[23]

Reiterating one of his favorite themes—that it is idiocy to think that public opinion should determine national policy, he said, "The notion that public opinion can and will decide all issues is in appearance very democratic. In practice it undermines and destroys democratic government... It is not in fact possible for all the people to know all about all things, and the pretense that they can and that they do is a bad illusion."

Effective government could not be conducted, he said, by officials who ask themselves "What does the Gallup poll say?" and "What does the fan mail say?" and "How do the editors and commentators line up?" The people could not know, not even "the most conscientious newspaper reporters" could know the complexities and intricacies of the problems caused by the war. But the country, he said, "is full of argumentative committees and sincere men and women who think they know enough to know what should be done. I do not know why they think they know enough. For having studied most of the information which is publicly available and talked with a great many more people who have some first-hand knowledge of the facts, all I know is that I do not know enough to have an opinion."[24] (Making allowances for modesty, and the truth, in principle, of his professed ignorance, one still might marvel that Lippmann not only formed opinions but expressed them nearly every day.)

Lippmann's doubts about his own competence to make correct judgments in the area of foreign affairs were again expressed in one of the books he published in the 1940's—*United States Foreign Policy.* He said he realized that "with the advantages of hindsight I am criticizing others for holding views which at the time I may myself have shared, or for a lack of foresight of which I was also guilty." In retrospect, for example, he said, he was aghast at his own folly in writing dozens of editorials for the New York *World* favoring naval disarmament. "I was too weak-minded to take a stand ... In fact I followed the fashion ... and celebrated the disaster as a triumph and denounced the admirals who dared to protest."[25]

Though he believed that the Great Beast, amongst whose hordes he sometimes deferentially included himself, was incapable of charting a day-by-day course to follow, it still needed, Lippmann felt, rudimentary information about the prevailing winds, and this, for reasons good and bad, often was unavailable during the war. Soon after the Japanese attack on Pearl Harbor, Lippmann attended a White House press conference and wrote: "Much better ways will have to be worked out if the American people are to exercise their inalienable right to understand the war."

The day of the conference, in January 1942, was a day of big news—the report of the Pearl Harbor losses, American troops landing in North Ireland, MacArthur fighting in Luzon, German submarines raiding along the Atlantic Coast. And yet, Lippmann said, when he and the others lined up around the President's desk, Roosevelt told them, in effect, that he had nothing important to say.

"Half a dozen of the newspapermen," Lippmann wrote, "asked him questions bearing directly upon the big news items of the day. None of them got anything which could be described as responsive. They made as much progress as a man trying to climb a greased flagpole, and I do not think I was the only one who left the White House feeling frustrated and dispirited, not wiser for the trouble of attending the press conference but much sadder."

The trouble, Lippmann said, was that the President had forgotten the purpose of the press conference, which was to explain the news, not to hand it out. "The difference between news and explanation," he wrote, "seems to me not to have been grasped in war-time Washington. I believe this is the fundamental reason why the nation finds itself fighting a war without understanding it. Sooner or later the cry is going to go up that it is the fault of the censor . . . But it is not the fault of the censor; there is plenty of news. The trouble is that there is no continuing and patient explanation of the news."

People were troubled, for example, Lippmann said, by the sending of troops to Ireland rather than rushing reinforcements to MacArthur, by the failure to concentrate the entire fleet in the Pacific. To explain the reasons would involve no military secrets unknown to the enemy or to anybody who took the trouble to figure them out, Lippmann said. "But the fact is that most people do not figure it out for themselves, and there are demagogues and agitators who are quick to exploit and bedevil the innocence of the people . . ." Only the President himself and his Secretaries of State, War, and Navy could tell the authoritative story which would ease the bewilderment, Lippmann said. "They ought to be telling it, the good with the bad . . . The people can take it . . ."[26]

In the early months of the war, Lippmann believed that the government's publicity services were a failure, because a lack of candor produced a lack of trust, because the President failed to define clearly the authority and responsibility of the heads of the new civilian war agencies, and because there was too much reliance generally on public relations experts who used big words to conceal the absence of effective deeds.

Whatever the cause, the relationship between the President and the press deteriorated, and by October of 1942 Lippmann felt compelled to urge Roosevelt "to clarify his ideas about the relations in this war between the government and the independent press. For it is painfully clear that he is so much annoyed with so many of us that his displeasure, like the rain, falls equally upon the just and upon the unjust."

The source of the difficulty, Lippmann said he suspected, was the absence of a loyal opposition whose leader, privy to all the secrets, could offer responsible, constructive criticism of the war effort. (A little later Lippmann endorsed a resolution by Estes Kefauver, then a representative from Tennessee, that the government in effect adopt the "question period" procedure of the British House of Commons and have the members of the President's Cabinet appear regularly before Congress to answer oral and written questions. Lippmann also found interesting a proposal by Thomas K. Finletter that the President and Congress create a Joint Executive-Legislative Cabinet, composed, in equal numbers, of the members of the President's Cabinet and the chairmen of Congressional Committees. Another suggestion of Mr. Finletter, that the President, in a time of protracted stalemate with the legislative branch, be permitted to dissolve Congress and call a general election, Lippmann regarded dubiously, though, he said, the time might come when it deserved serious consideration.)[27]

But with little well-informed criticism within government —Lippmann conceded that a few Congressmen occasionally had been good critics of some phases of the war—the press had to serve as substitute, with reporters, editors, and commentators bearing almost the whole burden. "Of course, as the President keeps telling them," Lippmann said, "they do not know nearly so much about everything as he knows . . . and that must be very annoying and not at all the way things ought to be in a more perfect world."

Much of the criticism to which the administration had been subjected was uninformed and sometimes even malicious, Lippmann said, but the President, however great his vision and initiative, was capable of making all the immense decisions required of him only with the help of a critical opposition. "The time could come," Lippmann said, "when Mr. Roosevelt could wish that, instead of resenting the critics, he had responded to such grains of truth as may be found in all their chaff."[28]

During the first months of the war Lippmann felt that the government's information program was ineffective. When there was nothing but bad news to report "the government flinched and then handled the bad news badly," he said, and thereby created what in much later days was called a credibility gap. It was true, he said in June of 1942, that the full extent of the damage at Pearl Harbor and the disaster in the Philippines could not at first be disclosed without aiding the enemy, but the attempts "to discount the somber reality of the opening phase of the war by magnifying and ballyhooing small tactical successes" were, he believed, unfortunate. To restore credibility, he urged "a candid disclosure of the defeats we suffered, of the perils we faced . . ."

The work of Elmer Davis, who directed the Office of War Information, of Archibald MacLeish, who headed the Office of Facts and Figures, and the other heads of the new agencies was needlessly impeded, Lippmann believed, by the President's failure to shelter them within his cabinet and thus give them firm protection and authority. How could MacLeish or Davis, whose authority rested "on vague executive orders and on personal contact with the President, . . . edit and vet the speeches of those who outranked them?" Lippmann asked. A babel of voices was predictable and the babel arose, he said. "We shall, I suppose, muddle through," he concluded. "But if we do, it will be because the press, understanding the plight of the orphaned experts, takes them under its protection and sees them through their ordeal."[29]

On the subject of governmental publicity in general, Lippmann felt obliged, as he put it, to get "something off my chest." There was growing distrust of public relations experts, he said, due to the fact that they operate on a theory which is inherently insincere. A people at war, facing "the issues of life and death," found this insincerity, he said, becoming more and more repugnant. The insincerity stemmed from the assumption, he said, "that the public aspect of a person can be fabricated by men who have specialized in the art of manipulating public opinion."

To be specific, he said, "let us consider the extraordinary and, to my old-fashioned mind, the astounding thing that now happens when the announcement is made that the President will deliver an important address. The papers report that a number of professional writers, men not responsible for shaping or carrying out the policies he will discuss, are gathering at the White House to write the words the President will utter." Indisputably, he said, the President needed help in preparing speeches, but the help should come, as it had in the earlier days of the New Deal, from his official family and not from outside ghost writers. The style of the President's recent speeches, he said, had been synthetic. "It does not require training as a literary critic for the people to feel this and to be put off by it." A public man, he said, need not be "bright, clever, ingenious, entertaining, eloquent or even grammatical." Lacking sincerity, he said, all was lacking. And then, speaking, it may seem to some, quite unprophetically, he said that the people "will not stomach a fabricated, manipulated, synthetic public mask covering the faces of their leaders."[30]

(Although he was averse to outsiders helping to formulate or draft policy statements, Lippmann had taken part in preparing an official interpretation of the American position during the London Economic Conference of 1933. In a column which Roosevelt read, Lippmann carefully argued the proposition that the United States abandon the gold standard in order to stimulate recovery from the depression. The President and his advisers had been debating the problem for months, and on the evening of April 18, 1933, the day the column appeared, Roosevelt, in a dramatic meeting at the White House, announced that he had made up his mind to devalue the dollar.

(The conference in London, which had been planned during the Hoover Administration, after Great Britain left the gold standard in 1931, gave the adherents of a return to gold, a chance, as they saw it, to "save Western civilization" from financial chaos. The American delegation to the conference was a mishmash, ranging from the Secretary of State to a Texas oilman. Raymond Moley, assistant Secretary of State, persuaded Roosevelt that Herbert Swope, who had acquired a sudden interest in currency stabilization, should go along, and presumably it was the presence of Swope, his former *World* colleague, that led to Lippmann's involvement.

(When the conference bogged down over proposals to fix the ratio of the dollar to the pound and the franc, Roosevelt sent a message denouncing the "old fetishes of so-called international bankers," and urged the conferees of the sixty-six nations involved to get on with "the larger purposes" of curing basic economic ills. The message was described as a "bombshell" and a "torpedo." The Manchester *Guardian* called it "A Manifesto of Anarchy," and King George V accused Roosevelt of wrecking the conference.

(With the hope of mollifying those whose personal and national esteem was affronted, Moley called in Lippmann, Swope, and Keynes—Keynes and Churchill both praised the message—to try to compose a conciliatory interpretation of what Roosevelt said. They worked until 3:30 in the morning, with Swope at the typewriter, on what was called "an urbane and masterly rendition of the new American policy.")[31]

Synthetic news—"soft publicity" as he called it—as well as synthetic speeches was an aggravation which the public ought not to have to endure, Lippmann believed. It was one thing to defend suppression of bad news and unpalatable fact on the basis of military censorship, Lippmann said; concealment to protect mediocrity and incompetence was quite another. The nation must be assured, he said, "that behind the curtain of secrecy" men were being held accountable for their mistakes. When the President delivered a radio address ridiculing armchair strategists who wanted to direct the course of the war, Lippmann said he evaded the real issue. "The President was everlastingly right," he said, "in insisting that these [military] decisions cannot and must not be made under the prodding of civilians." But what Roosevelt failed to distinguish was the difference between criticism of military activity before and after the event, Lippmann said. After operations were concluded, well or badly, public and press had a right to know about them, to criticize them, and to be confident that those who conducted them were held fully accountable for their decisions, Lippmann said, and concluded that "the assurance that all this would give is not present today . . . ."[32]

It would be a long war, Lippmann said, and the longer it lasted "the more important it will be to see to it that the press and the radio are able to keep the people informed about matters like rationing, price and wage fixing, the draft, taxes, salvage, priorities and allocations which touch directly the daily lives of everyone." In these areas censorship ordinarily should not play a part, he said, and though there was a twilight zone between civilian and military affairs—for example, facts about the nation's oil supply—the government's problem was "not how to conceal a few facts but how to explain the whole situation."

And then, paraphrasing the distinction that he had made twenty years earlier between news and truth, he said: "My own impression is that in the civilian field the government has fixed its attention on spot news to the neglect of the difficult business of enabling the newspapermen who must inform the public to inform them-selves . . . The government has never realized fully what every working newspaperman knows—that newspapers are not pro-duced by telegraphing official announcements to be set up by printing presses." The fragmentary facts need context, he said, adding that "news in the narrow sense of the term is like the visible part of an iceberg, which, in fact, is nine-tenths under water; a free press as distinguished from a government bulletin board cannot do its part unless newspapermen . . . have a substan-tial working knowledge of the iceberg under the water."

The solution to the problem, he suggested, would be for officials in charge of new policies, like rationing, for example, to prepare "comprehensive briefs" for newspapermen, and then, several days later, hold press conferences in which intelligent questions could be asked and answered.[33]

With respect to war plans, Lippmann believed that secrecy should be as tight as possible and that, if need be, deliberate confusion should be created about them. The risk of inadvertent disclosure in the press or on radio of something that the writer or speaker did not even know he knew troubled him. What was being published in England and in the United States was almost instantly available to the enemy, whose problem, Lippmann said, was "to watch warily for the unconscious disclosures and inspired guesses," and he warned that "an American writer or editor is not merely matching wits with the American public but with the smartest officer on the German or Japanese general staff."

American diplomats, admirals, and generals were not, of course, taking the press into their confidence, and the enemy realized this, Lippmann said; but public discussion of possible war plans was dangerous nevertheless because the writer "may see nothing in what is written, but all that matters is what one intelligence officer may see in it." He recalled that Churchill had said, speaking of the British expedition to Madagascar in 1942, that he "felt a shiver every time I saw the word Madagascar in the newspapers."

Perfect secrecy for a great military operation was impossible even in a totalitarian state, Lippmann said, because so many persons had to be involved in it; but Hitler and the Japanese had still managed to achieve the element of surprise by creating confusion, planting information and spreading rumors composed of truths, half-truths, and falsehoods. Lippmann suggested that this was also "the only method of concealment for free and talkative countries like Britain and America . . . For when you cannot black out the target you may have to blind the enemy with too many colored lights."[34]

Next best to knowing the whole story, Lippmann said, is realizing that one does not know it, and the temptation, though almost irresistible, to appear to be knowledgeable in spite of the absence of relevant facts still ought to be resisted. "A very considerable part of the mischief and rumor that are brewed in Washington," he said, "comes from not wishing to spoil a cocktail party by confessing to the inquiring lady that General Marshall has not consulted you about our war plans and that you do not receive carbon copies of the messages exchanged by Stalin, Churchill and Roosevelt."

Military factors, especially in American relations with Russia, controlled almost everything, Lippmann said, and in the absence of information about them it was foolish to base a story upon "ideological and political theories which are a dime a dozen." Future relations with Russia, he said in the Fall of 1943, would be determined by "the time when and the manner in which the war is concluded."[35] One of the proposals for post-war agreements was that all nations adhering to the United Nations must guarantee in their own constitutions freedom of speech and information.

Lippmann agreed that this condition should be imposed and predicted that the Russians would approve of it.

"We need not be embarrassed in raising this question," he said,
"because our Russian ally, not to speak of certain of our other
allies, has not in practice had this freedom of the press. The
Russians themselves . . . in all their recent utterances, have shown
that they are not embarrassed by it. This must mean that having
consolidated the results of their revolution, and seeing the sure
prospect of an invincible security against their external enemies,
they do not fear the inauguration of those common liberties which
in the past the Russian national . . . has never enjoyed."[36]

Lippmann soon grew less confident about this. In *U.S. War
Aims,* published in 1944, he said that we must ask the Russians
to "give proof" that they will make "free, equal and reciprocal
the exchange of news and opinion . . ."

No nation should tell another how to edit its newspapers, Lippmann said, but without a reasonably free flow of information
among peoples there could be no effective collaboration of their
governments. And America should not pose to the rest of the
world as the apogee of perfect freedom of the press but should
seek to set an example, he said, by raising its own standards of
"competence, responsibility, fairness, objectivity, disinterestedness, and indeed of charity, chivalry and good humor . . ."[37]

(This was written on December 23, 1943. On April 14, 1968,
the New York *Times* reported that a capitalist newspaper was being
sold for the first time at Moscow newsstands. The paper, which
the *Times* described as a bourgeois German-language newspaper,
was the Swiss *Neue Zurcher Zeitung.* It was sold from under the
counter, only to foreigners, for 66 cents a copy, 20 times the
price of Soviet dailies. The *Times* also reported that Aeroflot, the
Soviet airline, was "reported to be toying with the daring idea
of distributing non-Communist newspapers to passengers on its
international flights.")[38]

Freedom of the press, Lippmann always believed, was not essentially impaired by closed meetings in which heads of states or
their representatives sought to negotiate agreements. But to bar
the press from big international conferences, which he believed
did more harm than good unless they were called to ratify decisions
reached in advance, was an absurdity, he said. When one of the
big war-time meetings at which all the United Nations were rep-

resented convened at Hot Springs to discuss food problems in 1943, Lippmann said that in excluding the press Roosevelt was attempting to have a mass meeting behave like a small executive committee. A secret mass meeting, he said, was an impossibility, because "it will leak news in all directions" and result in distortions which the presence of trained, responsible correspondents could prevent.[39]

The official leaking of propaganda disguised as news corrupted the press, Lippmann said, and he suggested that the American Society of Newspaper Editors investigate it and attempt to stop it. Taking as his topic a secret agreement made and then broken to exclude the British and followers of de Gaulle from assisting the American expedition to North Africa, Lippmann carefully explained how the propaganda apparatus worked.

"The mechanics of the propaganda," he wrote, "are these: access to the data about our French policy is under strict control, on the ground of military secrecy, in Algiers and in Washington. Then news and opinion is fed out in several different ways. It is fed out through reporters who in the ordinary routine of the newspaper profession publish the selected news and opinion, ascribing it to 'high officials, unimpeachable authorities,' etc., etc. Exciting tidbits are also fed out to the professional rumormongers. Finally a journalist of standing is selected, given special access to information; in return for this special privilege, information which has to come out because it can no longer be concealed, is presented to the public in a form most agreeable to those in authority."

Reporters who accept special privileges must pay for them, he said, by being agreeable, by "singing for their supper," by helping to manipulate public opinion. (The incident which Lippmann denounced was the publication in the *Saturday Evening Post* of an article by Demaree Bess, who was given access in North Africa by General Eisenhower to official files.) Other journalists, Lippmann said, had known about the deceitful agreement with General Giraud but had kept a discreet silence "because they hoped and believed that the embarrassment of the disclosure could be avoided. But now Mr. Bess has spilled the beans," and, he added, contributed to the official American propaganda against de Gaulle.

Lippmann absolved Eisenhower of blame, saying that he acted on instructions from Washington.[40] The same issue arose in cruder form when Eisenhower as President made available to Robert Donovan of the New York *Herald Tribune* minutes of cabinet meetings and other confidential papers of the executive branch. Journalists were quick to point out that this precedent opened "a Pandora's box" and that, having bared the files to a mere reporter, the Executive would find it hard to resist Congressional requests for similar records.[41] And in 1955 when Secretary Dulles released for general publication detailed proceedings of the Yalta Conference, Lippmann objected, saying that this "treats the intimate conversation of public men as if it were a part of the official diplomatic record. It is as if every diplomat should be required to travel around with a tape recorder attached to him."[42]

The private sale or publication of public papers was so outrageous that it should be made unlawful, Lippmann had said in 1938 when Roosevelt announced that he would compile his official papers in a series of books to be published by Random House and that excerpts would be published by *Liberty* magazine and by newspapers. The President's pledge that neither he nor Judge Samuel Rosenman, who was to do the compilation, would derive any personal profit from the publications did not unruffle Lippmann or other critics.

"The proper rule, it seems to me," Lippmann said, "is to enact a law declaring that all the papers of any official bearing in any way whatsoever on public issues are the property of the nation and that their sale or publication at any time, except under official auspices, is prohibited." And the law should be supplemented by custom, he added, which would make it as indecorous for the President to sell his papers or opinions as it would be to sell "oil or gunpowder" from the White House.

The press had a special interest in seeking some restraint, Lippmann said, for one of the volumes was to contain transcripts of press conferences. Would these include, Lippmann asked, "some very merry jokes at the expense of one correspondent or another? Out of respect for the office the jokes are all one-way jokes; no one ever really replies to the President's quips. Is it really possible that these one-way jokes are to be sold?"

The controversy over the sale of the public papers subsided a few months later when Roosevelt announced that he planned to use the proceeds as the nucleus of a fund to establish a national library at Hyde Park. And in the summer of 1939 Congress passed a bill to create the library. *The Public Papers and Addresses of Franklin D. Roosevelt* were compiled by Judge Rosenman and published in a series of thirteen volumes beginning in 1938 and concluding in 1950.[43]

Attempts to manipulate the news, often by casting friends in a good light and present or former foes in a bad one, were regrettable, Lippmann believed, but worse was the fact that the news almost inherently slanted itself in the direction of trouble and pessimism. "Every . . . newspaper man is like a doctor," he said. "He spends most of his time hearing from people who have a pain, and if he is not on guard he is likely to think that the entire country consists of people who have a pain in the neck." By definition, news consists of the extraordinary, he said, and, though the people who were without pain or grievance were in the majority, they went unnoticed. "The 10 per cent or so of the chiselers, operators of the black market, hand wringers and breast beaters, precisely because they are out of the ordinary, have to be reported as news . . . But somehow we have to keep in mind the fact that the behavior of the wise and the honest . . . must be reported and celebrated . . ."[44]

More troublesome still, Lippmann believed, was the fact that the millions of Americans engaged in the war in Europe not only were deprived of the confidence that good news from America would give them, but they were not getting any news at all. On a visit to Europe in November of 1944, Lippmann wrote that he had come to realize "how very nearly complete is the blackout of news from the United States. The British hear a little, very little, American news, the French none at all, and for all practical purposes the American Army is cut off from regular and intelligible information about what is happening, what is being said and thought, what is being decided and why, in the United States. Even our diplomatic officers abroad are like men marooned . . ." And he issued a dire warning that because American information services were so inadequate "we are making the future more difficult than it needs to be."[45]

Although he wrote that "a lot more . . . can and must be said on this subject," Lippmann did not return to it until after the war, and then only indirectly, by attacking official attempts "to sell America" to the world by propaganda, especially through the "Voice of America." He believed that the question of whether there should or could be a "Voice of America," especially in time of peace, had never been closely examined, and that to counter-attack foreign propaganda by "fighting fire with fire" was not necessarily the best or even a particularly good procedure. Even if a "Voice" were required, Lippmann argued, it should not be an official organ of the Department of State . . . "heard round the world singing songs, cracking jokes, entertaining the kiddies." What the State Department needed, he said, was not "a selling or an advertising agency, but an intelligence service . . . oriented inward and not outward . . ."

It was arguable, he said, that the government should facilitate, perhaps through the Federal Communications Commission, the broadcasting of news summaries to the rest of the world. "My own view is that the Voice of America to the outer world [generally] should be the voice of the President of the United States and the Secretary of State. But I do not believe that this country can conduct an official propaganda of ideology, doctrine, and opinion. For this country, being a truly free country, does not have any such thing as an official ideology, an official doctrine and an official set of opinions."[46]

Official misunderstanding of the role of a free press and its operations sometimes approached the edge of nonsense, Lippmann believed. When Congressmen sought to justify refusal to appropriate relief funds to the United Nations because American newspapermen were not permitted to report how the funds were used, Lippmann called it demagoguery. The press needed no instruction from Congress, he said, about the importance of freedom, and the proposal that correspondents gain access to the rigidly censored countries under the threat of having "destitute people suffer and die" was a foul blow which editors repudiated.

And the idea of having an army of foreign correspondents cover the distribution of relief in Greece, Czechoslovakia, Poland, Korea, China, and ten other countries was a manifest absurdity, he said, deriving from abysmal ignorance of the way the press gets most of its foreign news. "They get it from American officials and the officials of friendly governments . . . and it would be the exception rather than the rule that a foreign correspondent obtained significant news that officials do not already know . . . Where the press comes into it is to report to the people what the officials are reporting, and to watch, which they can do, whether these officials are making competent reports."[47] His belief that the press can do or has effectively done even this much would seem to some rather sanguine.

As he had in 1940, Lippmann hoped that Roosevelt would feel no compulsion, political or otherwise, to seek another term in 1944. He conceded that without Roosevelt the Democrats would probably lose the Presidency, but he believed that if the Republicans could demonstrate, with a candidate and a platform, competence to finish the war and structure a durable peace, then the Democrats, with Roosevelt leading the way, should voluntarily go into retirement.

Of the Democratic party, he said that "its mandate has run out, its time is up and that to overstay its time . . . is to invite a catastrophic defeat at the next [1948] election." Though Roosevelt must keep the option of running until the Republicans showed their fitness, he said, the risks of a fourth term—the strain of sixteen years in the White House, the danger of being defeated and thus discrediting the war effort, the predictable bitterness of the campaign—weighed heavily against the President.[48]

Lippmann opposed the nomination of Henry A. Wallace as Vice President, though he admired him greatly, because of the danger that Roosevelt might die and the Presidency pass to a man "who divides the people so deeply and sharply." Wallace was a prophet and a mystic, he said, and although he did seem to see correctly the shape of things to come, his view of the "real world" was cloudy, "his heart so detached from the realities that he has never learned to measure, as a statesman must, the relation of good and of evil in current affairs." (This feeling about Wallace resembled that about Eugene McCarthy in 1968, and the question arises whether a man who sees even dimly what the future portends may not be the best choice for President.) Lippmann was unworried about the Republican's selection for the Vice Presidency. In choosing Governor John W. Bricker of Ohio to run with Dewey, the Republicans knew, he said, that they were picking a "Throttlebottom" who was most unlikely to enter the White House. "If the country thought that there was a serious possibility of his being President," Lippmann said, "there is little doubt that virtually all but the rank and file of the habitual Republicans would bolt the ticket."[49]

After the 1944 conventions, Lippmann said that the two-party system, in spite of all the weasel words, horse-trading, and buncombe, had again performed its great function of uniting the people and preventing the divisions within the parties and between the parties from erupting into sectional or ideological conflicts. "The contest for Vice President at the Democratic convention," he said, "showed the system at work. Mr. Wallace undoubtedly had the largest and most fervent personal following. But it was a faction within the party, and this faction would have divided the party, and at the same time it would have sharpened the division between the two parties. Senator Truman's nomination damps down these factional differences . . ."[50]

As the campaign progressed Lippmann came to believe that Roosevelt had been right in deciding to run. Two weeks before the election Lippmann reluctantly wrote: "I cannot feel that Governor Dewey can be trusted now with responsibility in foreign affairs. He has so much to learn, and there would be no time for him to learn it, that the risk and cost of a change during this momentous year seems to me too great."[51] Just before election day, with Dewey's views on the role of the President as commander-in-chief uppermost in his mind—Dewey believed that the President should keep his hands off the war and let the commanding generals and admirals finish it—Lippmann said that Dewey was not "even as well informed as Washington newspapermen on the military conduct of the war." Dewey has shown the nation, Lippmann said, that he "is a relentless prosecuting attorney . . . not that he is fit and ready to be a war President."[52]

Obituary editorials, as everyone in the newspaper profession knows, are difficult to compose, because it is unseemly to offer anything but praise, even though the writer, if the subject of his editorial were still alive, might be condemning him for sins of omission or commission. Poets have attended to the problem: Shakespeare in the lines, "The evil that men do lives after them. The good is oft interred with their bones,"[53] and Emily Dickinson's "The admirations and contempts of time / Show justest through an open tomb."[54] Shakespeare, speaking ironically—saying the opposite of what he meant—stated the obituarist's task correctly. Miss Dickinson seems to have misjudged it. The *World* solved the problem clumsily in a Lippmann editorial in 1924 on the death of Senator Henry Cabot Lodge. "The *World* refrains from comment," the editorial said. "It would be impossible for the *World* to offer praise without hypocrisy or dispraise without offense."[55] Why comment on the fact that there will be no comment?

Lippmann's praise of Roosevelt after his death on April 12, 1945, might have been discounted because of the requirement to be conventional. But five days before the President died, Lippmann, responding to the critics who were saying that Roosevelt and his staff had been duped by Churchill and Stalin at Yalta and elsewhere said: "For cool objective realism about what really matters most, the President has been quite the equal of the other two." And he added that "since the summer of 1940 his [Roosevelt's] estimate of the vital interests of the United States has been accurate and far-sighted. He has served these interests with audacity and patience . . . and he has led this country out of the greatest peril in which it has ever been to the highest point of security, influence, and respect which it has ever attained."[56]

In his "Roosevelt Is Gone" article, Lippmann repeated his praise of the President's conduct of foreign affairs and said that under his leadership the nation had debated and finished the debate of the question whether its human and natural resources should be used to advantage all its people. "Here lay the political genius of Franklin Roosevelt," Lippmann said: "That in his own time he knew what were the questions that had to be answered even though he himself did not always find the full answer. It was to this that our people and the world responded, preferring him instinctively to those who did not know what the real questions were. Here was the secret of the sympathy which never ceased to flow back to him from the masses of mankind . . ."[57]

The probability of the President's death, Lippmann said, was uppermost in the minds of the men and women who nominated Harry Truman for the Vice Presidency. Therefore, Lippmann said, Truman had a mandate, both from the party and from the balloting in November of 1944. "He is where he is today," Lippmann said, "because of all the men available, he was deemed best fitted to be Roosevelt's successor." Truman was by sincere conviction committed to the Roosevelt domestic policies, Lippmann said, and there was no other man available "who knew so much about how this country was organized for war . . ." But Lippmann warned that Roosevelt had been so unbeatable that irresponsible opposition could not stop him. Lacking Roosevelt's prestige, Lippmann said, Truman might fail "if the party politicians, the agents of special groups, the members of the press and radio . . . put out stumbling blocks in his way."[58]

American preparations for and participation in the post-war conferences, including the San Francisco meeting to draft the United Nations Charter, were appallingly inept according to Lippmann's view, and some of his columns exasperated and angered the State Department. *Life* magazine reported that Secretary Edward L. Stettinius accused Eugene Meyer, publisher of the Washington *Post*, outlet in the capital for the "Today and Tomorrow" column, of permitting Lippmann to sabotage the United Nations Conference. (Twelve hundred correspondents, six for every delegate, reported on the meetings, including Elsa Maxwell and Walter Winchell.)[59]

Before the conference began, Lippmann issued his customary warning against "fish bowl" diplomacy. "An assemblage of more than forty governments working under the scrutiny of the press and radio of the whole world, including that of our enemies, cannot possibly be a deliberative body," he said. The American Constitutional Convention of 1787, he pointed out, was closed to the press, and it proved to be "the most successful deliberative body of its kind the world has ever seen . . ." Unless basic agreements on the charter could be reached before the conference began, he said, a security system should be imposed. To do otherwise, he said, would permit publicity to magnify the issues until they became insoluble or "to bury them in ambiguities."[60]

The greatest issue, Lippmann said, was how to achieve continuing collaboration among the Big Five—the United States, Britain, France, China and Russia—and the greatest danger was to regard the new international organization as a weapon to curb the Soviet Union.[61]

When Secretary Stettinius refused a Soviet request to delay voting on the admission of Argentina to the new organization (the Russians contended that Argentina was a Fascist state), Lippmann deplored the American use of superior small-nation support within the conference. "On this question Mr. Stettinius, to the astonishment and dismay of every experienced observer I have talked with," Lippmann said, "took the position that his diplomacy was exhausted and that there must be a showdown. He got the showdown and he won." But such "victories—God save the mark—" Lippmann said, were too costly to continue to seek, because they negated diplomacy and negotiation.[62]

Yet the angry disputes which the press reported of Stettinius and Anthony Eden with Secretary Viacheslav M. Molotov, especially over the question of Poland's future, were not so serious as they seemed, Lippmann said. The political and military realities of American and Russian power, he said, required that the conference continue, and "if one set of diplomats could not find a diplomatic solution, others would have to be appointed . . ."[63] The work of drafting the charter, which Roosevelt had regarded as the only real task of the conference, was proceeding smoothly enough, Lippmann said. The cause of the other frictions, which he said Roosevelt would have averted, was that the foreign ministers rather than the chiefs of state were being permitted to improvise high policy, and to do it in the limelight of publicity.[64]

Although he was optimistic that the series of conferences which followed the San Francisco meeting would produce a durable peace and that President Truman was assuming a firm grasp of foreign policy, Lippmann soon came to entertain doubts that American diplomats could distinguish between the trivial and significant issues in the post-war world.[65] After the Potsdam and London conferences in the summer and early fall of 1945, Lippmann said that the President and his new Secretary of State, James F. Byrnes, "had been handed a bad case which was badly prepared. At Potsdam and London Mr. Byrnes had been like a lawyer who had to argue ten separate cases in the Supreme Court on the basis of briefs which were written in law offices other than his own, which in fact he had scarcely had time to read on his way to the court room." Not only were the cases badly prepared, Lippmann said; they were the wrong cases to take up. Focussing attention on free elections in Bulgaria and the disposition of the "miserable" Italian colonies in Africa, he said, was a ludicrous way to spend four weeks of discussion at the end of a great world war. Discovering the western allies unprepared, "Mr. Molotov found the opening, and then ran with the ball through the broken field . . .," Lippmann said.[66]

Lippmann was on leave from his column from July 12 to September 11, 1945, and hence did not comment immediately on the A-Bomb and the end of the war with Japan. After the Japanese surrender he urged that the United States adopt the British proposal for an Allied Control Commission for Japan, with Americans supplying the only occupation forces.[67]

In an event which foreshadowed Truman's recall of General MacArthur from Korea in 1951, Lippmann praised Secretary Acheson for restating the principle of civilian control of military forces. MacArthur had exceeded his authority, Lippmann said, in speaking about "the size and character of our Pacific forces," and Acheson's statement that "the occupation forces are the instruments of policy and not the determinants of policy," was timely and necessary. Evidence from Germany also indicated, Lippmann added, that subordinates of General Eisenhower were assuming an arrogant role. But along with a firm civilian control, Lippmann said, should come precise instructions from Washington. Lack of them, he concluded, "is the real reason why among the conquering generals and their colonels there is a tendency to act as independent potentates."[68]

In spite of the diplomatic and political problems which had accumulated as part of the war's debris, Lippmann foresaw a Golden Age for the young men who were returning from the battlegrounds of Europe and the Pacific Islands. "Never before have the young men of any American generation had spread before them such a prospect of a long peace . . . There has never been a better time than this to be an American and to be young, nor a more interesting one to be alive." Yet the opportunity to inaugurate a timeless era of peace and plenty might be missed, he said, if the United States, a parvenu among the great powers on earth, used its power and influence arrogantly. To attempt to dictate to any nation, even the smallest, how it must conduct its social and economic life, would be folly, he said, and to brandish the A-bomb in arguments with our allies would be monstrous. It was no more conceivable, he said, that we could use the bomb, than that we could employ assassins against foreign statesmen whom we disliked. To behave arrogantly, he said would simply convince "the rest of the world that their own safety and dignity compel them to unite against us."[69]

During the war years the famous column was written in a big upstairs room in the Lippmann house in Georgetown. His study was spacious enough to include a big desk (always rather tidy), comfortable but shabby armchairs often piled with books and magazines, hundreds of books in floor-to-ceiling shelves, a terrestial globe, and a short-wave radio set. The Georgetown house was once owned by Alexander Graham Bell, and in the backyard was an annex which the inventor used as a laboratory. The annex, still containing some of the equipment of Bell's son, was the working quarters of Lippmann's secretaries.[70]

In 1946 the Lippmanns moved to a larger house on Woodley Road across from the Episcopal Cathedral. A big upstairs room was reconstructed, using the best sound-proofing materials available, into Lippmann's study, and his secretaries—two, plus a research assistant—moved into the attic above him. Autographed pictures of Woodrow Wilson, Churchill, Justice Holmes, Clemenceau adorned one wall of the study, sharing space with the cartoon in which Thurber's woman says to Thurber's man, "Lippmann scares me this morning."[71]

The columnist's daily routine usually began with waking at about 6:45, breakfast at 7:15 in his wife's bedroom, a quick look at the New York *Times,* Washington *Post* and the New York *Herald Tribune,* then, by 8:30 or 9, to the study, wearing pajamas and bathrobe or slacks and sweater, to write his column. Though not so Proust-like in its insulation as the study in New York, "the pool of silence" which Lippmann insisted every writer must have was still maintained. James Reston wrote: "Even his chimney is padded to muffle the melodic repertoire of a noisy mockingbird which he doesn't want to disturb and doesn't want to hear." His secretaries were under strict orders not to disturb him until summoned, usually a little after 11.

By then the column—800 to 1,200 words—was written in longhand, then sometimes rewritten, and recorded on a Dictaphone, ready for typing. In the half hour that his secretary, back in the attic, took for this task, Lippmann dressed, read his mail and returned to the Dictaphone to begin answering letters. By about 12:45, the column corrected and ready to be telephoned to New York, Lippmann left for lunch, driving his own car, usually to the Metropolitan Club.

Estimates of the number of readers the column attracted in the 1940's varied, but it always appeared in at least 150 papers with a combined circulation of more than ten million—including newspapers in most of the world's big cities. (In 1954, perhaps with some exuberance, the *Herald Tribune* syndicate estimated that

Lippmann's American audience might number 38 million and that his foreign papers commanded a circulation of 10 million—including London, Paris, Tokyo, Athens, Brussels, Bombay, Madrid, Oslo, Rio de Janeiro.) The fact that this audience included Presidents and Prime Ministers troubled Lippmann not at all. "I do not think about that," he said. "It would be ruinous, like an actor always worried about applause." And the suspicion that millions who had access to the column did not read it was of no concern to him, either. "I do not assume," he said, "that I am writing for anybody of a lower grade of intelligence than my own."

In his working schedule Lippmann set a difficult pace. His companions at lunch invariably were personages and the talk was serious for an hour or an hour and a half. In the early afternoons he spent more time on his mail, on background reading, in conference with his research assistant about the column or a magazine article or the book he was writing. The rest of the afternoon was spent walking with his wife and their two French poodles (there was a succession of them named Courage, Brioche, Vicky, Coquet), or golfing, or working on a piece of furniture in his carpentry shop.[72]

In the evening there was a cocktail party, sometimes two, to attend between 6 and 7:30 and then dinner at 8, out or at home, and, if at home, usually with guests. *Time* in its ormolu prose once reported on "Dinner at the Lippmann's": "When the guests step out of their cars, the Cathedral rises behind them, hazy above the street lights. In the long drawing room they find drinks, a very important person seated before the fire, respectful black poodles tethered under the piano. At dinner it is on Mr. Lippmann's right that the very important person sits, and the charming intellectual lady on his left. After dinner . . . the ladies flow into the drawing room. The men find themselves in a small parlor with brandy in glass balloons in their hands. The less important guests listen . . . The columnist gravely nods . . . Eyebrows bristle to little points, bags appear under the eyes: There's a touch of the croupier in evening dress. The ball starts rolling. Everything is delightfully off the record. The very important person outlines succinctly a few things he would like the public to know . . . They can't come from him, you understand . . . The columnist's eyebrows bristle with portent . . . Time to join the ladies. After a short Scotch fizzed with generalities, the wife of the very important person rises to her feet. Once they have gone, there is nothing left to say. As if the house were on fire, the less important guests are handed their wraps and hurried to the door."[73]

So by 10:30 or 11 the Lippmann day was over, except for some escapist reading for bedtime relaxation, and the lights were out on Woodley Road before midnight. Next day, whether there was a column to do or not, the regimen would be much the same. Social life—lunch, parties, dinner—always, at least around the edges, merged into professional life where the weight of the world had to be shouldered. The exigent schedule was varied by frequent trips abroad and every year by a long summer interlude in Maine, near Bar Harbor. (One of the big canvas mail bags used for the Maine post office trips is in a glassed bookcase in the Lippmann Room at the Yale Library. Close to it is another memento: his letter of appointment as secretary to George R. Lunn, Socialist Mayor of Schenectady, in 1912.)

During the 1940's criticism of Lippmann slackened, but there were some who remembered the old Lippmann and wanted him back and others who thought his new great fame was bogus. An editorial in John L. Lewis' *United Mine Workers Journal* called him a "natural-born word juggler and a baloney peddler" who made "$40,000 a year for passing out whangdoodle to the snobby readers of the daily press who like to think of themselves as highbrows."[74] Lippmann's claim to the title of Great Clarifier was growing shaky, said an article in the *American*, because the increasing passion and emotion of public affairs baffled him. "When sophistry, huffiness, and hauteur creep in, you know that the unreasonable human race has got him up a tree."[75]

"Walter Lippmann these days is as tremulous as a maid on her wedding eve," wrote Barbara Giles in the *New Masses*. Then, getting her metaphor a little mingled, she said there were two brides involved, the British Empire, which the U.S.A. was to marry, and Big Business, which the federal government was to take to the altar. Lippmann's jitters, she said, arose from his fears that Roosevelt might prevent both weddings. "The liberal yesterday of Lippmann's youth," she said, "is too far past to even echo . . . Mr. Lippmann does not only 'represent Wall Street,' as Steffens predicted he would; he works both sides of it."[76]

Efforts to parody Lippmann were not particularly successful, perhaps because his prose is autoparodic. In a series of "Impossible

Interviews," *Vanity Fair* reported an imaginary conversation between Winchell and Lippmann.

"Lippmann: The world, Mr. Winchell, is in a position where only confidence in the ability of its leaders and the conviction that a comprehensive program for recovery is to be resolutely pursued can avert international catastrophe."

"Winchell: That's the trouble with you, Lipp, you take the world too serious."[77]

Another *Vanity Fair* parody presented Lippmann as the "Enigma of Equilibrium" in a tight-wire act, supporting the House of Morgan on his shoulders while quoting Bergson, Spinoza, and Adam Smith.[78] And *Colliers* depicted Lippmann as the Apotheosis of the Antithesis: "In any consideration of the heat wave, we must remind ourselves that heat or cold, depends upon weather or not . . ."[79] Readers of *Colliers* and *Vanity Fair* presumably were amused.

From the *American Mercury,* in an article by Fred Rodell of the Yale Law School, came criticism as totally adverse as Amos Pinchot's attacks in the 1930's. Sapient and profound, lucid in style, liberal in philosophy—this was the Lippmann legend, but it had no basis in fact, Rodell said. The "real" Lippmann's talents were "something far more rare than mere wisdom, mere clarity, mere liberalism," he continued. Then after reciting Lippmann's bad guesses about Hitler's intentions and the probability of war, the threat of a Japanese attack on the West Coast, his vacillations about Tammany Hall, Roosevelt, and Woodrow Wilson, Rodell said that "the wisdom of Today" all too often became "the unwisdom of Tomorrow." Quoting from some of the columns ("But without a steering gear, the car could not be driven rapidly on a winding road"), he said the supposedly lucid style masked "a muddiness of meaning" or cloaked the obvious with false profundity. On the question of Lippmann the Liberal, Rodell recited the opposition to the New Deal and the praise, even as early as 1914, of big business. "Closely examined, the legend of Lippmann the liberal, or even the once-liberal," he said, "is on a par with the legends of Lippmann the sagacious and Lippmann the lucid."

Warming to his task of explaining why, in the absence of all the qualities that were supposed to account for it, Lippmann's reputation had become colossal, Rodell said, "What, then, is Walter Lippmann's unique talent? . . . Briefly stated, it is his almost uncanny knack of using words in such an impressive way as to *appear* sapient and lucid and even liberal. He has mastered to an extraordinary degree a species of distinguished and high-grade double talk."

And the achievement of this, Rodell suggested, had not been easy, and it had been costly. "It has required a complete forswearing, as to himself, of all humor and all true humility. It has required a kind of Olympian omniscience coupled with a sort of patient pedanticism that condescends now and then to words of one syllable in order to clear things up for the class. It has required the trappings of learning casually interjected—a philosopher referred to, an economist quoted. Above all, it has required the temerity to state the disputed as though it were obvious and to intone the obvious as though it were profound."[80]

To Rodell, Lippmann's major book of the war years, *U.S. Foreign Policy,* which Lippmann began in the summer of 1942 and finished in the winter of 1943, was merely an elaboration of a platitude—that "The United States shouldn't bite off more than it can chew." But the book gained prominent attention and praise. Secretary of War Stimson told Lippmann that he had been "recommending a reading of your book to everybody that I can."[81] The *Saturday Review* placed Lippmann's picture on the cover of the issue in which it received an essay review. *Newsweek's* review said that Lippmann was "perhaps the foremost editorial voice of enlightened conservatism in this country." The reviews were lavish with accolades—"masterful summary," "brilliant pamphleteering," "eloquent," "persuasive," "learned," "cogent."[82]

The essence of the foreign policy which Lippmann proposed was a "nuclear alliance"—the phrase had nothing to do with nuclear weapons, though it must have created great apprehension among those who were secretly working on the bomb—between the Atlantic Community, consisting of England, France, the United States, and Canada on the one side, and Russia and, if possible, China on the other. With "enlightened interest" and "cold calculation," the alliance would keep peace throughout the world.[83]

An elaboration of this thesis, which Lippmann said William Allen White urged him to make, was published in 1944—*U.S. War Aims.* In this book Lippmann spelled out the details of the nuclear alliance or alliances, outlining the orbits that the great powers would control and recognizing the need for regional alliances within North Africa, the Middle East, and Southern Asia. He warned particularly that "we must not repeat the error of counting upon a world organization to establish peace." Saying that "the great experiment at Geneva" failed because it sought to "build a universal society from the top downwards," he urged that the United States should recognize that "the Age of Innocence" was over. "We can advance toward a universal society. But should we fail to arrive, we can stand with great advantage upon the order which the United States, Britain, the Soviet Union, and China can establish by maintaining the coalition they have formed in this war." And if that failed, he said, "We can still find a large measure of security within the Atlantic Community." But he said hopefully, not dreaming of the dreadful meaning of the word "nuclear," that the geographic separation of the two great powers, the United States and Russia, made the risk of a third World War remote. "Not since the unity of the ancient world was disrupted has there been so good a prospect of a settled peace . . . We have come again to an age when the two leading powers capable of waging great war are, as respects to one another, invulnerable."[84]

Simplified in a cartoon that Rollin Kirby might have drawn for him in the old days, Lippmann's view of the post-war world would show the Russian Great Bear and Uncle Sam, both walking softly and carrying a big stick, patrolling the perimeters of their two worlds and policing the inhabitants, confident that they themselves would not collide.

The influence that Lippmann exercised on official thinking about war and peace is imponderable. Some said he mirrored the thinking rather than affected it, but his books and his columns were read by Secretaries of State and War and even by generals in the Army. Writing in 1944 of his friend and contemporary, the exiled French journalist Pertinax (André Géraud), Lippmann said, perhaps with himself in mind, though it would have been immodest to say so: "Now Pertinax [became] so well-informed that he became eminent, he exercised a power and influence in France, and indeed in Europe, which enabled him to be ever more intimately and definitively informed."[85]

Chapter VI

THE COLD WAR,
AND
THE PUBLIC PHILOSOPHY

EVENTS AND THE ISSUES WHICH THEY PROVOKED DICTATED, AS always, the subject matter of "Today and Tomorrow," and the big issues of the next decade were the two national elections, the loyalty program and McCarthyism, scientific secrecy, devising a foreign policy to chill the Cold War and keep the war in Korea limited, and, paramount on the domestic scene, procedures to ensure equal rights and liberties for Negroes.

Accommodations and changes within the press, in order to help the public exert a beneficent influence on the solution of these problems, Lippmann believed to be necessary. Discussing his own role and that of columnists in general, he said that the syndicated column, which was developed during the crises that began in 1929, might disappear. "There are reasons for thinking, so it seems to me," he said, "that as time goes on, the country gets used to having a great national government and to being a world power, the number of men who have training in these fields will become so large that the leading newspapers in each community will take back under their own control the whole responsibility of editorial writing."[1]

The influence of editorial pages, contrary to the general belief, he said, was increasing, because newspapers had come to realize that explanation and interpretation of the news, rather than argument and advocacy for a man or a cause, led people to abandon their prejudices and change their attitudes. "Argument alone, advocacy alone, however brilliant, usually means," he said, "that the editor ends by preaching only to those who already agree with him ... and they can take the editorials for granted ..."

Although the columnists might still be regarded, within the profession, as the Army and Navy regarded members of the Air Force—"amateur upstarts and spoiled darlings"—the best of them, he said, were simply good editorial writers who had educated themselves to write authoritatively about the problems arising in the centers of world power, Washington in particular. And to do this they had "to make their own personal contact with events and with the leading figures who shape those events ... They have to get to know what public figures are like behind the build-up, behind the facade of their public reputations ... behind the communiques and the handouts."[2] (Lippmann could "go on making perfectly good sense about current news when he is taking a long semi-vacation in Maine," Joseph and Stewart Alsop wrote. But even he, they added, needed "frequent, direct contact with people and events. Not even the most astute analyst can possibly know what the news means by sheer mental telepathy.")[3]

The Lippmann prediction that the syndicated political columnists might fade away has not, of course, come to pass. Even though all big-city newspapers have their own Washington reporter or bureau, few except the New York *Times* rely entirely on their own staffs for political comment. The *Times* syndicates Reston and its other stars, but it is export trade only. It would not import opinion, even Lippmann's, which partly explains why, after the *Herald Tribune* expired, New York City readers encountered difficulty in finding "Today and Tomorrow."

When the *Wall Street Journal* reported in 1966 that the *Times* was considering publication of Lippmann's column, Turner Catledge, executive editor, said that the *Times* "is not now and never has been interested in publishing syndicated columns." After the *Herald Tribune* was absorbed in the short-lived *World Journal Tribune*, the Justice Department filed an anti-trust suit to compel the new paper to let the New York *Post* and others bid for Lippmann, Joseph Alsop, Art Buchwald, and lesser luminaries. When the new paper consented to do this, the *Post* made no offer for Lippmann and the others. The *News*, richly endowed with two million subscribers, never displayed an interest in acquiring them. Subsequently fifteen suburban papers in the metropolitan area began publishing the Lippmann column. Finally, when the *World*

Journal Tribune expired in May of 1967, the *Post* decided to publish Lippmann—precisely at the time he announced he was discontinuing his regular column.[4]

The pressure to meet deadlines, even the rather leisurely schedule of a thrice-weekly column, and the need sometimes to offer comment and interpretation without adequate information worried Lippmann, but he concluded nothing could be done about it except to keep one's guard up. "There are many signs that big things are happening in the world," he wrote, "and every sensible man must want above all to wait and see, to keep his eyes open and his mouth shut. I must postpone the luxury of being that sensible until I finish this piece." (This was written soon after the death of Stalin, when everybody had to have a theory about its consequences.)

Even if it were possible to wait and see, there still would be the problem of where to look, Lippmann said. "The human eye, and particularly the mind's eye, will not see everything at once, as a whole, and in its full significance, but rather it will see what it is trained to see in those places where it has chosen to look . . . If . . . we do not keep clarifying and defining to ourselves what we are looking for, our open minds will have no defenses against our wishes and our fears."

And then in 800 words of dazzling virtuosity he discussed the implications of Stalin's death. Should we look for a change in tactics or a change in strategy? If tactics, how define tactics? If strategy, how define strategy? It would be best to look for tactical change, but change in strategy should not be ruled out. And furthermore we should consider, not only from our point of view but also that of the Soviets and of the satellites what any change, strategic or tactical, might, if indeed it eventuated, portend.[5] It was a marvelous example of the Lippmann style and substance, and, depending on what one was looking for, either brilliant or banal. The legerdemain of the Stalin column excited the admiration of A. J. Liebling, who kept an eye on "The Wayward Press" for the *New Yorker* during the 1940's and 1950's. Lippmann, Liebling said, was "the greatest on-the-one-hand-this writer in the world today."[6]

Reverting to the problem of how to write a column that would be timely and timeless, readably controversial and yet incontrovertible, Lippmann said facetiously that there were several tricks of the trade which would accomplish this—especially for the pieces to be published a week after the writer had gone on vacation. Lesser men might take the easy, safe way and denounce crime or the man-eating shark, but the best way, he said, was to adopt the device of rewriting "history in order to show that if something had happened which did not happen, many things, which unfortunately did happen would not have happened."

Then, in another coruscating *tour de force*, this time of 1500 words, he "proved" that Dewey's failure to get elected in 1948 was responsible for: national disunity, premature disarmament, the Korean War, the rise of Red China, Franco-German irreconcilibility, and the enfeeblement of the Eisenhower administration. "Something went wrong with our political order when the normal system of our parties became deranged in 1948," he said. And he concluded, tongue at least in a crevice of the cheeks that once were described as cherubic, "That at least is my story."[7]

As Critic-at-Large-and-in-Chief of men and institutions everywhere, Lippmann was sensitive to the fact that the press as watchdog of democracy had no watchman of its own performance. When the Commission on Freedom of the Press issued its report in 1947, Lippmann agreed with its conclusion that regular, searching, serious criticism of the press was lacking and that it was essential that it should be forthcoming. He said that "criticism ought not to be so much as it is a one-way street—the uncriticized press criticizing all other institutions and activities . . . what is sauce for the goose—that is to say for public men, business men, bankers, labor leaders, artists—must be sauce for the gander, for reporters, editors, commentators, book reviewers, dramatic critics."

Free expression, unique among all liberties, was diminished, he agreed, by the absence of criticism of the critics. "The lack of it deprives the press itself of the very principle of which the press is, in relation to everything else, the chief exponent." But he strenuously disagreed, as has been pointed out earlier, that the criticism should come from within the profession. "The good critic must be an outsider . . . [with] personal detachment."[8]

It is perhaps ironic that the major criticism by the press of the Commission's report was the fact that all the Commissioners were outsiders and therefore did not know what they were talking about. Robert Hutchins, who was chairman of the Commission—Henry Luce financed it with $200,000—told the annual meeting of the American Society of Newspaper Editors eight years after the report was published that the press still suffered from a pathological sensitivity to criticism.

The quality of the performance of television and the movies, which the Commission also studied, drew Lippmann's attention. When parts of the proceedings of a Senate investigation were televised in 1951—the Kefauver inquiry into crime—Lippmann felt that Pandora's Box had been opened again. The questions of public policy which television raised, Lippmann said, were "subtle, complex, and elusive." And though the future of television was unpredictable, decisions had to be made, at least provisionally, about this new way of exposing public affairs and influencing public opinion.

He said that "the selection of what is to be televised invites the exercise of a power over what people shall know that no editor of a free newspaper could, or would dream of exercising." It was true, he said, that newspapers exercised editorial selection, but professional standards required that they publish every day the essential information about important public affairs. "But with television," he said, "an event is broadcast or it is ignored: either it is in enormous headlines or it is nowhere at all. This power to choose what the great mass of people shall see . . . is altogether too great to be left to the judgment of a few television companies and to private arrangements made by committees and commercial sponsors . . ."

To formulate a policy and a code of rules to solve the legal, political, and ethical problems which the televised hearings suddenly created would be, Lippmann admitted, asking for too much too soon. But he said that given the choice between "let her rip and see what comes of it" or adopting the extremist position of prohibiting any broadcasting of hearings, he would choose to be an extremist.[9]

Kefauver, Lippmann said, might avoid the "dreadful fate" awaiting him: that "long after only the oldest reporters can still remember who Frank Costello was, or even Virginia Hill, Senator Kefauver's name may remain connected, like Lord Sandwich's and a quick lunch, with the grandeur and the miseries of conducting public affairs in front of the television audience." The senator could avert this ignominy, Lippmann said, by taking the lead in working out a public policy for television.[10]

Later Lippmann kept a television set, and a news ticker, in a closet close to his study, but he watched television only for the big events, like the national political conventions.[11] Television, he conceded, when it departed from dreary or spectacular concentration on the formal proceedings of the conventions and went behind the scenes, could do "what no other journalistic medium can do... bring the real business of the convention out in the open." Beginning in 1944 he had stopped attending the conventions.[12]

Television, the movies, and comic books were at least partly responsible for an increase in juvenile crime and immorality, Lippmann believed. All three media, he said, were "purveying violence and lust to vicious and intolerable degree." He was convinced, though there is still no conclusive proof of it, that portrayals of violence and sadism taught the audience how to gratify violent and sadistic desires. Admitting that censorship "is no doubt a clumsy and usually a self-defeating remedy...," he said that he saw "no objection in principle to censorship of the mass entertainment of the young."[13]

When the motion picture industry responded to his criticism by saying that the films were not pandering to sadism but rather were reflecting the community's concern about sadism, Lippmann said: "That, it seems to me is a tall story." The sophistry of the argument, he said, was exposed by the fact that the industry had an elaborate code of morals for which there would be no need if the movies were mere reflections of the state of public morality. Argument that "the peddling of a high-powered kind of celluloid dope... has no bad effects" was an irrational delusion, he said.[14]

During the quiz-show scandals of 1959, when it was disclosed that some of the extraordinarily knowledgeable contestants were knowledgeable only because they were fed in advance the answers to obscure questions, Lippmann began to advocate a non-profit public service television network to supplement the commerical squalor of the vast wasteland. Punishing the quiz-show cheaters under existing laws, even passing stronger laws to try to compel the networks to improve programming, might be palliative but would not be curative, Lippmann said.[15]

"The regulatory method runs counter to the facts of life," he said. "It supposes that the broadcasters can function permanently as schizophrenics, one part of their brain intent on profits and another part of that same brain intent on public service and the arts."[16]

So, though he contested the argument of the broadcasters that the government had no more right to regulate television than it did newspapers, Lippmann said that the broadcasting industry had become too powerful to submit to effective regulation. (Lippmann used two arguments in contending that radio and television were not entitled to the full protection of the First Amendment: the air waves belong to the people; and the networks operated a virtual monopoly.)[17]

The "age of innocence," when it was assumed that the profit motive was not supreme in the industry, came to an end during the 1950's, Lippmann said, and the government, aware that self-regulation was a failure, began a new effort to cajole and coerce better programming. The crusade of the Kennedy administration, led by the chairman of the FCC, Newton Minow, was, Lippmann said, "a noble idea, but it proved to be wishful."

The Kennedy administration's proposal to charge commercial stations rent for use of the air waves was sound in principle, Lippmann said, but would provoke such wrangling in Congress that proceeds to finance a public television network would not be forthcoming. Consequently, Lippmann endorsed the Ford Foundation proposal that satellites like "Early Bird" rather than expensive cables be used to relay commercial television programs and that the savings produced by this be channeled into a fund for a non-commercial TV network. If this failed to produce enough revenue, taxes on broadcasting revenues and on broadcasting sets should be levied, he said.

Non-commercial television in competition with the "mediocrity and blah" dictated by advertisers, he said, had become as essential as non-profit churches, libraries, and universities. "Such a network, which could be governed by disinterested citizens and operated by the frustrated and unhappy professionals of the existing networks could become a powerful competitor," he said, "and by the competition of its example a powerful regulator of the existing commercial networks."[18]

The government's own information services continued to aggravate him—from presidential press conferences to American propaganda abroad. In 1946, when Truman had been in office a little more than a year, Lippmann said that the press—"for

compassionate and patriotic reasons"—had protected him "from
the consequences of blunders which would have shaken to its
foundations the administration of a stronger president." But,
Lippmann warned, "the fund of good will and good nature, of
charity and chivalry" was close to exhaustion.

President Truman, Lippmann suggested, was trying to conduct
his press conferences in the Roosevelt style without Roosevelt's
style. "Moreover, as one who had been to presidential press conferences for more than thirty years, I should like to say that even
if Mr. Truman could imitate Roosevelt, he ought not to try."
Roosevelt's conferences, after his early years in office, had deteriorated, Lippmann said. "Less and less came out of them which
gave substance to the freedom of the press. More and more they
degenerated into persiflage"—a battle of wits in which the President, protected by the respect due his office, could always score
a cheap or easy victory.

Truman's conferences, Lippmann said, mentioning reliance
"upon hunches and chitchat," were becoming dangerous and
needed to be reformed. "The President is frequently asked questions which he is unprepared to answer." (This complaint—that
he had not done his homework—later was made frequently of
Eisenhower.) "He may catch the point of the question," Lippmann
continued, "or he may miss the point. He can then give no answer.
Or he can make a quick guess. Or he can give the wrong answer.
This system is bound to produce confusion and consternation
throughout the world."

The remedy was simple, Lippmann said: "to make it a rule
that on matters of high policy, touching foreign affairs, the armed
forces, government finance, questions should be submitted in writing, and answered when the President has had time to have prepared a considered reply." There might be "a smell of censorship
and regimentation" in this, Lippmann said, but the odor was too
faint for him to detect. A more serious objection might be that
the prepared answers "would be ghost-written and would, therefore, conceal from the public the quality of the man who is President." But that could be met, he said, by continuing the practice
of random questions and spontaneous answers about domestic
policies and internal affairs.[19]

(Although the format of the conferences changed somewhat,
especially after the coming of television, Lippmann's suggestion

was not adopted. James Hagerty resisted it for Eisenhower, and Kennedy rejected it for himself.)[20]

Lippmann was so confident that the Republicans would win the Presidency in 1948 that his main concern was control of Congress. Governor Dewey (Lippmann's first choice for the nomination was Senator Vandenburg) would carry in enough Republicans to organize the House, he believed, but a G.O.P. Senate was doubtful. The solution which Lippmann proposed, in order for the nation to have a unified government, was for a half dozen Democrats whose terms were not expiring to announce that they would abstain from voting on organization day and permit the Republicans to control committees. "Such a move would shock the party hacks," he said, but it would produce better government and in the long run would help the Democratic Party by forcing the Republicans to assume total responsibility and depriving them of alibis for mistakes that might be made.[21] The Lippmann proposal was similar to one made by Marshall Field III, who suggested after the Democrats lost control of Congress in 1946 that Truman resign as President after appointing as his successor a Secretary of State acceptable to the Republicans.[22]

The anti-Truman "Today and Tomorrow" columns in 1948 were often phrased in terms which their author usually considered immoderate: "gives no evidence of his ability to perform the functions of the commander in chief"; "not only divides the Democrats, he disintegrates them"; "disrespect for the dignity of his office and the proprieties of the Constitution"; "a weak President and at heart a jingo . . ."[23]

After the election, in which the Democrats regained control of the House and Senate, Lippmann, like the pollsters and almost all the other columnists and commentators, distastefully ate his crow. Truman's surprising victory, he said, was a tribute to the strength of the Democratic Party which Roosevelt put together. "It can be said with much justice . . . that of all Roosevelt's electoral triumphs, this one in 1948 is the most impressive." The Democrats who were elected as Governors and Senators—Chester Bowles in Connecticut, Adlai Stevenson and Paul Douglas in Illinois, Hubert Humphrey in Minnesota, Estes Kefauver in Tennessee—were conspicuously Rooseveltian both on foreign and domestic issue, Lippmann pointed out. (In the 1948 campaign Humphrey, whom Lippmann was to fail to support for President in 1968, fared badly in the printing plant. Once he was "Humphreys," once "Humphries." Mistakes of this kind were a rarity in "Today and Tomorrow" columns.) Oddly enough, Truman, who had been a "jingo" to Lippmann during the campaign, now received credit for attempting to restrain jingoism in the State Department and in the Pentagon. "Both Truman and Dewey, as they made contact with the mass of the people, became aware," Lippmann said, "that the professional soldiers and diplomats who have been dominant in policy were going too fast and too far ... and that somehow it has become necessary to reassert the supremacy of civilian and popular control of the conduct of foreign policy."[24]

That there was increasing dislike and distrust of the United States and that its "image" to the world needed repairing was a prevalent belief in the late 40's and early 50's. Lippmann agreed that distrust was increasing, but the notion that better American propaganda would solve or even help to solve the problem he regarded as naive.

Critics of the propaganda apparatus, including some Congressmen, believed that a lack of skill impaired it, and that America could be successfully "sold" to the world simply by hiring more skilled writers and speakers to sell it. This, to Lippmann, betrayed an ignorance of the nature of propaganda.

"The first principle of all the arts of managing people's minds," he said, requires that there be "a monopoly of publicity ... The indispensable piece of operating equipment in the kit of the propagandist is a curtain. Without a curtain the beauty, the charm, the terror, the cleverness of what he says will be undone or neutralized by the knowledge of what he does not say."

Without censorship a nation cannot have even a veil, let alone a curtain, Lippmann said, and added rather sarcastically that in the United States there was "not even at the moment much discretion ..." Generals holding press conferences, cabinet officers making ghosted speeches, Congressmen talking through their hats, were all part of the many voices of America, some of them cuckoo, that were heard through the land and the world, Lippmann suggested; and so it was ridiculous to suppose that "the American story" could be told to "our loving friends, much less our skeptical friends, not to speak of the very unfriendly people with whom we are just managing to co-exist."[25]

By 1953 Lippmann's recipe was: abolish the Voice of America altogether, and broadcast overseas only the same news which Americans receive, and leave the selection of this up to the press associations and the networks.

The story of how the government got into the peacetime propaganda business, Lippmann said, was an incredible and unfunny joke. At the end of the war, he said, Congress wanted to abolish the war-time propaganda agencies and the Administration wanted to keep one. "The leaders on the Hill were consulted, and the word that came back was that the only executive department which Congress trusted, the only one that was not overrun with New Dealers and whatnot was—believe it or not—the Department of State."

So, Lippmann said, Secretary Byrnes, who did not want to do propaganda but was "a compassionate Democrat," provided "a refuge and asylum for the displaced persons of the war-time propaganda services." And once ensconced, Lippmann continued, they thought "of new worlds to conquer . . . and began broadcasting throughout the world, to all the races of mankind in all the languages . . ." In the summer of 1946 Byrnes offered him the directorship of the U.S. Information program, Lippmann said later. "I told him I couldn't do it. I didn't want to be involved in formulating American propaganda." Congress could never trust the Voice and yet could never find a way to reform it, Lippmann concluded; so the time had come, especially since it was becoming the "Voice of McCarthy," to kill it.[26]

The spectacle which America presented to the world during the investigations by and of Senator Joseph McCarthy and his committee Lippmann found execrable, and he blamed Dwight Eisenhower, whose nomination and election he encouraged, for failing to awaken the country from the Washington nightmare. Although Lippmann came to share the belief of the Supreme Court that Congressional investigations must have a legislative purpose and that inquiries conducted to expose evil and evil-doers violate due process of law, he condoned the need for the House Committee on un-American Activities when it was first established. After the committee, headed by Martin Dies of Texas, reported in 1940 that it had no legislation to propose but wished to continue investigating, Lippmann said: "It is plain that the Dies committee cannot be abolished and must be continued since it offers a center

of resistance to evils which could not otherwise be brought to
light and checked."

The nation was faced, he said "with the ancient moral dilemma
of whether the end justifies the means," and, though the commit-
teemen were vigilantes "often lawless in spirit and disorderly in
their methods," they were protecting the American system from
subversion. The only solution, Lippmann said, was to proceed,
but with safeguards to protect the innocent.[27] After the war, when
Congressional committees began investigating wartime espionage
and publicized testimony of Elizabeth Bentley and other confessed
and professed reformed ex-spies, Lippmann changed his position.
To argue, he said, that "the national interest is being served so
well that it justifies the sacrifice of a few innocent persons . . .
is profoundly immoral." The Bentley ring, he said, dealt with
gossip, rumor, and fabrication, and the committees were incompetent to sift the truth from the revelations, or to do more than
"lock the stable door with a loud bang long after the horse has
been stolen." The safeguards of law, developed patiently through
the centuries, he said, were in danger of disappearing.[28]

When a spate of investigations of the protection of military
and scientific secrets was being conducted in 1949 and 1950, Lippmann said that "these investigations are running hog wild." For
senators to assume that they were competent to protect the secret
of the atomic bomb was as absurd as assuming that they could
censor Chinese newspapers, Lippmann said. "The effort of
laymen, who know virtually nothing about nuclear physics, to
determine what is a secret and how to guard it, is rather like
what would happen if say Senator Hickenlooper woke up one
morning and found he had been appointed the censor of the
Chinese Nationalist press." Illiterate in Chinese, how could he
protect Chinese secrets from disclosure to the Communists? Lippmann asked. One way would be to stop publishing newspapers,
or possibly to get all newspaper employees to take an oath not
to disclose secrets. But this would not work, Lippmann said,
because how could Chinese reporters distinguish what was secret
and what was not? In the end, Lippmann said, the senator would
have to rely upon some Chinese who knew all the Chinese military
secrets, and this is what he suggested be done with the scientists.
"They are the best, in fact the only judges of what is really
secret . . ."[29]

By telling the world that the atomic program had been mismanaged, that we were building bad airplanes, that the government was riddled with spies, we were providing the Communists with superb propaganda, Lippmann said, and were scaring our allies into believing that we had lost the strength to help protect them. "End this disorderly uproar," he said [or] "freedom will perish in its own home."[30]

In May of 1950, when McCarthy's charges of subversion and perversion in the State Department were being broadcast, Lippmann said that the government was "virtually paralyzed by corrosive suspicion" and that there was no way out of "the horror . . ." In England or France, he said, the substance of charges like McCarthy's could be dealt with in Parliament, and the government, demanding vindication and failing to get it, would be dissolved. The essential weakness of the American system of government, he said, lay in the fact that there was no way of forcing such a showdown.[31]

McCarthy posed in a form more extreme than ever before, Lippmann said, the question of whether laws regulating free speech apply to Congressmen. Article I, Section 6 of the Constitution, he pointed out, says that "for any speech or debate in either house they shall not be questioned in any other place." But this does not mean, Lippmann said, tracing the question back to a conflict between the King and the House of Commons in 1629, that senators are immune to reach of the law—it means only that the Senate alone can punish senatorial speech which violates the law. By failing to apply to McCarthy "rules of justice, or the canons of decency," the Senate, Lippmann said, was violating one of the great principles of the Constitution and was letting liberty degenerate into license.[32]

With McCarthy unchecked and the nation and the world taking it for granted that it was "quite proper, some even say patriotic, to summon the military and civilian leaders of a nation . . . and then to proceed publicly and officially to strip them naked," Lippmann said that he had begun to marvel at senatorial omniscience. Some senators, he said, were fully confident that they "can remake the past and fasten down the future." He suggested that they might "meditate on Santayana's saying that not even God can change the past."[33]

When Eisenhower and the Republicans took office in 1953, and McCarthy, now chairman of the Permanent Investigations Sub-Committee, showed some reluctance to attack his own party, Lippmann expressed pleasure. With "the trials and errors" of the Truman administration past, and the executive branch presumably back in control of the loyalty and security program, Lippmann said he was confident that: "Under the firm and clearheaded administration of Mr. Brownell (the new attorney general) there should be no reason, as Senator McCarthy has in fact already recognized quite handsomely, why committees of Congress should attempt to take over the Executive responsibility."[34]

Before the year was over, however, McCarthy began to charge Eisenhower with being "soft on Communism" and commenced what Lippmann called his "formidable effort to seize control of the powers of the President . . ." Lippmann blamed Herbert Brownell, and Governor Dewey, too, for opening the way for McCarthy's attack by the "violence and venom" of their own attacks against former President Truman and his administration. In drawing upon the secret files of the F.B.I. in an attempt to discredit Truman's loyalty, Brownell, Lippmann said, "planted seeds of irreparable discord" and made it almost impossible for any Democrat to continue bipartisan support of the President.[35]

Denouncing McCarthy and his supporters in the Senate, Lippmann said that "the power of the law to protect the liberties of our people" was being threatened by "lawless behavior" in Congress. When McCarthy began what Lippmann called his "bullying brutality" of Army officers, Lippmann accused Eisenhower of appeasement and of condoning "this essentially totalitarian assault . . ." The people were becoming afraid, he said "not only of the cold war and not only of McCarthy's exploitation of their fears of the cold war. Our people are being made afraid of McCarthy himself."[36]

The notion that the press itself was responsible for the McCarthy phenomenon, that without publicity he would wither away, Lippmann disdained. "In the early stages of his adventure," Lippmann wrote, "it may have been true that the attention he got from the press helped to build him up. But it is not true now . . . The national obsession which is giving him the fullest kind of attention is [finally] having the effect which true believers in the freedom of the press have always counted upon. It is that given prolonged and uninhibited reporting, it is not only impossible to fool all the people all the time, but it comes progressively more difficult to fool even some of the people all the time."

Lippmann credited television with contributing greatly to what he called "the breaking up of the spell," because, he said, when people actually saw the persecution of witnesses and "the filling of our air with poison and stink," they experienced a revulsion. "For one reason and another people are realizing that advertising yourself as the world's champion anti-Communist and being the world's champion anti-Communist are not necessarily the same thing."[37]

But the spell was not yet broken, or at least the hearings were not over. When President Eisenhower gave the American Newspaper Publishers Association a lecture on the need to balance bad news with good news, Lippmann gave the President a lecture on the nature of news. Eisenhower had brought into the open, Lippmann said, the undercover grumbling that the newspapers had magnified McCarthy's importance by giving him too much page-one space. Describing himself as "an old newspaperman, who had worked with news editors but has never been one himself," Lippmann said, "I think General Eisenhower is quite mistaken."

McCarthy was a senator, chairman of a big committee, Lippmann said, and he added sarcastically, "a politician until recently at least in good standing at the headquarters of the Republican party." When a man of this stature makes charges of treason, subversion, perversion, and spying, it constitutes news which cannot and must not be suppressed or played down, Lippmann said. Eisenhower wanted "good news" for balance. What kind of news would this be? Lippmann asked. "Not, I take it, news of inspirational talks to the Girl Scouts." Presumably, then, the "balancing" news would be news that McCarthy's charges were false, Lippmann said, or even that they were true.

But this was precisely the news that editors could not get and had no way of getting, Lippmann said. They could, to be sure, print denials from those whom McCarthy accused, but the denial of an accused man does not balance an official's charge, he said, so the balancing news must be the news that the charges—or the denials—were either true or false. And this news, he pointed out, could not be manufactured by the press serving as substitute for full, fair, judicial inquiry. The news that such an inquiry was to be made, or at least that McCarthy's "perverted inquiry" would cease, would be good news that the President had the power but not the inclination to make, Lippmann said. "General Eisenhower is right in realizing that the news . . . is not uniting the American people. But the remedy, the only sure and prompt remedy, is in his hands, if only he would use it, and not in the hands of news editors."[38]

When President Eisenhower said that "the world is suffering from a multiplicity of fears . . . the men in the Kremlin . . . unwise investigators . . . depression . . . the loss of jobs . . ." and that the fears, all with some basis, were producing an almost hysterical reaction, Lippmann agreed that this was true, and that the President's panacea for hysteria — faith in the destiny of America—was undoubtedly the right prescription. But he said an essential fact was missing from the President's diagnosis—the breakdown of leadership and authority.

Both as "the Chief Executive and the Commander in Chief," Lippmann said, Eisenhower had been "giving ground here, there and almost everywhere . . . He has been accepting without more than spasmodic resistance and without serious protest the public humiliation of the Foreign Service . . . and of the officers of the Army . . ." Forced to conclude that "Eisenhower is manifestly unprepared by experience and by education" to deal with the McCarthy challenge, Lippmann said that the President nevertheless might overcome this handicap if he would face the problem as a basic Constitutional issue—the necessity for the separation of powers.[39]

Lippmann's prescription for the President was: give orders to everyone within the jurisdiction of the executive branch to refuse to appear before the McCarthy committee. "This is the true medicine of the Constitution for the disease with which this country is now afflicted," Lippmann said, for even if a Senate majority should support McCarthy, there was no power in Congress to compel witnesses to appear—"to go up to Camp Kilmer and arrest General Zwicker."[40]

(Richard Rovere has an amusing account of McCarthy's encountering two reporters in a Capitol corridor and asking, "Do you want a story, boys?" This being rather like asking a hungry dog if it wanted a hamburger, they said "Yes," and thereupon the senator pulled from his pocket one of the blank subpoenas that he always carried and filled in a summons for former President Truman to appear. There is also an account in a remarkable book by Charles Potter, an unsympathetic Republican member of McCarthy's committee, about Potter's conversations with Eisenhower during this period, in which the President asked, "Charlie, what can be done right now?" and then added ruefully, "It was different in the Army. If a man was guilty of rebellion, we just put him in the stockade.")[41]

The hearings, including the televised investigation of the McCarthy committee investigating the McCarthy committee, continued into June, and it was not until October that the Senate voted condemnation of McCarthy—not for his conduct in the investigations—but for his refusal to testify before the Sub-Committee on Elections and Privileges. Its condemnation of McCarthy (condemn in this context, oddly enough, is weaker than censure) restored the dignity of the Senate, many of whose members had seemed to believe, Lippmann said, that "the cheapest and easiest way not to look red or pink was to be yellow."[42]

Reviewing the affair on December 27, 1954, after the elections were over and the Republicans lost control of Congress, Lippmann said that "our reputation in the world . . . has been grossly tarnished" and that damage at home would take a long time to repair. "The effect has been," he wrote, "to clamp down and in a degree to smother the full exercise of the traditional American freedom of thought and of speech. There is a kind of smog in what should be the clean and open air of this free land, a smog which makes men nervous, makes them afraid to speak their minds, makes them not sure they dare to keep their minds open."[43]

Given a choice between Dwight Eisenhower and Adlai Stevenson for the presidency, Lippmann, one might have surmised, would have found Stevenson to be his man. Many of the qualities which Lippmann possessed—articulateness, a liberal education, and a love of intellectual life—Stevenson had in high degree. And the qualification for the office which Lippmann placed highest—long experience in politics and especially the experience derived from being the successful governor of a big industrial state—was Stevenson's, not Eisenhower's. Besides, there was Stevenson's humor and humility, his detestation of the traditional generalities and buncombe of politicking. But once there was a chance of Eisenhower's availability, Lippmann believed that he would make the better President. In spite of the fact that he thought that Stevenson could unify his own party and attract the support of independent Republicans, Lippmann felt that the need for a change of parties, urgent in 1948, was imperative in 1952, and that only a Republican President could successfully end the Korean War.[44]

To say that Lippmann's high hopes—that Eisenhower would reunify the country and redesign its foreign policy to make commitments more nearly equal to capabilities—were unfulfilled would be an overstatement. But neither aspiration was fulfilled in large measure. Especially in domestic affairs—the McCarthy imbroglio, the wrecking of Robert Oppenheimer's reputation, the pusillanimous reaction to the Supreme Court desegregation decision—Lippmann found the executive branch timorous, indecisive, evasive, muddled, disoriented, to use a few of the adjectives that he applied.

Part of the blame for Eisenhower's failure to deal forthrightly with domestic political problems might rest with Lippmann, whose columns Eisenhower read and pondered when the pressure to seek, or at least to submit to, the Republican nomination began early in 1952. David F. Schoenbrun, CBS correspondent in Paris, who was close to Eisenhower and his staff at SHAPE, reported that the *Herald Tribune* editorial page, and especially Lippmann's columns, influenced him greatly in the months while he was trying to make up his mind. "The General read and re-read Lippmann's columns," Schoenbrun said. "They fitted his own concept of his unwilling mission in politics. And he began to sound, when he spoke, as if he were quoting from Lippmann."[45]

What Lippmann was telling him was that "the disunion and distrust in American politics are becoming insufferable," that Eisenhower could put an end to "the partisan and factional warfare" and dispose of "all the many issues that Truman and Taft have managed to snarl up." With a truly national President, Lippmann said, the presently irreconcilable conflicts could be resolved. "We cannot carry the burden of protecting and leading the free nations of the world if every policy and every measure we have to take must be dragged through the stinking mass of shyster politics," Lippmann told the General and the world.[46] One could ask whether a man persuaded that it was his mission to do what Lippmann said Eisenhower could do might be reluctant to stoop to intervene in the political brawling that McCarthy and his faction produced.

An interpretation of Lippmann's view of the Eisenhower role appeared in *The Freeman.* Saying that the General's "mission, in other words, is to abolish politics," the editorial accused Lippmann of "a complete loss of faith in the American character" and said he served as spokesman for the élitists who "see the people as poltroons, and their elected representatives as shysters..." (A copy of the editorial in the Lippmann Collection at Yale is initialed "W.L." and the initials are followed by a bold exclamation point of astonishment. *The Freeman,* it should be said, did not dislike McCarthy.)[47]

Eisenhower's first press conference as candidate drew Lippmann's admiration. "I find it deeply reassuring," Lippmann wrote, "that without any evasiveness he has left himself entirely uncommitted for the great issues of war and peace which lie ahead of us." To survive the ordeal of a press conference and emerge with one's personality intact was a great accomplishment, he suggested. In a conference such as the one at Abilene, he said, it is "virtually impossible in such a specially sophisticated audience to pretend to know more than you do know ..." The press conference, he said, had become an institution "for overcoming that growing threat to honest journalism, the ghost-written speech and the public relations facade."[48]

Late in 1951 and in the early months of 1952 when he was extolling Eisenhower in the kind of phrases that irritated the editor of *The Freeman,* Lippmann's fear had been that Taft and Truman might be the rival nominees. After the convention, with a relatively safe choice confronting him, and hence the country, his enthusiasm for Eisenhower bubbled a little less.

In phrases reminiscent of what he had said about Willkie, by October Lippmann was writing that Eisenhower had failed to unify the party and that he "was not in control of his candidacy." His friends needed some gesture from the General, Lippmann said, to indicate that he would resist Old Guard pressure—something "to sustain them against the growing suspicion in the country that that man Stevenson may not only be speaking in the accents of greatness but that he may perhaps embody some of the qualities of a great American leader."[49]

The Nixon affair, the charges that the Vice-Presidential candidate's campaign funds were tainted, and the famous appearance of the Nixons and their dog on television, Lippmann found disturbing. It was an attempt to settle a legal and moral question by appealing to mob law, he said "with all the magnification of modern electronics." The decision to keep Nixon on the ticket or to drop him was for Eisenhower to make, not the public, Lippmann said, and waiting to improvise a solution on the basis of public opinion was "off the cuff," "ad lib," and "disorderly."[50]

When the election was over, Lippmann said that the people had decided on a change of parties long ago and wanted Eisenhower regardless of the Republican factional disorder. Eisenhower's great majority 6,600,000 votes—was conclusive. "He is the captive of no man and of no faction. He is free, as few men in so high an office have ever been, to be the servant of his own conscience."[51] By the time he wrote his memoirs, Eisenhower had forgotten his earlier debt to Lippmann, who, he said, "consistently opposed me." And Sherman Adams reported that "Mr. Lippmann's influence on the Eisenhower administration was nil."[52]

Ruminating on the American electoral process, Lippmann said that the primaries, the conventions, the campaigning were often "inelegant, tiresome, annoying and embarrassing," but the result was "a process by which the diversities of sections, of classes and sects are assuaged and mollified, are purged and cooled, so that the nation can live with them . . ." Some smaller nations, he said, presumably with Britain in mind, protect individual liberty more securely, are more efficiently and honestly and representatively governed, but nowhere except in the United States is a free society maintained for a vast and heterogenous people sprawled across a continent. And he added that "the tremendous uproar" of the electoral process, seeming iniquitous, is rather "an enormous virtue."[53]

Though the political process may have sutured the nation's wounds (to paraphrase, or perhaps to metaphrase Lippmann), bloody bandages remained and needed changing. The war in Korea had to be ended, McCarthy silenced, the loyalty and security policy adjusted, the segregationists confronted.

Lippmann took the position that Truman and Dean Acheson, badly advised by General Douglas MacArthur, made a fatal mistake in attempting to occupy North Korea. The time for an armistice was September of 1950, he said, when South Korea was cleared of aggressors. After that the war became indecisive and unnecessary. He predicted, correctly, that Eisenhower would seek an armistice and try to get the struggle with the Communists back on a political basis of co-existence.

The terms for co-existence, Lippmann said, should be fixed in a settlement between Russia and the Atlantic community—a settlement which would set boundaries between the two worlds, make modest trade agreements, and "reduce the propaganda war from . . . volcanic hatred to icy dislike." More than this could not be achieved, he said, because collaboration between democratic and totalitarian states was impossible. All parties to the settlement should understand, he said, that if the terms could be safely and profitably violated, i.e., without provoking war, they need not be observed.[54]

When Ilya Ehrenburg, the Russian critic and historian visited the United States soon after the second World War, and wrote about the "spiritual possibilities" of the American people, Lippmann reminded him that the Russians had spiritual potential too, but it could never be realized until the Soviet gave Mr. Ehrenburg the same right to criticize Russian institutions as he enjoyed here to denounce "Bilboism" and other blights on American civilization. Ehrenburg overlooked, Lippmann said, one of the greatest virtues of the American people—"that they regard the exposure of their vices and their failings not only as a right to be guarded jealously but as a duty which, as they perform it proves their manhood." Until the Russians could say the same about themselves, Lippmann said, "the shrewd common sense of mankind and its instinct of liberty will not permit men to trust them, to like them, or to follow them."[55]

When Stalin intimated in an answer to a series of questions from James Reston late in 1952 that there might be a possibility of negotiations, Lippman praised Secretary Dulles for the formality and politeness of his reply. Stalin's rare utterances to newspapermen, Lippmann said, were "unlike anything to which mankind has listened attentively since the priestess on her tripod at Delphi delivered the oracles. The Greeks then, as we today, found the prophecies puzzling—but also fascinating—because they could mean so many different things." And American journalists in Moscow should remember, Lippmann cautioned, that the rule for them was the same rule for the suppliants at Delphi: No questions were answered except those the oracle wished to hear. "There is, therefore," he said, "no way of telling which of these occasional interviews is intended to bring about a negotiation and which is for propaganda."[56]

The question of negotiating with Russia was of such subtlety, Lippmann felt, that it needed exploration in "talks about talking." Those who argued that the absence of negotiations proved that all the press conferences, speeches, interviews on both sides were mere dalliance viewed the problem too simply, Lippmann said. It was true that psychological warfare had become a plague and that public opinion throughout the world had been debauched by propaganda, he said, and the argument for "a retreat into secret diplomacy and an abolition of informative and inspiring public utterances" had a certain plausibility. But, for adversaries who found their big problems unnegotiable, to "talk about talking" was preferable, he said, to "glaring ominously at one another and shining up their weapons . . ." better than "leaving the field of public attention vacant and open to all the mischief makers . . . the demagogues and the diplomatic racketeers."[57]

The mischief makers included politicians and journalists who gave the impression, Lippmann said, that they were discussing the actual foreign policies of the President and the Secretary of State. Even when they knew what they were talking about, which, he implied, was not often, their disclosures might be premature, he said, and when they spoke from ignorance the harm was incalculable. For example, he said, it is often impossible officially to deny any untrue report without running the risk that the denial will be distorted into something worse than it means. Everyone has a constitutional right to criticize everything the President says or does, but nobody has a constitutional right to do his talking for him, Lippmann said.[58]

And Lippmann found it deplorable that the official exposition of foreign policy often was lacking in clarity and candor. When Secretary Dulles broadcast a televised review of foreign affairs from the White House in May of 1955, Lippmann disliked both the form and substance of it. "These stage-managed shows with props made out of the White House furniture, with live officials reciting or reading the script, are not a new and advanced form of journalism and true reporting," he said. "They are fiction and

theater meant to give the illusion that they are true reporting."
Dulles' picture of the world, he said, "was true only as far as
it went, which was not very far."

The Dulles speech was optimistic, stressing Soviet and Red Chinese economic troubles and the growing strength of the West. If
there was a Soviet retreat from a tough cold war policy, Lippmann
said, it was based not on weakness but on a careful appraisal
of popular feeling in the smaller nations of the world. Their tendency to pull away from the American or Russian orbit and to
liquidate foreign or native oligarchies was being appraised correctly by the Soviets, Lippmann said. And he added that having
discerned "a wave of the future," Russia might well attract support
in the smaller nations of Europe and Asia. To accentuate Soviet
weaknesses and to denounce Russian pretensions of benevolence
as hypocritical was "wishful and indeed highly conceited thinking . . . ," Lippmann said.[59]

In the midst of the McCarthy uproar the Administration was
embarrassed by its own failure to deal clearly and fairly with the
charges brought against J. Robert Oppenheimer. The nuclear
scientist, who was called "the father of the A-bomb," was accused
of having been a fellow traveler from 1936 to 1942 and of exercising bad political judgment after the war during the controversy
over whether to seek to develop the H-bomb.

The administration appointed a board consisting of Gordon
Gray and Thomas A. Morgan to investigate the charges and the
general question of Oppenheimer's loyalty and his fitness to continue to share atomic secrets. The board found no evidence of
disloyalty, praised Oppenheimer for "an unusual ability to keep
to himself vital secrets," but concurred with the Atomic Energy
Commission decision to discontinue his security clearance.

Lippmann accused the Administration of "using a bulldozer
to sweep a carpet," of ordering "a trial to chop off Dr. Oppenheimer's head." There were a dozen decent ways of ending Oppenheimer's services as AEC consultant, Lippmann said, without subjecting him to public humiliation. "But all the decent ways of
doing it required the exercise of executive power instead of the
tiresome and demoralizing process of avoiding decisions, of evading responsibility."[60]

The respect of the scientific and academic community for the
administration—never very generous, reached a nadir as a result

of the Oppenheimer verdict. Speaking later about President Johnson and his lack of prestige in the intellectual community, Lippmann said no man could be a great president without the support of the scientific and academic élite.[61]

In the Ladejinsky case, which developed soon after the Oppenheimer affair, Eisenhower's lack of sensitivity to what Lippmann called "the inviolable rights of the human person" alienated the intellectual community still further. After an investigation had cleared Wolf Ladejinsky, a career employee, of security-risk charges, Eisenhower permitted himself to be trapped into a long discussion of the case during a White House press conference. The substance of the President's "soliloquy" to the press, which filled a column of newspaper space, was that perhaps Ladejinsky was trustworthy and perhaps he was not. The President's recklessness in discussing a case about which he admitted he was uninformed appalled Lippmann. Accusing Eisenhower of perpetrating a "cruel injustice," Lippmann said that the minimum requirement for the conduct of press conferences was that the President be briefed about questions which were sure to arise and be humble and discreet enough to reserve answers to unexpected inquiries.[62]

When a similar attempt to engage the President in a discussion of the loyalty of two State Department employees was made in 1962, President Kennedy sharply rebuked a reporter who asked the question. He was familiar with the records of both men, Kennedy said angrily, and added that he hoped they could continue to serve their country "without detriment to their characters by your question." Both men had been cleared to perform their assigned duties, Kennedy pointed out, and suggested that a reporter using "the very strong term" security-risk should be prepared to substantiate it.[63]

Charitably, Lippmann blamed most of Eisenhower's weaknesses on the Old Guard of the Republican Party, particularly on the chairmen of Senate Committees. He rejoiced when the Democrats gained control of Congress in 1954, and urged the election of a Democratic Congress in 1956 to complement the second Eisenhower administration. Freed from the pressure to appease powerful recalcitrants in his own party, Lippmann said, the General could be "the only kind of President which by training and temperament he is made to be: a President who stands above and not in the middle of the party struggle."[64]

And now reconciled to the kind of federal support and control which he had deplored during the New Deal, Lippmann said that a Democratic Congress would permit the President successfully to propose a "new plateau of Federal expenditure" for schools, hospitals, roads, and housing which were desperately needed by the exploding population.[65]

Except for some rather severe criticism of *The Public Philosophy*, one of his "big" books, which was published in 1955, Lippmann's work and reputation during the 1950's escaped the vigorous detraction encountered in the two preceding decades. Indeed the praise bestowed upon him was sometimes a bit slathering.

In 1951, reviewing Lippmann's work from the time of his graduation from Harvard, Richard Rovere said: "The remarkable thing about his career ... is the number of summits he has ascended—or, more accurately, descended upon ... The radiant and reigning genius of the editorial page of the New York *World,* the meeting place of the greatest congress of journalistic intellects in American history ... In all of American daily journalism, Lippmann's column is the one continuous act of cerebration ... that second noblest work of God, a thinking man ... at the summit of his influence." Although Lippmann was and had been intimately associated with members of the cabinet, his influence on policy, Rovere said, was exerted through his writing rather than through personal discourse. Public officials in America and abroad, he said, "have been giving wings, wheels and fire-power to Walter Lippmann's words." Rovere's explicit reference was to Lippmann's insistent persuasion that America's basic commitment was defense of the Atlantic community and that attempts to suppress Communism all over Asia would prove disastrous.

The caution which Lippmann advocated with respect to foreign policy, Rovere said later, was only one exemplification of the basic maxim that permeated all his beliefs: "Don't make a bite larger than the mouth ... Grasp only what your hand can hold ... Stay within the realm of the possible ..." The stately newspaper articles and the statelier books which elaborated this creed, Rovere said, were the product of a stylist whose control of the language was always admirable, and, in the books at least, without the slightest flaw.[66]

In a 1954 series of three articles entitled "A Preface to Lippmann," John Mason Brown stressed the same themes: calmness, restraint, lucidity. Over the years, Brown said, Lippmann had come to function as a one-man State Department, sometimes to the distress of secretaries of state, whose policies could not be as flexible as Lippmann's opinions. Brown also credited him with considerable influence on domestic affairs, mentioning particularly his constant concern for the protection of the individual against encroachments of the state.[67]

Curiously enough, it was Lippmann's interest in the obverse of this problem—the need to protect government against the encroachments of the individual, or against the masses of individuals whose opinions lead government astray—which prompted him to engage in public controversy with one of his critics, a venture always distasteful to him. Soon after the publication of *The Public Philosophy*, Archibald MacLeish wrote a 6,000-word essay about it for the *Yale Review* in which he accused Lippmann of conducting "a retreat from the idea of freedom as that idea has been understood in this Republic."

Lippmann's thesis, MacLeish said, was that democratic governments had suffered since World War I a catastrophic decline in power, that the decline was due to too much democracy and too little government, that radical measures were needed to counteract the pressure of the masses, that dissent and dispute should be encouraged only within the limits of a universal philosophy on which all reasonable men were agreed. These ideas, MacLeish said, were neither novel nor particularly significant. But both significant and novel was the fact that Lippmann, "a writer whose career has been closely associated with the development of democratic ideas . . . one of the most habituated of democratic journalists," was promulgating them.

"It is one thing," MacLeish said, "for an American, thoroughly familiar with the American situation, to assert that our position is dangerous and our society far from perfect . . . It is another thing altogether for such a commentator to assert that the ideas which have made a nation of us—the ideas which have shaped our development since the beginning of the nineteenth century—are pernicious ideas which should now be renounced: that the modern democratic belief in the greatest possible individual freedom itself is false doctrine."

What galled Lippmann especially was MacLeish's assertion that he epitomized the loss of the love of freedom and that the loss had permitted McCarthyism to flourish. In MacLeish's view, Lippmann wrote, "I have become an extraordinary example of a dual personality: while Mr. Hyde was writing a sinister book retreating from freedom, Dr. Jekyll was writing column after column for the New York *Herald Tribune* syndicate about the menace of McCarthyism to our freedom..." And as a matter of fact, he added, McCarthyism was an example of "the derangement of powers" which democracy had suffered, and the columns attacking him were reaffirmation of the idea of the book.

It was curious, Lippmann said, that he and MacLeish, "each believing he is on the side of the angels, appear to differ so much on what is the idea of freedom as it has been understood in this republic." The difference appeared to derive, he said, from the failure to distinguish the two abodes of freedom—the realm of essence in which the liberty of the individual human spirit was boundless, and the realm of existence in which the freedom of individuals must be kept within bounds.

"With Mr. MacLeish," Lippmann said, "I believe in 'the boundless liberty of the human spirit.' But I do not believe, and neither can he, that boundless liberty is 'possible' in the public actions of everyone." In the inward and private country of the mind, he said, freedom could be boundless. But in the outward, public country it could only be as great as possible. The founders of our republic were aware of the distinction between the two realms, Lippmann said, but their successors, having lost sight of it, had placed democracy in peril.[68]

MacLeish's condemnation of Lippmann's view of freedom is difficult to understand, except on the impossible assumption that he was a newcomer to the works of Lippmann, for the distrust of popular rule was made explicit at least as early as 1925 in *The Phantom Public*. The new theme in *The Public Philosophy* was the insistence that "a universal order," "a natural law" objectively exists and must be obeyed, that there are "certain principles which... only the willfully irrational can deny... and that only the willfully subversive can reject..."[69] The earlier Lippmann was content to base his hope for social and political sanity on a procedural foundation—"the maintenance of a regime of rule, contract and custom." The Lippmann of 1955, as Arthur M. Schlesinger, Jr., pointed out, apotheosized conformity into transcendental faith. "Lippmann's conception of natural law," Schlesinger said, "cannot help seem an artificial construct," and he suggested that Lippmann was caught in a position that he himself had warned against twenty-five years earlier—"flight from the human problem . . . search for perfect adjustment . . ."[70] Heinz Eulau, who published a series of articles about Lippmann, said that in *The Public Philosophy* "Walter Lippmann has reached the end of a long and lonely intellectual road." The book, he added, "is Mr. Lippmann's final rationalization of his dislike of the masses, distrust of democratic processes, and dislike of the main currents of American life." In essence, he said, what Lippmann advocated was no less than a return to aristocratic power.[71]

In a letter praising the book, his old friend Bernard Berenson wrote to Lippmann: "I fear there is no remedy . . . unless we return to a graduated, a pyramidal, i.e. hierarchical and even oligarchical society . . . The people now as hitherto care only for *panem et circenses,* are indifferent to our ideals and our values and will not listen to us . . . to return to a Public Philosophy would be conceivable in an aristocratic community that temporarily had got off the rails or lost its North Star but scarcely in this kind of community to which we are now being reduced."

Berenson noted that the response to the book had been immediate—it was published in eight languages, including Korean and Arabic—but he added wistfully that it "would be hopeful if those who read and understand it had the power and authority."[72]

Chapter VII

CIVIL RIGHTS,
AND A CREDO
FOR JOURNALISTS

IN 1919 LIPPMANN WROTE THE INTRODUCTION TO *Chicago Race Riots*, a book by Carl Sandburg. The race problem, Lippmann said, "is really a by-product of our planless, disordered, bedraggled drifting democracy." The only solution, he said, was to learn how to clean up what he called "a dirty civilization" and to guarantee the Negro and white alike decent housing and wages, civil liberties, and educational opportunity. Once all this was attained, he said, "the ideal would seem to lie in race parallelism," which would free the whites from the fear of amalgamation and give the Negro "complete access to all the machinery of our common civilization."[1]

This proposal had the ring, presumably especially to Negro ears, of the 1896 Plessy doctrine of "separate but equal," which the Supreme Court overturned in 1954. Commenting on the 1954 decision, Lippmann said that though the Plessy doctrine had aided the Negro substantially it sanctioned a caste system which had become repugnant to the conscience of the country. Lippmann praised the "statesmanlike" decision of Justice Earl Warren and his colleagues, predicted that the states would loyally accept the new principle, but cautioned that a radical increase in educational appropriations, particularly in the southern states, would be needed to implement it.[2]

When compliance with the decision proved to be negligible, Lippmann opposed coercion, including the withholding of federal funds to segregated school districts. To do so, he warned, would lower the level of education and harden the temper of resistance.[3]

When Adlai Stevenson was asked if he would, as President, use the Army to enforce integration, Lippmann was horrified. In replying that he would not do so, Stevenson gave the only conceivable answer, Lippmann said. "It is ominous, however, that the question should have been put to him at all . . ." It might well be, Lippmann said, that in the deep South, for a long time to come, integration would be impossible except for college and university students in graduate and professional schools.[4]

When *Life* magazine published William Faulkner's famous letter appealing for gradualism and for northern sympathy toward southern moderates, Lippmann said that "we can have no great hope that mutual warnings like Mr. Faulkner's and mine, that these pious exhortations to reason and moderation, will in themselves be heeded." The weakness of his own position, he conceded, was the absence of "a consensus of enlightened opinion" about the pace at which integration should proceed, and he suggested that President Eisenhower might exert his leadership to produce a solution.[5]

But the President disappointed him once again. After Governor Orval Faubus of Arkansas used the National Guard "to maintain law and order" at the Little Rock High School—and thus blocked the enrollment of Negro children—Lippmann approved the President's dispatch of federal troops to suppress state defiance. However, when Eisenhower told a press conference that he was obliged to "execute" court decisions but not obliged to say whether he agreed with them, Lippmann said that this was "a weird view" of the presidential office—a view which "would have horrified all his predecessors, all, at least since Buchanan." Eisenhower was not even able to perceive the nature of the problem, Lippmann said. "He thinks of it as a problem of maintaining law and order against violence . . . But what we have today in Arkansas and elsewhere is the defiance of Federal law, not by mobs but by the State government . . ." In such an impasse, Lippmann said, internal diplomacy, i.e., negotiation between Federal and state authorities of a policy for gradual integration, was the only solution. The alternative, resort to the use of overwhelming force to crush the resistance, he said, "of course, is ruled out."[6]

Although he despaired of success, Lippmann continued to advocate "a negotiated program to modify, reduce, restrict and eventually to dissolve the principle of segregation." Outside the

South, he said, no political leader was willing to call publicly for a gradual solution, and in the South no influential politician dared risk an appeal to reason. The drab prospect of massive resistance and an occasional federal foray against some particular southern school would continue, he said, unless the northern and southern Democrats were driven to a compromise in the 1960 national convention. "This might well engage," he said, "the fixing abilities of Senator Lyndon Johnson and the broad nationalism of Governor Stevenson."[7]

Doubting the wisdom of instant integration of the schools, Lippmann entertained no doubts about the desirability of integrating the ballot box, though he did express reservations about the Supreme Court's efforts to weigh all votes approximately evenly. Attempts to continue to disfranchise the Negro and to suppress demonstrations against denial of the right to vote he regarded as abhorrent. "This time and in this case," he wrote—the time was 1965 and the incident was the brutal dispersal of marchers in Selma, Alabama—"the issue of civil rights is clear as crystal. There are no fuzzy edges as there were and are on the problem of the desegregation of the schools and of public accommodations . . . Because the basic issue is so clear-cut, the human reaction of the American people to the outrage in Selma is not sicklied o'er with any pale cast of intellectual doubt."[8]

But on the question of "one man—one vote," Lippmann, quite predictably, agreed with the need for reform but cautioned against a crash program to achieve it. Lippmann defended the Supreme Court against charges of usurpation of power, saying that when there is no other legal remedy for substantive evil in the democratic process, intervention of the court is indispensable. But he added that "it is nevertheless true that the problem here, unlike that of the civil rights bill a few months ago, is not such a present danger that delay is intolerable . . . Very great things are at stake, and it would be a bad sign if those of us who favor reapportionment were not made to debate the plan and justify our case."

There were two principal arguments to justify the continuing domination of state legislatures by rural voters. The first, that "stable and virtuous farmers . . . should . . . prevent the urban masses from ruling the State," could no longer prevail, he said, in a nation two thirds urban and suburban. The second argument, that the senate in a legislature should be so constructed as "to moderate the impulsiveness of the house of representatives," he found persuasive, and suggested that even under the one-man, one-vote rule this could be accomplished by continuing the custom of making the senates smaller, by giving senators longer terms and by permitting them to delay but never to veto legislation passed by the house.

Lippmann took the position here, as he had in the school desegregation controversy, that too big a burden was being placed on the Supreme Court, that Congress and the Executive should assume responsibility for the redress of social and political grievances. A year before the reapportionment dispute, when President Kennedy asked Congress for civil rights legislation, Lippmann wrote: "At long last, a President has recognized that the law of the land as defined by the courts must be enforced by executive action under a legislative mandate from the Congress... It is a late beginning. The principle should have been applied nine years ago... in the school cases."[9]

Writing of the march on Washington in the summer of 1963, Lippmann said: "The American Negro movement is not at all revolutionary... We must never forget, however, that... if the redress of grievances is denied too long, it could and probably would become clandestine, violent, and ugly." The Negroes' new demands, for better jobs and housing, he feared, would not be met. The necessary measures, he said, "are distrusted and opposed in Congress and, it would seem in the country as well."[10] More pessimistically, after the riots during the summer of 1967, Lippmann said that the young Negroes could no longer live "on promises, on small tokens, and samples of better things to come." The only way to reconcile them and assuage their grievances, Lippmann said, was to abandon the idea that the uplifting of the Negro is a separate enterprise rather than a part of the central problem of reconstructing the entire social order. "But this undertaking," he concluded... "is possible only if it becomes the main preoccupation of the whole nation. And that is impossible while the nation is distracted and preoccupied by a foreign war it does not understand and does not believe in."[11] Lippmann saw some virtue even in what he described as "the irrationality and wildness of black power." The feeling among Negroes that they must help themselves rather than rely on white governmental philanthropy was, he said, "one of the bright spots in a somber picture."[12]

But massive riots in northern cities and American involvement in an Asian civil war were but spectral possibilities in 1956, when Lippmann was obliged to advise his 20 million potential readers about the choice of a President, the Suez Canal crisis, the uprisings against the Soviets in Poland and Hungary.

Eisenhower's decision to seek a second term in spite of his age and illness confronted the country with "a big gamble," Lippmann said. "The risks of the gamble could be somewhat reduced if the Congress will clarify the constitutional puzzle of what happens if the President is disabled or seriously diminished," he said. "But in any case the gamble remains and the stakes are very high."[13]

Lippmann disliked "the device of the regency," the administration of the Presidency by Sherman Adams during Eisenhower's two illnesses, and urged that in any future emergency the Vice-President should discharge the powers and duties of the President. The President's illness, he believed, had had an unfortunate effect on the conduct of foreign affairs. Secretary Dulles, he said, had "enlarged his own personal operations to take in propaganda and psychological warfare." This new role, he said was "bad for our diplomacy and our propaganda as well."[14]

A secretary of state or a foreign minister, Lippmann said, must operate on a moral plane much higher than that of a propagandist. "He must be known as a man of his word, as one who uses words precisely which mean genuinely what they say . . . Words are used by the propagandist not to convey the whole truth as he knows it but to work an effect on other men's minds . . ." A secretary of state who practices propaganda, Lippmann said, was "like a doctor who sells patent medicine." All governments, Lippmann continued, discounted their own propaganda and that of others, refusing to regard it as the expression of serious intention and policy.

Dulles, he observed, was making it difficult to play the game by the traditional rules, and was playing it badly by his new rules. The upheaval within the Communist world caused by Khrushchev's destruction of Stalin's reputation was being exploited by Dulles, Lippmann said, as the product of American intervention. "Mr. Dulles," he added, "has provided the most obvious pretext for the repression of the upheaval—that it is the work of an anti-Communist underground backed by the United States Government."[15]

As the presidential campaign of 1956 began, Lippmann urged that the Democrats nominate Stevenson again and ridiculed former President Truman's attempt to deny him the nomination. Truman was living in the past, he said, "forever wanting to fight again the old battles of the New Deal and of the Fair Deal and of the Stalinist era of the cold war." The old formulae and slogans were useless, he said, and Stevenson knew it and was capable of reevaluating them. "The fact that Stevenson has brains and that he knows how to use them will . . . count heavily in his favor."[16]

Lippmann praised the Democrats for conducting an open convention and said that the excellent work of the television reporters permitted the public to view the struggle for leadership and the controversy over civil rights. The Republicans, on the contrary, he said, met only to ratify decisions already made. With Eisenhower's nomination, and presumably his election, already assured, Lippmann said, the key position for the professional politicians was the vice-presidency and they "used the steamroller to flatten out the opposition" to Nixon. "The President," Lippmann noted, "though he has shown faint signs of regretting that the convention has nothing to do, has not objected seriously . . . As a result, the convention has had nothing to do but listen to ghost-written speeches, and to watch a stage-managed show, and to vote yes."[17]

As the campaign progressed, Lippmann said that the big television speeches were redundant, a contrived performance which concealed rather than revealed the candidates. "Hence the demand," he said, "for personal appearances, for the candidates in the flesh . . ." There were no national issues dividing Eisenhower and Stevenson sharply, he said, and the human issue, whether to entrust the Presidency to a man who had suffered serious illness could not, in good taste, be publicly discussed. The contest, he said, was not between two parties: It was between Eisenhower and the Democratic party. "But for Eisenhower personally, the Republicans would not have a chance to elect the next President."[18]

Toward the end of the campaign, when the Suez crisis developed, Lippmann castigated Eisenhower and Dulles severely for failing to keep in touch with developments in the Middle East and for devising no policy except to frustrate Britain and France. "General Eisenhower . . . reacts peaceably when a crisis reaches the point where a war might come," Lippmann said. "He does not react much sooner. He reacts to what is happening, and does little to foresee and little to prepare for what is going to happen. The result is that his solutions are stalemates in which he accepts the status quo . . . teaching his countrymen to live in the present with no serious concern about the future."[19]

After the election, Lippmann said that "a great contented majority" had given Eisenhower, but not his party, "an enormous vote of confidence," and attributed it to "the prosperity of the country, his personal prestige both in war and peace, and his achievements as the healer of the internal divisions of the country." But Lippmann predicted that Eisenhower's political influence would decline in his second term and that "Mr. Nixon's power and influence will be enormously greater."[20]

When the President was exposed to press conference questions about the conduct of Sherman Adams, his *alter ego* who presided over White House affairs, Lippmann said that it "must have been as unpleasant an experience as Mr. Eisenhower has passed through in his charmed and lucky career." (Sometimes Lippmann referred to Eisenhower as "Mr.," sometimes as "Gen.," and though a pattern of the use of the civilian term when domestic affairs were involved and of the military term in connection with foreign affairs seems to emerge, it is not consistent. Perhaps it was one of Lippmann's rare addictions to "journalese," in which the compulsion to use synonyms is strong.)

The President tried to evade the issue in the Adams affair by contending that though Adams had accepted gifts they had never caused him to exert his influence on behalf of the donor. James Reston of the New York *Times* pinned Eisenhower down by inquiring whether the extenuation applied to all other federal officials. It was the crucial question, Lippmann said, and predicted that Eisenhower must reconcile himself to letting Adams resign. It was true, Lippmann said, that Eisenhower's dependence on Adams was unprecedented, even greater than Wilson's need of Colonel House or Roosevelt's of Harry Hopkins, but Adams could not be kept on, he said "without making a shambles of his [Eisenhower's] standards of public propriety and public virtue."[21]

Lippmann accused the administration of attempting to control the press and to suppress information about the declining position of the country in the arms race with the Soviet Union. His main target was Secretary Dulles, one of his old friends. When a clamor arose in 1957 for the State Department to rescind its prohibition against American correspondents traveling to Red China, and Dulles relented to the extent of offering to let twenty-four selected correspondents go there, Lippmann reacted with unusual vigor. The proposal was both spurious and dictatorial, he said—spurious because it failed to provide reciprocity for Chinese correspondents traveling to America and dictatorial because it usurped the right of the press to decide where and by whom news should be reported.

Under the circumstances, Lippmann said, the Red Chinese were unlikely to swallow their pride and grant visas to Americans. "But then," he added sarcastically, "as Mr. Dulles may conceivably have foreseen, he can argue that it is the Red Chinese and not he who prevent the American press from gathering news on the Chinese mainland. He can even be disappointed and indignant at these totalitarians who do not believe in freedom of the press."

Dulles was attempting to establish "a new and hitherto entirely un-American conception" of the press, Lippmann said—to treat it as an instrument of his own policy, to decide when it became "desirable that additional information be made available to the American people . . . We have here the unprecedented and impertinent assertion that the right to turn off and the right to turn on the tap of news is one of the prerogatives of the Secretary of State."

The government had only the right to warn newspapermen where it might be dangerous to go and to tell them they could expect no help if they encountered trouble, Lippmann said. But to go or not to go anywhere in the world, he said, was for editor and reporter to decide. "All this," he concluded, "discloses the fact that Mr. Dulles has an imperfect grasp of the principles of a free press in a free society."[22]

After the Russians launched their first satellite, and fears of American danger and vulnerability arose, Lippmann accused the administration of telling only a half truth when it began to deny rumors, based on leaks to the press, of the secret Gaither report on national defense, that the country was in peril. It was undoubtedly true, Lippmann said, that we were still stronger than the Russians, but in the development of new weapons our technology had become second-best. There was, he said, "a grave impairment of confidence" because of a widespread belief "that intelligence

reports on the real position in the race of armaments have somehow been ignored by the President or suppressed before they
reached him."[23]

In the Russian satellite achievement Lippmann saw "a profound
challenge to our cultural values" and cautioned that the way to
meet it was by neither propaganda nor a spectacular feat of arms
to outmatch the Soviets. Our great prosperity, he said, had led
our people "to believe in the enormous fallacy that the highest
purpose of the American social order is to multiply the enjoyment
of consumer goods." Equally fallacious, he said, was the popular
distrust of intellectuality—the suspicion that to be a highbrow
was to be subversive. "With prosperity acting as a narcotic," he
said, "with Philistinism and McCarthy rampant, our public life
has been increasingly doped and without purpose.With the President in a kind of partial retirement, there is no standard raised
to which the people can repair." Though the challenge to our
military power must be met, he concluded, the fundamental challenge was to restore the scientific and intellectual superiority of
the West.[24]

Applauding a Senate speech by John F. Kennedy, warning of
our weakness, Lippmann said that neither the Republican nor
Democratic leadership in Congress was responding to the alarms
that men like Kennedy, Stewart Symington, and Henry Jackson
were sounding in the Senate and Joseph Alsop was sounding
in the press. " . . . we turn over and go to sleep again."[25]

When Russian propaganda began to exert pressure in 1958
for suspension of testing nuclear weapons and for a summit meeting, Lippmann found the American response ineffective, partly
because of adverse events and partly because of a lack of candor
in the war of words. Although the points made in a propaganda
contest could not be scored precisely, he said, "we know on no
less an authority than Mr. Dulles himself that at this stage in
the game the Russians are leading."

Always distrustful of summit meetings unless an agreement were
reached in advance about what was negotiable, Lippmann won-
dered why "this wrong-headed idea is winning such popular support in the Western world." The answer, he believed, was that
Dulles, the British and the West German leaders had "given the
impression not only that they do not want to negotiate at the
summit but that they do not want to negotiate at all." Although

it was true that on the big issues of the cold war, such as reunification of Germany, there could be no successful negotiations, Lippmann said, the West was missing an opportunity, purely propagandistic, to offer to negotiate below the summit some small specific issue like limiting arms to the Middle East. As long as the Western governments continued to say no to everything, Lippmann said, "they are surrendering the diplomatic and the propagandistic initiative to the Soviet Union." Elaborate proposals for general disarmament or "metaphysical negotiation . . . in the vast reaches of outer space," were, he said, ludicrous gambits in the propaganda game.[26]

To regard the Russian proposal to suspend nuclear testing as a "gimmick" or a "propaganda trick," Lippmann said, missed the point. The Russians had concluded, he said, that the world balance of power was shifting in their favor, that a freeze in the development of nuclear weapons would accelerate it, and that therefore they could sincerely offer an agreement on which they would not need to cheat.[27] When the Russians did suspend testing and Dulles told a press conference that it was a propaganda stunt, Lippmann said, "This theory may comfort him, but it is, I venture to believe, a dangerous form of escapism from the hard realities of the world situation."

The notion that America's declining prestige was due not to any defects in our position but to superior Soviet propaganda, was a comforting self-delusion, Lippmann said. "The whole world would agree with John Foster Dulles if it were not that the world is so gullible that it is being taken in by the Russians. This is flattering to our pride, but it is not true."

Dulles should have stated candidly, Lippmann said, the reason why we could not risk suspension of testing instead of advancing the fiction that America wanted "to eliminate nuclear weapons effectively from the international arsenals." To tell the world that the threat of the use of nuclear weapons against Russia was our only strong defense might not make Dulles "beloved in the world," Lippmann said, "but it would make him believed."[28]

American propaganda worked badly in general, Lippmann said, because it was based on a congeries of fictions which the opinion leaders of the world could not believe—the fiction that Formosa was China, the fiction that the Soviets might invade the Middle East, the fiction that West Germany would absorb East Germany.

Policies based on such misconceptions, Lippmann said, could not be "sold" by the cleverest propaganda to informed people, or even to the masses.

Sympathizing with the troubles of the Secretary of State, who had to conduct delicate negotiations with friends and adversaries, and at the same time felt compelled to talk about them in press conferences, Lippmann said that Dulles was too much concerned about saving face and too little concerned that his word should be trusted. "It would be a great relief, and it would enhance the prestige of this country," Lippmann said, "if the Secretary of State announced that the situation had entered a phase where the issues are too delicate and critical to be discussed in public statements. Most people would believe him."[29]

In spite of this criticism, much of it rather severe, Lippmann and Dulles remained warm friends, and in a later column Lippmann explained why. "Long experience has taught me," he wrote, "how rare it is in public men to accept public criticism without private resentment, which only too often spreads to their wives and their sisters and their brothers and their aunts. To be free of that kind of resentment is the mark of a thoroughbred, and the Dulles family are thoroughbreds..." It was true, Lippmann said, that, "Like most men, he [Dulles] preferred praise to criticism and agreement to opposition. But... he respected debate and the practice of free journalism."[30]

The United States lost another round in the propaganda contest with Russia, Lippmann believed, when Khrushchev was interviewed for an American television program. "Like all very high personages," Lippmann said, "he was questioned, but he was not cross-questioned. Protected in this way, he was able to take full advantage of the strong positions which the Soviet Union has staked out for itself and has preempted in the propaganda contest." Khrushchev could make attractive proposals—for nuclear disarmament and for withdrawing foreign troops from all countries—confident that the West could not accept them. "Here it is heads he wins and tails we lose," Lippmann said. "He gains by making the proposal, and he gains when we refuse it. Sooner or later the government's public relations experts... will have to find a way to deal with this dilemma."

The technique of the interview interested Lippmann especially. He himself was soon to interview Khrushchev and to win a Pulitzer

Prize for it, and he was soon to be the subject of a series of television interviews. "The real reason for interviewing public men on television," Lippmann wrote, "is not to communicate news but to reveal what they are like . . . The trouble on Sunday, so it seemed to me, was that one could see Khrushchev but could not listen to him. There was a baffling distinction between the picture of Khrushchev talking and the English words that the translator was uttering." Perhaps, he said, the problem of translation, particularly in an unrehearsed interview without a script, was insoluble. "Yet the problem of translation is all important . . . What was lost was the way Khrushchev was saying it, why he was so often smiling about something he was saying, and how he really put it . . ."[31]

When it was arranged that Khrushchev and his family should visit the United States in the Fall of 1959 and that the Eisenhowers should go to Russia in the Spring of 1960, with a summit meeting in Paris spaced in between or afterwards, Lippmann reacted tepidly to the program, nearly two-thirds of which came to be blown to bits in the U-2 spy plane incident. The notion that by receiving Khrushchev America would be endorsing Communism, Lippmann regarded as doltish.

Former President Truman's objection that "the power and leadership of the Presidency should not be dissipated in ceremonial visits" he found basically sound but, since the normal channels of diplomacy had become frozen, impractical to accept. Informal exchanges of visits between heads of state were a manifestation of the declining influence of foreign ministers, Lippmann said. The old theory that the foreign ministers "were the skilled lawyers who would negotiate the contracts which their rich clients, the heads of government, would sign" became unworkable in the United States after the death of Dulles, Lippmann said, and was unsuitable to the needs of West Germany, France, Russia, and even Britain, because of the rise of personal government. "In the new approach," he said, not without misgiving, "the heads of government conduct parleys to determine whether they can find ground on which they can instruct the foreign ministers to negotiate."

Truman's fears that Eisenhower's journey to Moscow would lead "the world to expect that peace can be advanced by the mere exchange of visits" were unfounded, Lippmann felt, because the world, including the newspaper press, was too sophisticated to entertain false hopes. "The most serious objection to personal Presidential diplomacy in foreign countries is that when the President himself is the negotiator he has no backstop who can instruct him, warn him and overrule him."[32]

The Khrushchev visit included a tour of America, and as it drew to a close, Lippmann expressed relief that the risk of conducting the Soviet leader through our big cities was safely past. "There have been some embarrassing incidents," he said. "These were bound to happen once both governments accepted the half-baked idea that the great issues which divide us can be dealt with by face-to-face catch-as-catch-can encounter." (The "news mob," as it was called, followed Khrushchev through the country, and during a visit to an Iowa farm, the crush of reporters and photographers so irritated him that he aimed a kick at the shin of Harrison Salisbury, one of the New York *Times* experts on the affairs of the Kremlin.)

Resuming his rather disdainful review of the cross-country tour, Lippmann said, "Mr. K. does seem to have embarked on the journey with the odd notion that he could alter American policy by haranguing the people. The President seems to have toyed with the idea that a sightseeing tour of the United States might make a new man of Mr. K." Dismissing all this as "the trivialities and the irrelevancies of the pitter-patter of the propagandists and of the exhibitionists," Lippmann suggested that the President and Mr. Khrushchev would do well to get on with some serious discussions.

As the visit ended, Lippmann confessed that he had been too apprehensive about the risks to Khrushchev and too pessimistic about the success of the adventure in personal diplomacy, and he looked forward hopefully to the new negotiations which were to flow from the visit: a Foreign Ministers' and a summit meeting and the Eisenhowers' trip to Russia.[33]

Spying is "a dirty business, outside the law and outside the moral code," Lippmann said. But it is a business which all governments conduct, with the tacit agreement that the spy's only crime is to be caught and that when he is caught his employer will disavow responsibility for him if the employer can do so without being caught in a lie. When a Russian missile disabled an American spy plane, forced it down, and captured its pilot just before the scheduled summit meeting was convening in Paris, the American government first denied it was a spy plane and then, caught in a lie, denied that it was authorized to fly over Russia. Then, caught in this lie, the government admitted the spying, attempted to justify it as necessary, and vowed that it would continue.

This series of blunders, which wrecked the summit meeting, led the Russians to cancel the invitation for the Eisenhowers' visit, and induced Khrushchev to denounce the President publicly, Lippmann analyzed for his readers in a series of "Today and Tomorrow" articles. Since Eisenhower knew about the flights, he said, it was incredible that he should not have suspended them once the summit meeting was scheduled. When Khrushchev sought to de-emphasize the incident by saying that he did not believe Eisenhower was responsible for ordering the flight, it was beyond belief, Lippmann said, that the President rejected this "diplomatic exit from his quandary." Eisenhower's statement that he was responsible for the flights and that they were necessary was "a direct challenge to the sovereignty of the Soviet Union," Lippmann said, for it sought to compel the Russians to concede that their territory was violable. "No statesman," Lippmann said, "can live in any country after making such an admission."

To say, as some were saying, that the Russians welcomed the spy plane fiasco as a chance to make successful propaganda was naive, Lippmann wrote. "For the Soviet Union there is in this much more than propaganda." Morally and legally, he said, the Russians had been given an opportunity to exert demands that Norway, Iran, Pakistan, Turkey and Japan must neutralize American air bases because they might be used for spying.[34]

After Eisenhower conceded that the U-2 flights had stopped and would not be resumed and Khrushchev suggested the possibility of new summit negotiations in six or eight months, Lippmann said that "the emotions drummed up by propaganda and counter-propaganda" had led to a "breakdown not of diplomatic relations but of diplomatic communications between Moscow and Washington." Even communications would be difficult to restore, Lippmann said, and when they were restored the United States would indubitably have a new President who would be unlikely to go to a summit meeting unless he were certain of avoiding the treatment that Eisenhower—even though he seemed to ask for it—received from Khrushchev. Summitry having failed, Lippmann said, not quite with an air of "good riddance to it," perhaps the Soviet and Western foreign ministers could meet once a month or so under the auspices of the United Nations and quietly discuss "our open skies proposal, disarmament, and, above all, what have you."[35]

One of the greatest dividends accruing to a free society, Lippmann said, was the opportunity to deal with error: to criticize, debate, and investigate blunders. Only through dissent and opposition, he said, could we prove to the world that we were not satisfied with the bad government and political incompetence that prevailed during the U-2 affair. "These are harsh words," he said, mindful that they would be read by the Secretary of State and the President. "But in what other words shall we describe the performance . . . ?"

The proof that we could investigate our own fiascos without giving either aid or comfort to the adversary came during the Senate Foreign Relations Committee inquiry into the spy plane incident, Lippmann said. Praising Senator Fulbright for his "high-mindedness" and "sagacity," Lippmann said that the investigation dealt with a question never before scrutinized in any country. "The question was the competence of the President and his principal advisers in dealing with an entirely illegal . . . operation which is, nevertheless, necessary to the security of the country." The inquiry disclosed, Lippmann said, that the President and the Secretary of State failed to keep in close touch with the operations of the Central Intelligence Agency, failed to keep the "cover" statements in the hands of high officials who knew what was going on, and failed, because they themselves were ignorant of "the conventions and practices which have always surrounded the black art of espionage," to refrain from panic.[36]

When the outcry arose in 1967 against the Central Intelligence Agency for secretly paying students, professors, and journalists to conduct anti-Communist propaganda, Lippmann said that "the CIA operation has begun to smell like a backed up cesspool." The revulsion against the deception, corruption, and lying proved once again, he said, that a free society could not tolerate, except under conditions of panic and fear, behaving as if it were a totalitarian state.[37]

The cloud of suspicion generated at first abroad and belatedly in the United States by all the clandestine operations of the CIA could be dispelled, he said, only by divorcing the agency from all activity except intelligence work, i.e., "espionage, research and analysis." Other activities, especially propaganda, he said, "should not be under the same roof, they should not be manned by the same men and they should not be under the same cloak of secrecy." All American propaganda should be open and avowed, he said, so that students, professors, journalists, trade union members who travelled abroad need not be under suspicion.[38]

Activities such as intervention in the affairs of foreign governments, if intervention was vital, could be managed by the Defense Department, Lippmann said. "As to the dirty tricks, like bribing a politician somewhere abroad, the American Republic will survive if such dirty tricks are not performed."

To argue that all the CIA activities were conducted by able, courageous, patriotic Americans and that what they did was sanctioned by Truman, Eisenhower, Kennedy, and Johnson was perfectly true, Lippmann said, but it missed the point: that most of the activities were self-defeating. Black propaganda, intervention, and intrigue, he said, "are the methods of a totalitarian state and without a totalitarian environment of secrecy and terror, they are unworkable."[39]

As the U-2 incident continued to reverberate in the developing campaign of 1960—particularly with statements from Khrushchev that he would not seriously negotiate with Eisenhower or with Nixon—Lippmann said that Khrushchev's endorsement of the Democrats would not be of consequence. "For their basic position—as defined by Stevenson, Kennedy, Symington, and in some measure by Johnson—is quite invulnerable to the charge that they are softer on Communism," Lippmann said. But it was nevertheless embarrassing, he said, to be the beneficiary of a Russian propaganda campaign which insulted the President and defamed his office.

What Khrushchev sought to do—and Lippmann said he had to do it—was to destroy the world image, to which he had contributed greatly, of Ike the Peacemaker, and to purge himself of an association with it. Khrushchev had "played Eisenhower as his trump card" in his efforts to persuade the Communist world that a detente with the West had become necessary, Lippmann said. "He staked his prestige on the personality of the anti-Communist head of an anti-Communist state, a deeply conservative General presiding over a highly capitalistic administration. After the U-2 affair . . . Mr. K. was in a position which is intolerable for a dictator. He had been made to look ridiculous, gullible, and weak, in the presence of the Communist world." Hence, Lippmann said, Khrushchev's "prolonged fury."[40]

When Dr. Gallup asked voters, "Who can do the best job of dealing with the Russians?" Lippmann said that, though the pollsters had not come to interview him, he would like to ruminate on the question. Once a Presidential candidate had established his general qualifications, Lippmann said, among the first questions directed to him might be to inquire whether he played chess—not poker and not golf, he said, perhaps with Truman and Eisenhower in mind. In poker a bluff might win, he said, and in golf "what you are trying for is a bloodless and mindless abstraction, something better or not much worse than par for the course." In chess, which is, he noted, the national game of Russia, one uses exactly equal forces to try to outmaneuver the adversary by intelligence and imagination. You can't win, he observed, by proclaiming that "your own white pieces are obviously purer and nobler than his sinister black pieces." Bluffing, getting stubborn or getting tough, trying to sweep the board, do not prevail, he said, in chess or politics; and in politics "good intentions, sincerity, charm and magnetism are, so to speak, only the adjectives; they are not the nouns and verbs . . ."[41]

Continuing the games analogy, Lippmann said that the good newspaper reporter had to be adept in solving jigsaw puzzles rather than at playing chess. In a speech to the National Press Club, which honored him on his 70th birthday, September 23, 1959, Lippmann attempted to analyze the qualifications that a political correspondent needed to perform his task successfully in a world which he said had grown fantastically complex since the depression of 1929. The modern Washington correspondent, he said, "is a product of the world-wide depression and of the social upheaval which followed it, and of the imminence of war during the 1930's." His generation, he said, had "had to find its way through an uncharted wilderness . . . to be explorers of a world that was unknown to us and of mighty events which were unforeseen."

Reporting no longer could be regarded as it was in simpler days when a crude but workable distinction could be made between fact and opinion or fact and interpretation, he said. Even assuming that the relevant facts were obtainable—which they often are not: a first-hand report of what is going on in China, a correct assessment of the mood of the voters, a look at what goes on inside Khrushchev's head—to give the reader only the news of happenings, he said, "would be like the pieces of a jigsaw puzzle thrown in a heap upon the table. The unarranged pieces of raw news would not make a picture at all, and fitting them together so that they do make a picture, is the inescapable job of the Washington correspondent."

But, he hastened to add, the analogy was imperfect. "Our job is harder than it implies. In real life, there is not as there is in every jigsaw puzzle, one picture and one picture only into which all the pieces will eventually fit."

Next Lippmann gave his audience—the Washington press corps and their guests, including members of the Cabinet and Vice-President Nixon—a credo for liberal journalism and an *apologia pro vita sua*.

"It is the totalitarian mind," he said, "which thinks that there is one and only one picture. All the various brands of totalitarianism, as violently as they differ among themselves, have this in common. Each holds that it has the key and pattern of history, that it knows the scheme of things, and that all that happens is foreseen and explained in its doctrine.

"But, to the liberal mind, this claim—like any other human claim to omniscience—is presumptuous and it is false. Nobody knows that much. The future is not predetermined in any book that any man has written. The future is what man will make it; and about the present, in which the future is being prepared, we know something, but not everything, and not nearly enough.

"Because we are newspapermen in the American liberal tradition, the way we interpret the news is not by fitting the facts to a dogma. It is by proposing theories or hypotheses, which are then tested by trial and error. We put forward the most plausible interpretation we can think of, the most plausible picture into which the raw news fits, and then we wait to see whether the later news fits into the interpretation. We do well if, with only a minor change of the interpretation, the later news fits into it. If the later events do not fit, if the later news knocks down the earlier story, there are two things to be done. One is to scrap the theory and the interpretation, which is what liberal, honest men do. The other is to distort or suppress the unmanageable piece of news.

"Last summer, while walking in the woods and on the mountains near where I live, I found myself daydreaming about how I would answer, about how I would explain and justify the business of being opinionated and of airing opinions regularly several times a week.

" 'Is it not absurd,' I heard critics saying, 'that anyone should think he knows enough to write so much about so many things? You write about foreign policy. Do you see the cables which pour into the State Department every day from all parts of the world? Do you attend the staff meetings of the Secretary of State and his advisers? Are you a member of the National Security Council? And what about all those other countries which you write about? Do you have the run of 10 Downing Street, and how do you listen in on the deliberations of the Presidium in the Kremlin? Why don't you admit that you are an outsider and that you are, therefore, by definition, an ignoramus?

" 'How, then, do you presume to interpret, much less criticize and to disagree with, the policy of your own government or any other government?

" 'And, in internal affairs, are you really much better qualified to pontificate? No doubt there are fewer secrets here, and almost all politicians can be talked to. They can be asked the most embarrassing questions. And they will answer with varying degrees of candor and of guile. But, if there are not so many secrets, you must admit that there are many mysteries. The greatest of all the mysteries is what the voters think, feel, and want today, what they will think and feel and want on election day, and what they can be induced to think and feel and want by argument, by exhortation, by threats and promises, and by the arts of manipulation and leadership.'

"Yet, formidable as it is, in my daydream I have no trouble getting the better of this criticism. 'And you, my dear fellow,' I tell the critic, 'you be careful. If you go on, you will be showing how ridiculous it is that we live in a republic under a democratic system and that anyone should be allowed to vote. You will be denouncing the principle of democracy itself, which asserts that the outsiders shall be sovereign over the insiders. For you will be showing that the people, since they are ignoramuses, because they are outsiders, are therefore incapable of governing themselves.

" 'What is more, you will be proving that not even the insiders are qualified to govern them intelligently. For there are very few men—perhaps forty at a maximum—who read, or at least are eligible to read, all the cables that pour into the State Department. And then, when you think about it, how many senators, representatives, governors, and mayors—all of whom have very strong opinions about who should conduct our affairs—ever read these cables which you are talking about?

" 'Do you realize that, about most of the affairs of the world, we are all outsiders and ignoramuses, even the insiders who are at the seat of the government? The Secretary of State is allowed to read every American document he is interested in. But how many of them does he read? Even if he reads the American documents, he cannot read the British and the Canadian, the French and the German, the Chinese and the Russian. Yet he has to make decisions in which the stakes may well be peace or war. And about these decisions, the Congress, which reads very few documents, has to make decisions too.'

"Thus, in my daydream, I reduce the needler to a condition of sufficient humility about the universal ignorance of mankind. Then I turn upon him and with suitable eloquence declaim an apology for the existence of the Washington correspondent.

" 'If the country is to be governed with the consent of the governed, then the governed must arrive at opinions about what their governors want them to consent to. How do they do this?

" 'They do it by hearing on the radio and reading in the newspapers what the corps of correspondents tell them is going on in Washington, and in the country at large, and in the world. Here, we correspondents perform an essential service. In some field of interest, we make it our business to find out what is going on under the surface and beyond the horizon, to infer, to deduce, to imagine, and to guess what is going on inside, what this meant yesterday, and what it could mean tomorrow.

" 'In this we do what every sovereign citizen is supposed to do but has not the time or the interest to do for himself. This is our job. It is no mean calling. We have a right to be proud of it and to be glad that it is our work.' "[42]

Lippmann was also honored on his 70th birthday by the publication of the book called *Walter Lippmann and His Times,* a series of essays written for the occasion by his colleagues and old friends. Foremost of the book's many virtues was the fact that among its dozen authors were men who had known Lippmann at one time or another from the day he was seven to the day he was seventy. Carl Binger, who was a classmate of Lippmann's from elementary school through college, remembered his precocity. ("I don't suppose that he got less than an A on any examination in his life.") His French was excellent, he could translate Ovid at sight, and he was the only boy in school who learned enough Greek to satisfy the principal. At Harvard the achievement was the same, sampling the potpourri of courses which President Eliot's free elective system permitted and breezing to an A.B. degree *cum laude* in three years.

George Kennan supplied for the book the story of Lippmann's *New Republic* days; Allan Nevins, the account of the New York *World* editorship; Marquis Childs, Arthur Krock, and James Reston their estimation and appreciation of the author of "Today and Tomorrow." Foreign journalists, including Iverach McDonald of the *Times* of London and Raymond Aron of *Figaro,* wrote of what they called Lippmann's unique place in international journalism. Harry Ashmore contributed an essay on Lippmann's position in the journalistic political spectrum. ("He will show liberal on one issue and conservative on another . . .") Though Lippmann was not a southern hero like David Lawrence, who, Ashmore said, "evokes a mighty chorus of rebel yells," the moderation of his views made his column acceptable on southern editorial pages. He added that even in "the great American journalistic deserts," like Texas and California, the traveler might be reminded by the Lippmann column that a world exists east of the Rockies and north of the Red River Valley.

Reinhold Niebuhr and Arthur Schlesinger, Jr., evaluated Lippmann's work as moral and political philosopher, with emphasis on the books rather than on the journalism. Schlesinger saw Lippmann the intellectual veering always away from the popular course, gravitating now towards pluralism, now toward monism, and then back again. "When the crowd has boasted a common faith, as in the twenties, Lippmann has stressed pluralism; when the crowd appears to have no faith at all, as in the fifties, he stresses monism; ... when the crowd is overcommitted to drift, he stresses mastery; when the crowd is overcommitted to mastery, he stresses drift." The problem of the One and the Many, Schlesinger suggested, had been around for a long time, and Lippmann was scarcely to be blamed for having failed to solve it. His contribution, Schlesinger said, was to contribute "urbanity and intelligence" to the long dialogue.

With Lippmann the pragmatic journalist-educator, Niebuhr said he always agreed. With Lippmann the political and moral philosopher, he found himself in disagreement. Lippmann's political prescription for the ills of democracy—exercise of greater executive power by an élitist government—would lead to irresponsibility, Niebuhr said, and his moral prescription—restitution of natural law—was too abstract and unrealistic to "allow for the endless contingencies of history and the variety of its configurations."[43]

Newsweek, the magazine for which he was soon to write a twice-monthly commentary, interviewed Lippmann at 70 and asked him to gaze into his crystal ball. "Nobody knows anything about the future of a mass society where everyone can read, write, and vote, and yet where everyone remains undisciplined by events," Lippmann said. "In the long run, I believe the Soviet system will inevitably be softened by the affluence of luxury. But you will have to live 50 years to know what will happen to America."[44]

Chapter VIII

THE CREDIBILITY GAP
AND GOODBYE
TO WASHINGTON

WHAT BEGAN TO HAPPEN TO AMERICA IN 1960, SUPERFICIALLY AT
least, encouraged Lippmann. The candidate of his choice, who
seemed in many ways to approach his ideal of an élitist executive,
was elected President, and there appeared to be hope that the
"drift" and "defeatism" of the Eisenhower years might be
arrested.[1] After the Congressional elections of 1958, Lippmann
said that an old rule of politics was beginning to work—that
about fifteen years after the end of a great war a new political
generation began to take power. The political class of 1946, which
took control after World War II, had been defeated or was retiring
in favor of new men, Lippmann said, because the people had
become weary of old slogans and old ruts—even of Eisenhower,
who was "living in the past." Vice-President Nixon, Lippmann
said, was in a peculiar position: his age placed him in the new
generation, but his politics seemed irretrievably to align him with
the generation that was passing from power. "While he is not
a man of deep and abiding principles and can shift his position,"
Lippmann said, "it is not easy to see how he can now remake
the public image of himself."[2]

As the 1960 campaign opened, Lippmann found it listless, lull-
ing and drugging the people into "apathy and complacency." The
two-party system was throttling debate and stifling innovation,
he said, because the Democrats were perverting the role of the
opposition, opposing Eisenhower where they should be aiding
him and deferring to him where they should oppose him. In

foreign affairs, he said, the Democrats in Congress placated Truman and Acheson, who opposed the administration's attempts to find accommodations with the Soviets, and on domestic affairs they deferred to Lyndon Johnson, their Senate majority leader, who agreed with Eisenhower that federal spending should not be increased. So on the foreign front, Lippmann said, the Democrats had handed Eisenhower a "monopoly on peace" and on the domestic front they had disqualified themselves from criticism.[3]

Before the 1960 convention, Lippmann believed that Stevenson should be the Democratic nominee. His qualifications in foreign and domestic affairs were superior to Kennedy's, Lippmann said, and his nomination would not produce virulent debate and unwholesome division over the issue of a Catholic president. Kennedy should be content to seek the Vice-Presidency, he advised.[4] But when Stevenson declined to work for—"scramble for"—the nomination, Lippmann found Kennedy wholly acceptable and predicted that he could best rally "the large diverse masses of the Democratic party." Among Kennedy's strengths, Lippmann cited "his youth, his sharp and trained intelligence, and his undoubted popular magnetism." If he were nominated, Lippmann said, and "if it comes down to infighting, Nixon will know that he has been in a fight."[5]

The Republican party had an opportunity to offer the country a choice between two men capable of leadership, Lippmann said, "if the party had the sense to nominate Rockefeller" in spite of the fact that Nixon had become Eisenhower's "one and only heir." Though he regarded it as inevitable that Nixon would be chosen by the convention, Lippmann warned that Eisenhower could not bequeath him his "exalted position" or continue to invest the office of President "with the attributes of a constitutional monarchy." As candidate and, if elected, as President, Lippmann said, "Mr. Nixon will be down in the dust and the heat of the battle, not above it in the clear blue yonder." The prospect of a divided government under Nixon, without Eisenhower's prestige to overawe the Democrats controlling Congress, Lippmann found frightening. It would seem, he said, "far less benign than it does under the Eisenhower-Johnson regime."[6]

Lippmann welcomed Kennedy's choice of Johnson as the vice-presidential candidate. "Johnson is a Southerner, but not a sectionalist," he said. "More than any other man in the public life, more than any politician since the Civil War, he has on the race problem been the most effective mediator between the North and the South." So even with a Southerner on the ticket the Democrats assumed a stronger posture on civil rights than the Republicans could, Lippmann said, because of Nixon's need to appease the Old Guard, which was determined to preserve the Republican coalition with southern Democrats and stall both welfare and civil liberties measures.[7]

On one of the big issues of the campaign—the need to restore America's power and influence throughout the world—Nixon had to walk warily, Lippmann said, because to admit that there had been a decline would reflect on Eisenhower. The Republican tactic, therefore, had to be to blame all our troubles abroad on "the wicked machinations of the Communists." It was true, Lippmann said sarcastically, that the Republicans could point with pride to the fact that they had protested against all the Soviet misdeeds "regularly, frequently, solemnly, and softly. The President has protested almost every hour on the hour." This fudging and smothering of the issue was ingenious, Lippmann said, but he doubted that it would succeed, even though it put Kennedy, when he sought to tell the truth, in the unpopular position of being the bearer of bad news.[8]

The television debates between Nixon and Kennedy were a bold innovation, Lippmann said, and predicted, incorrectly, that no future candidate for important public office could avoid engaging his opponent in such a confrontation. Synthetic candidates who relied on ghost writers and public relations men would be exposed for what they were by TV's "truth machine," he said. But he cautioned that the cameras, "which can also be cruel and at times unfair," must be made technically impartial. Failure to correct for his "photogenic defects" made Nixon look sick, old, and worn, he said.

The format of the debates, in which a panel of newsmen addressed the questions to the candidates, was susceptible to corruption, Lippmann feared. The format was that of a quiz show, he said, and the temptation to rig the show as the quiz shows had been rigged might become irresistible. The only sure guarantee to the voters of the integrity of the performance would be for the candidates to question each other, he said. "To let the panel ask the questions is to rely too much on the judgment and on the unconscious bias of the members of the panel."⁹

Although the debates may have gone badly for Nixon partly because he lacked telegeneity, the campaign apart from the debates disclosed to Lippmann weaknesses which neither the application of greasepaint nor improved camera angles could cure. Nixon's proposal that if elected he would institute a series of conferences and committees at home, in Latin America, Asia, Europe, and Africa to deal with the world's problems was famous, Lippmann said. "The oldest and the most hackneyed device of a weak government is to appoint a committee and call a conference." Nixon was confirming, Lippmann said, the impression created in the television debates—indecisive, weak, infirm, inaccurate.

"The contrast with Mr. Kennedy has become very sharp," he wrote. "It has been truly impressive to see the precision of Mr. Kennedy's mind, his immense command of the facts, his instinct for the crucial point, his singular lack of demagoguery and sloganeering . . . And through it all have transpired the recognizable marks of the man who, besides being highly trained, is a natural leader, organizer and ruler of men."¹⁰

When the religious issue was openly raised in the campaign, Lippmann found it salutary. "The black propaganda" could not be stilled entirely, he said, but it was being allayed by legitimate discussion. When a group of Protestant ministers asked Kennedy whether he could as President escape being influenced by the Catholic hierarchy, Kennedy might have responded, Lippmann pointed out, that merely to raise questions about religion violated the spirit of the Constitution. Kennedy's decision to treat the issue as relevant in fact if not in theory was both wise and courageous, Lippmann said. When the clergymen were dissatisfied with Kennedy's statement: "I do not accept the right of . . . any ecclesiastical official to tell me what I shall do in the sphere of my public responsibility as an elected official," and expressed their doubts that he could be as independent as he professed to be, Lippmann was impressed with Kennedy's rebuttal: He was not stating a position of his own, the candidate said, but "a position of the American Catholic Church in the United States with which I am associated." Lippmann said that the way Kennedy dealt with "this loaded question" marked him as "a brave and truthful man."¹¹ It was Kennedy's speech to the ministers, Lippmann said later, which convinced him that Kennedy was "a thoroughbred." He also said that he believed the Catholic issue cost Kennedy five million votes. But, he added, "All that's finished now, and, I suspect, forever."[12]

For more than a month after the election, newspapers continued to print articles that charges of vote fraud in Illinois and other states, if substantiated, might reverse the result and make Nixon the winner. Lippmann praised Eisenhower for disassociating himself from the controversy and arranging for an orderly transfer of administrations. But he said that the partisan charges tended to cloud the validity of Kennedy's title to the Presidency, and he sought to prove that there was no way in which Nixon could be declared the winner.

Citing constitutional authorities and precedents, he pointed out that the 12th Amendment required the Electoral College to choose as President the person having a majority of the appointed electors—not a majority of the electors. The practical result of this requirement, Lippmann pointed out, would be to shrink the number of votes required for election by half the number of votes being contested at the time the Electoral College ballots. In Illinois, for example, he said, it would be impossible to complete the litigation of a challenge and conduct a statewide recount of the vote before January 20, when a new President must take office. "The most that can happen in Illinois is to prevent Kennedy from getting the twenty-seven electoral votes. Illinois, in other words . . . would be unable to participate in the election of the President." Thus, he concluded, the number of votes required to win would be cut from 269, which is a majority of the Electoral College, to 256. (Lippmann's article explaining this helped to end the reports, which should never have been taken seriously, that the election result might be reversed.)[13]

The country could have survived a Nixon administration, Lippmann said, but it would have been an ordeal better averted than endured, because Nixon was mired in the old Eisenhower ruts of inertia and distrust of new ideas. "Nixon would not have attracted new brains to Washington," he said, ". . . brains, you know, are suspect in the Republican Party."[14]

Gadfly to Presidents always, Lippmann began early to lecture Kennedy on his failures. While it was true, Lippmann said on March 7, 1961, that Kennedy's personal popularity had increased because people admired his "style" and his political sophistication, millions who liked him lacked conviction that the programs of the New Frontier were necessary. "He will have to close this gap," Lippmann said; "he will have to persuade the large majority who like him that they must believe in him."

Lippmann's diagnosis of the communications failure was that Kennedy curbed the instinct, which he said all great leaders have, to teach his followers to be true believers in his cause. "There is a missing element," he said, "in his press conferences, his speeches, and his public appearances . . ." The press conferences were symptomatic of the general problem, Lippmann said he believed, for the President used them mainly to announce policies and developments rather than to explain them, and he permitted reporters to waste the precious television time in digging for "scoops." "The real use of the Presidential press conference," he said, "is to enable the President to explain his policies and, if necessary, to compel him to explain them." Kennedy had failed, he concluded, to establish "full effective communication with the American people."[15]

Part of the problem, Lippmann also felt, was the President's impatience with stupidity. Kennedy was "a very quick and intelligent man himself," Lippmann said. "Reads very fast, understands very fast; and it bores him to explain things . . . He ought to have the patience that a teacher must have, who is willing to start where the pupil or the hearer is, and explain it step by step as he goes along . . ." What needed to be explained, Lippmann said, was the urgency of increasing the gross national product in order to overtake the Communist world and of reducing America's moral and legal over-commitments around the rim of Asia.[16]

To Lippmann the very model of the politician as educator was Al Smith, whom he called "the foremost master in our time of the art of popular government." Smith had a superb ability, Lippmann said, to make the masses "share his own interest in problems that the ordinary public relations expert would say were too dull and over the people's heads."[17]

Kennedy was sensitive to the criticism that his public information program was floundering, but he believed the problem was subtler than the press saw it to be. Coupled with his innate distaste for being Messianic, evangelical, or dramatic, was his conviction that the nation was in no mood to listen to a hortatory President even if he wanted to be one. As Arthur M. Schlesinger, Jr., put it, the President believed that "there was no quicker way to dissipate presidential influence than to natter away when no one was listening." When Kennedy did occasionally succumb to the clamor "to carry his program to the people," some of his newspaper critics who had urged him to do so accused him of using "hippodrome tactics."[18]

The President sought Lippmann's views frequently and read the "Today and Tomorrow" column regularly. Before his inauguration Kennedy visited Lippmann at the house on Woodley Road and talked with him about cabinet appointments, and the columnist and the President met privately many times later. Lippmann was one of many who helped with Kennedy's inaugural speech. His principal contribution was to suggest that Kennedy use "adversary" instead of "enemy" in his references to the Soviet Union. Kennedy concurred and always thereafter used the softer word when speaking about Russia.

Kennedy, it was widely reported, read newspapers at breakfast, late at night and intermittently during the day, racing through them at 1200 words a minute. He attended to Murray Kempton (on the Left) and David Lawrence (on the Right) but focussed his attention on Joseph Alsop, James Reston, and Lippmann.

Newsweek reported on their contributions to Kennedy's thinking: "Lippmann, gentle, quiet, unassuming, with nearly 50 years of experience observing national and international affairs, provides reason. Alsop, elegant, precise, arrogant, with a knack for spotting trouble months away, provides warning. Reston, energetic, inquisitive, dignified, with an intricate network of news sources, provides information." One editor told the *Newsweek* reporter that all three columnists were good, but added, "I think Kennedy himself has greater intellectual depth. If Kennedy will write a column, we'll buy it."

The Big Three and other influential columnists, Marquis Childs, Doris Fleeson, Roland Evans, William S. White, Robert Novak, Joseph Kraft, Stewart Alsop, and Drew Pearson, got special treatment from the White House, Pierre Salinger reported. "A request from one of them to see the President personally was usually honored and White House staff members . . . made sure that they had the administration's views on prevailing problems," Salinger said.

"In any crisis situation, it was standard operating procedure to be in touch with these columnists to give them background on the government's actions. The President himself frequently took part in these background sessions. He would, for example, call Lippmann or invite him to the White House."[19]

Two of the great crises of the Kennedy administration, other than the confrontations of the governors of Alabama and Mississippi with federal power, were Cuba I and Cuba II. The Bay of Pigs adventure, Lippmann said, had been doomed to fail because it violated both law and conscience. For the invasion to succeed, he said, demanded a ruthless and unscrupulous use of American force on behalf of an un-American policy. Intervention of the forces of one nation in the internal affairs of another, unless it came at the request of a lawful government, was a violation of a rule of international law, which, he said, "is at the very heart of Western freedom." If we were to scrap the law in order to overthrow Castro, he said, we must henceforth be silent when Moscow or Peking intervene in the affairs of other nations. It was recognition of this on the part of both the President and the people, he said, which made the Cuban affair "hesitant and ineffectual . . . out of character, like a cow that tried to fly or a fish that tried to walk."

Many people found it "sissy" he said, to refuse to fight fire with fire and to adopt ruthless and unscrupulous tactics against a ruthless and unscrupulous adversary. But recalling his 1958 interview with Khrushchev, he said that American attempts to strengthen or restore small anti-Communist governments throughout the world were exactly what the Soviets wanted. "We have used money and arms," he said, "in a long losing attempt to stabilize native governments which, in the name of anti-Communism, are opposed to all important social change. This has been exactly what Mr. K.'s dogma calls for—that Communism should be the only alternative to the status quo with its immemorial poverty and privilege."

The quandary of the weak countries in Asia, Africa, Latin America, he said, seemed often to be that "they must stand still with us . . . or start moving with the Communists. This dilemma cannot be dissolved unless it is our central and persistent and unswerving policy to offer these unhappy countries a third option, which is economic development and social improvement without the totalitarian discipline of Communism."[20]

Although Western society must remain true to the spirit of international law and its own principles in the struggle to contain Communism, Lippmann conceded that law and principle were flexible enough to permit clandestine help to Castro's opponents and to anti-Communists elsewhere. Espionage combined with covert activity against each other was "the ancient and universal practice of great states," he said, and, if conducted according to the unwritten rules, might be employed wherever it was feasible. "It was not feasible," he said, "to overthrow Castro with 1400 refugees, and it was unlawful to attempt it. But it is feasible, and in the practice of states it is not prohibited, to give clandestine help, so long as it remains clandestine . . ."[21]

According to Pierre Salinger, Kennedy's press secretary, Lippmann seems to have vexed the Kennedy administration during the Cuban missile crisis by talking somewhat excitedly and by joining in the suggestion, made principally in Great Britain, that the United States should withdraw its missile bases from Turkey in exchange for a Soviet withdrawal from Cuba.

On October 20, 1962, six days after the government confirmed the presence of offensive missiles and two days before Kennedy disclosed the crisis in a television statement to the people, Salinger kept a record of what he called "the frantic pace of rumors and events." At 2:15 p.m. there was a call from the Virginia *News Pilot* asking about unusual activity at the Norfolk naval base. "2:35 p.m.: A call from AP reporting a large scale movement of marines from California to Florida." "3:45 p.m.: A call from Charles von Fremd of CBS. His office is convinced that a major crisis is at hand." "10:08 p.m.: A call from Eddie Folliard of the Washington *Post*. He informs me that columnist Walter Lippmann has just told *Post* editor Al Friendly at a party that we're on the brink of war. I call the President back. He's angry. 'This town is a sieve.' "[22]

Lippmann's suggestion of the missile base swap—Cuba for Turkey—entered the circuitous negotiations for a settlement of the crisis in a roundabout way. Kennedy made his speech announcing the quarantine of Cuba on Monday, October 22. As the days passed there were signs that the Russians were unwilling to risk war, but work on the missile sites continued and the American army prepared for an invasion of Cuba. On the afternoon of Friday, October 26, Alexander Fomin, a counselor at the Soviet Embassy in Washington, called one of his acquaintances, John Scali, the State Department correspondent for the American Broadcasting Company, and urged that they should meet immediately. If the Russians offered to remove the missiles and promised never to try to install them again, Fomin asked, would Kennedy publicly promise not to invade Cuba?[23]

Scali informed the State Department of the overture and was asked to tell the Russian that "real possibilities" existed for a negotiation but that time was short. At 7:30 p.m. Fomin had this word, and two hours later a long conciliatory letter from Khrushchev to Kennedy began to arrive by cable. But the hope for peace which this offered was blighted the next morning when Moscow radio broadcast another Khrushchev letter insisting on removal of American missiles from Turkey a proposal which Kennedy instantly rejected.

Scali felt, as he told the State Department, that the Russians had been "using" him and sought another meeting with Fomin. The Russian told him that he and the other embassy officials were "mystified" by the second Khrushchev letter. When Scali insisted that he had been double-crossed, the Russian replied that the proposal about the Turkish bases was not new. "After all, Walter Lippmann mentioned it and many other prominent Americans," he said. "I told him," Scali said, "I didn't give a damn if Walter Lippmann or Cleopatra mentioned it—that it was completely, totally, utterly and perpetually unacceptable." Scali also reminded Fomin, he said in a memorandum which he wrote for Secretary Rusk, that "everything Mr. Lippmann writes does not come straight from the White House, that he is frequently wrong..."[24]

To detect all the nuances in this upmanship game within the Washington press corps would require a connoisseur. Lippmann seems to have been better informed than Alfred Friendly about the crisis, though Friendly, as managing editor of the Washington *Post*, had a staff of reporters to keep him informed. Scali, though lower on the totem pole than Lippmann, who played badminton with Khrushchev and helped edit Presidential speeches, was the chosen intermediary. Remembering the caution which Lippmann expressed during World War II about talking too much at parties and about giving the appearance, though quite unintentionally, of knowing the presidential mind, it might be fair to ask whether in this crisis he neglected his own advice.

According to Robert Kennedy's memoir of the crisis, the importance of the proposal to remove American Jupiter missiles in Turkey in exchange for withdrawing Soviet missiles from Cuba was exaggerated. President Kennedy had asked the State Department to negotiate removal of the obsolete missiles from Turkey a year and a half before the Cuban crisis, his brother said. When he learned at the height of the crisis that the State Department, because of Turkish objections, had failed to act, the President was angry. He felt that accepting a Soviet demand for an exchange would cause America to lose face and rejecting it would appear unreasonable. The night before Khrushchev capitulated, Robert Kennedy said that he told the Russian ambassador that though no "deal" could then be made over the missiles in Turkey they should and could be removed within a short time.[25]

Lippmann wrote two post mortems to Cuba II. In the first one he questioned the adequacy of American intelligence information about Cuba during the time that Russian missiles were being installed. The loss of public confidence in the reliability of the information that it had been given would be difficult to repair, he said, since Senator Kenneth Keating had been correct in contending that the offensive weapons were there and the State Department and the President had been wrong in insisting that they were not. On two occasions, he said, high officials had privately assured him of the accuracy of the aerial surveillance of Cuba. And so, he said, "with others, I have had first-hand experience which enables me to understand how difficult it is to restore confidence once it has been shaken."[26]

The second post mortem dealt with the big controversy about the government's "management of the news" during the crisis, particularly from October 15, when the President was shown the photographs of the missiles, to October 22, when he told the world they were there. (During this week of secret discussion about how to deal with the Soviet threat, the White House tried desperately to keep a tight lid on the news, even to the point of personal requests from the President to the New York *Times* and Washington *Post* not to disclose the existence of the crisis until he made his own disclosure.)[27]

In the "managed news" dispute, Lippmann took the lofty position that news manipulation, like spying, is inevitable, and the cardinal sin is not to do it but to admit doing it. When Arthur Sylvester of the Defense Department said that in the interests of national security it was sometimes necessary for a government to lie to its people, he was guilty, Lippmann said, "of violating the first principle of managed news."

"As a matter of fact," he said, "with its large and expert press corps, there can be very little deliberate lying in a place like Washington. What lying there is comes for the most part out of the need of the armed forces and the intelligence services to hide their own secrets and deceive the adversary. It is not a pretty business, but deception is a necessary part of the unpretty business of preparing for and carrying on wars, both hot and cold."

He had thought long and hard, he said, about a general rule to distinguish between justifiable and unjustifiable deception but had been unable to formulate one. "We have to depend upon the game of cops and robbers played between public officials and keen newspapermen." Almost always when deception was used to disguise blunders, he said, it would come to light.

Actually, all news is managed somewhat, he said. "It is naive to suppose that in public affairs there is such a thing as one genuine, historically accurate version . . . If there were . . . we could dispense not only with the public relations industry, but also with most managing editors, correspondents, columnists, and the insiders of the inside." It was unlikely in a free and seldom neat society, he said, that the public could depend for truth on other than "the unending pulling and hauling between the good reporters wanting a true story and the officials who believe, as the saying goes, that they are protecting the public interest."[28]

When the Cuban crisis was over and what Lippmann described "as a faint resemblance to peace" had settled on the world, he predicted that Kennedy would find it difficult to generate support among the people or in Congress for his legislative program. "In our American constitutional experience," he said, "the power of a President to lead is generally speaking a function of some kind of national crisis, abroad in time of war and at home in a time like the great depression of the 1930's. President Kennedy's problem in this Congress is how to lead it when there is no apparent national crisis." The long-term problems of improving the decrepit educational system and stimulating economic growth were not vivid enough, he said, to arouse a satisfied people, but they were so crucial that the President must resort to "overwhelming persuasion" in his efforts to solve them. "Kennedy must," he said, "take the risk of boring the public by saying the same thing over and over again, if possible in different words. That has not been in the Kennedy style. But it may be indispensable."[29]

Kennedy was the first Keynsian President, as Arthur Schlesinger has said, but he was not Keynsian enough for Lippmann, who seemed in the early 1960's more profligate about federal spending than Harry Hopkins had been during the New Deal. When for political reasons Kennedy shied away from deliberate deficit financing (he could not afford to be tagged as a big spender, he said), Lippmann wrote that he was continuing the Eisenhower economic philosophy. "It's like the Eisenhower administration thirty years younger." Schlesinger reported a conversation which he and Lippmann had with Kennedy about the problem of achieving a five per cent annual increase in the Gross National Product. One of the few economists who told him precisely what needed to be done, Kennedy said, put a price tag of $5 billion a year in deficit spending for ten years on his program. Kennedy agreed that this would not be excessive, but said that politics precluded trying it.[30]

Lippmann saw the problem in terms of re-education of public opinion—the clearing away of the semantic confusion surrounding words like "spending" and "investment." One was a nice word, and it applied to business. The other was pejorative, and it applied to government.

"There is, for example, the notion that the public authorities . . . never invest. They only spend. On the other hand, private corporations and private individuals not only spend but invest. This leads to the blind prejudice that, since governments can only spend, whatever money they use tends to be wasted . . .

"This semantic muddle inhibits clear thinking about public questions," he said. "It takes good judgment to spend and invest wisely, be it publicly or privately. But that kind of judgment cannot be made at all if we react, like Pavlov's dogs, to the prejudiced sound of words." "The one thing Eisenhower has put over to the American people," Kennedy said, "was the sinfulness of spending and the danger of inflation."[31]

Lippmann accelerated his own program of public education with two new ventures—publication of a column in *Newsweek* and a series of interviews on television. The first of the television interviews was produced on July 7, 1960, by CBS, with Lippmann responding to questions from Howard K. Smith. Lippmann had rejected overtures to appear on the screen until Fred Friendly (Lippmann described him as a "tremendous salesman") persuaded him to take the risk. Although Lippmann did not have to be "dragged in kicking and screaming," as Friendly put it, he refused to appear unless he was given the right to scrap the film after it was made.[32]

The hour-long program was favorably reviewed, though *Time* found Lippmann's appeal for increased spending for public needs "one of his less persuasive remarks." "To have the sage of Washington up close at his ease, and ad-libbing, revealed not only his urbanity, which was to be expected, but yielded a bonus in the impression of kindliness and personal warmth never apparent in the intense concentration of his logical, impersonal prose," said the *Saturday Review*.[33]

Two interviews were filmed in 1961, one with Smith and the other with Walter Cronkite asking the questions, and in 1962, 1963, 1964, and 1965, David Schoenbrun, Charles Collingwood, and Eric Sevareid took a turn at getting Lippmann to elucidate about Presidents and the Presidency, Cuba and Khrushchev, desegregation, the Berlin wall, de Gaulle and Churchill, and Viet Nam. Edward Weeks of the *Atlantic* edited the texts of the interviews for the book *Conversations with Walter Lippmann*. "My God, my syntax," was Lippmann's comment when he read the text, Weeks said.[34] Although the programs were prestigious, many CBS stations made substitutions for them. For example, only 115 of 250 affiliates carried the second interview.[35]

The performance of American journalism in reporting the assassination of President Kennedy was so good, Lippmann said, that it made him wonder what it could be "if it were always as disinterested and as concentrated on the task of telling the true story as it was in those days." But the performance of the mythmakers and the sleuths who reconstructed the assassination and created the Kennedy legend were not so much to his liking, although he gradually succumbed a little to their persuasion.

When the Warren Commission report appeared in 1964, Lippmann said that "there is no ground on which any contemporary man, here or abroad, should question the verdict," which held that Lee Harvey Oswald alone murdered Kennedy and that there had been no conspiracy. "The commissioners are quite aware," he said, "that the truth, as they found it, is stranger than fiction." But having read a good deal of the literature about a "conspiracy," he was convinced, he said, that the report dealt "factually and authoritatively" with the objections raised against Oswald as a solitary assassin.[36]

But two years later as incredulity, especially in Europe, about the verdict increased, he said that since "a certain amount of reasonable doubt exists" it might be desirable to reopen the case unofficially. He suggested that "a reputable agency, politically and financially independent," might "examine new interpretations of the old evidence and any new evidence that might be brought forward in the future." He predicted, however, that there would not be, for a long time at least, conclusive answers to dispel the mystery and suspicion.[37]

In the long rows of closed black boxes of Lippmann correspondence in a vault in the Yale Library, there undoubtedly are letters to and from Jacqueline Bouvier and Jacqueline Kennedy. (She was a friend of Lippmann's close friend Bernard Berenson, who advised her and her sister Lee that they should marry American boys.)

And among the letters must be one from Lippmann expressing his grief over her husband's death. But in his public reaction Lippmann displayed scant emotion and was critical of the uncritical adulation of Kennedy after his death. William Manchester's story that he "collapsed" in an office at the Washington *Post* after he heard that Kennedy had been shot was untrue, Lippmann said. When he learned that the President was wounded but still alive, Lippmann said, he left the noisy and crowded newsroom and rushed for a taxi to go home, where he sat "glued to his television set." Lippmann disliked Manchester's *The Death of a President* intensely, finding in it "dumb and ruthless realism," "a gluttonous appetite" for anecdotes and tidbits, and, worst of all, a meretricious attempt to transfigure Kennedy into a successor to King Arthur. Manchester was a reporter, Lippmann said, "and as a reporter he had to agree that the murder was a ghastly futility. As a literary artist, however, he was compelled to shape the material to a main theme . . . that John F. Kennedy was transfigured by his death and thereby became a legendary hero." The true Kennedy legend would rest on what Kennedy accomplished, Lippmann said, not on his intolerable murder.[38]

Yet as the legend grew Lippmann was compelled to say that "I, for one, have learned a new respect for the myth-making process." Reciting the "prosaic fact," Lippmann said that Kennedy's record in foreign affairs had been fumbling until the Cuba II crisis, that he understood little of modern economics, that his record of accomplishment in adapting modern technology to the needs of men was not imposing. "But a passionate multitude all over the world," Lippmann said, "believes him to have been the herald of better things in dangerous and difficult times." And he concluded that although he had been "skeptical and often disappointed, now in retrospect, I am glad of the legend and I think it contains that part of the truth which is most worth having."[39]

Violence in word and deed and its exploitation by the mass media had become habitual in America, Lippmann said immediately after the assassination, and he looked with hope to "the healing arts" and the talent for consensus which he believed Lyndon Johnson possessed.[40] Kennedy himself, Lippmann reminded his readers, regarded Johnson "as the man, were he himself to fail, who was best qualified to be President."[41] Johnson's specific problems, Lippmann wrote, were to push the New Frontier program through Congress, which Kennedy through no fault of his own could not do, and to revise foreign policy to fit the fact that America was no longer *the* paramount power in the world.

"In my view," he said, "President Johnson will do well to begin with a confident acceptance of an accomplished and unavoidable fact—that our position in relation to Europe is no longer that of guardian and tutor." And in South Asia, he said, the role of the United States as protector of the status quo would have to be reappraised.[42]

To help the President achieve his goals, particularly his domestic program, Lippmann urged Congress to pass a rule that any measure certified by the President as important must be brought to a vote within a specified time. The frustration of the executive branch of government by recalcitrant legislative assemblies had grown intolerable in most of Western Europe and the United

States, he said. "I do not know what will happen if we cannot remedy the paralysis of the executive."[43]

Attempts both to paralyze and to intimidate the government were making national affairs unmanageable, Lippmann said in the Spring of 1964. Though the Negro protest movement could not be quieted by the passage of a civil rights bill alone, he said, the prospect of a long summer of filibustering was frightening. The one encouraging sign in the sectional and ideological conflict, he said, was that "a great prudent majority" had rallied behind President Johnson, but he feared that the Democrats might, as they often did, "snatch defeat out of the jaws of victory" by permitting a Robert Kennedy-Johnson struggle to develop at their 1964 convention.

Robert Kennedy, he said, had no claim on the Vice-Presidency and was not ready, should the President die, to be President of the United States. "But at his age and with his very remarkable political gifts he has every right and much reason to aspire to be President some day." What Kennedy should do, Lippmann suggested, was move to New York and run against Rockefeller in 1966 and, if he won, thus establish a claim to the Presidential nomination "in his own right."[44]

The unease between the Kennedys and the Johnsonians, he said, could be dispelled only by time, and the time required would be briefer "if the principals and the supporting casts, the mind-readers and the key-hole peepers, the inside dopesters and the tale-bearers" could be made aware that some degree of rancor was simply normal.

For the inner circle, he said, the consequences of the crime in Dallas were understandably unbearable. "It was a kind of disloyalty to say that the King is dead, long live the King, and to go on as if the unspeakable had not happened." But the Kennedy circle must realize, he said, "that the legend of John F. Kennedy, of which they are the custodians, is a great temptation to designing men." In the interest of keeping the dead President's reputation burnished, the Kennedys might consider "that they have a profound interest in the political fortunes of Lyndon Johnson," Lippmann said, for only Johnson could finish the unfinished business of the New Frontier.[45]

To repose any confidence in the Republicans' ability to lead the nation in 1964 was, Lippmann believed, impossible for an informed, adult American. Even Rockefeller, he said, during the New Hampshire primary campaign, was "trying to beguile the boobs." The New York governor and Barry Goldwater, Lippmann said, traveled all over the state mentioning the big issues, but never discussing them. "My own view," he said, "is that Senator Goldwater is just being natural and was on the level to which he belongs." But Rockefeller, he said, had succumbed to the advice of the public relations experts, whose research convinced them that effective campaigning should be pitched to a low level of interest and information.

"But in public life, and indeed, I would say, in journalism and the arts," Lippmann wrote, "it is essential to aim higher than the average of the mass audience." Though it was true, he said, that the interested and the well informed were a minority, "they have influence far beyond their numbers." The Republicans such as Henry Cabot Lodge, who were not talking at all, Lippmann said, might have a considerable advantage over Rockefeller and Goldwater, who were campaigning like mountebanks.[46]

Lippmann flirted in 1963 with the notion that the Republicans ought to nominate Goldwater, but he doubted that they would have "the nerve" to do it. He had been hearing for years, he said, that the reason the Democrats almost always won was that the Republicans invariably ran a "me too" man. It might be well, he said, to put up a "real Republican" and see what the country wanted.[47] But as the indications grew that Goldwater would be the nominee, Lippmann warned that if the "radical right" captured the party its "historic traditions" would be lost, and he turned to Governor Scranton of Pennsylvania as the man who could prevent this from happening. Lippmann hoped, but doubted, that "the Eisenhower of 1952" might join the struggle. But in "the Shangrilas at Gettysburg and Palm Springs," the General, he said, apparently had already surrendered. "Especially during his retirement," Lippmann said, "General Eisenhower has come to share with Senator Goldwater a profound distrust of the Federal Government, to which, incidentally, Dwight Eisenhower himself owes everything he is and has."[48]

It was impossible, Lippmann said, for Goldwater to conduct a rational campaign and win, and so, he said, "he appears to be gambling recklessly on racism and jingoism"—to exploit the white backlash and to promise to free the captive countries of

Eastern Europe. "The kind of campaign that this one is threatening to be," he said, "will put to the acid test the American conviction that there is in the great masses of the people enough common sense and good will to defeat the snares of the demagogues and extremists."[49]

What the extremists were attempting to exploit, Lippmann said, was the malaise which had overtaken the Western world two centuries ago and had become progressively worse. The disease had nothing to do, he said, with unbalanced budgets, bureaucracy, Communism, violence, or the corruption of politicians. "The malady is caused, I believe," he said, "by the impact of science upon religious certainty and of technological progress upon the settled order of family, class, and community . . . It comes from being lost in a universe where the meaning of life and of the social order are no longer given from on high and transmitted from the ancestors but have to be invented and discovered and experimented with by each lowly individual for himself."

Bureaucracy, Communism, and all the rest of it, Lippmann said, were merely symptoms—"pains of the recent freedom to which Western men are not as yet adapted and adjusted." What the "romantic and deluded reactionary" failed to see, Lippmann said, was that "modern liberal democracies are in the early stages of the vast creative effort to invent and make work the kind of authority and discipline and government under which free men can enjoy freedom."[50]

After the Democratic convention Lippmann praised Johnson and his choice for the Vice Presidency, Hubert Humphrey. "Both men have proved," he said, "that they know how to make our difficult system of government work." Of Humphrey, he said that "though he is a brilliant controversialist, he is by instinct a peacemaker, conciliator, and harmonizer." In the November election, he said, there would clearly be an opportunity to distinguish between "a choice and an echo." "It is Goldwater and Miller on the one hand and Johnson and Humphrey on the other hand. Some choice."[51] Johnson, he said, lived "in the daylight world" and Goldwater in the fantasy where there were only "the good buys and the bad guys of superman's imagining."[52]

As the campaign drew to a close in late October, Lippmann said that Goldwater and Miller had dragged it "down to the lowest level within living memory." Accusing the Republicans of attempt-

ing to destroy the character of the President, Lippmann said:
"Out in the open Goldwater and Miller have carried on a drumfire,
not of charges that were specific and could be met, but of innuendo
and insinuation, of sly hints and smirks . . ." Fortunately the public
opinion polls were showing, Lippmann said, that fewer than 20
per cent of the people agreed with the Goldwater picture of
Johnson as the cause of "crime, smut, sodomy, and all the other
vices . . ." It was "delicious" to await the results of the election,
but in the meanwhile, he said, "I think I shall now wash my
hands."[53]

The election proved, Lippmann said, that Americans were still
willing to follow a worldly leader in pursuit of the old American
dream of harmony—now called "consensus." To many people,
even to some "quite civilized and decent people," those who
dreamed this dream were "sentimental visionaries in the mushy
middle of American politics," he said. But to be visionary with
respect to goals—to believe that conflicts of race, religion, ideology
could be settled without extirpating the adversary—need not pre-
clude, he said, the use of none too fastidious politics in the attempts
to achieve the goals. And Lyndon Johnson, he intimated, was
not too fastidious.[54]

Considering the open hostility that soon developed between
Lippmann and the President, this evaluation of Johnson seems
prophetic. The President's tactics in dealing with his opponents
at home and his policy in dealing with the enemy in Asia came
to be, in Lippmann's view, almost totally lacking in decorum, and
even in decency.

Lippmann had been uneasy about the administration's Viet Nam
policy before the Gulf of Tonkin incident in the Summer of 1964.
The administration, he said, "has let itself be chivied into making
public declarations about our willingness and readiness to fight
a great war in hypothetical and undefined circumstances." He
realized, he said, that it was necessary to warn Hanoi and Peking
that America would not be forced out of Indo-China. "Such a
warning was useful," he said. "But it should have been delivered
privately through diplomatic channels."[55]

In late September of 1964 Lippmann wrote optimistically about
the prospect of a settlement in Asia, though, he said, "I have
no magic formula to offer." But American strategy clearly should
rest on two principles: The folly of becoming involved in a land

war in Asia (General MacArthur told Dulles in 1950, he said, "that any American who committed American troops on the mainland of Asia should have his head examined"), and the superiority of American sea and air power in all the Pacific Ocean. Patient adherence to the two principles, he said, could produce a negotiable settlement which would permit the United States to withdraw its 18,000 "advisers" from South Viet Nam.[56]

In 1965, as the Viet Nam war escalated and American marines were sent into the Dominican Republic, Lippmann foresaw the prospect of an endless series of futile interventions—"a global nightmare" which, he said, the administration was trying to dispel by promising that a victory in Viet Nam would mean the dawn of world peace. The theory that the Soviets and the Red Chinese were "masterminding" all the disorders in the world and that once we could expose and defeat their conspiracies permanent peace would descend on earth, was "a piece of mythology," he said. "The essential fact about all these disorders is that they are at bottom indigenous to the countries where the social order is broken down..."[57]

Even the Secretary of Defense admitted that all revolutionary wars were not "made in Moscow or Peking," Lippmann pointed out. In a speech to the American Society of Newspaper Editors early in 1966, Robert McNamara absolved the Communists of involvement in 98 of the 149 serious insurgencies which had erupted in the world since 1958. So "the Hydra of Revolution," Lippmann said, "had more heads than America was capable of cutting off."[58]

When the press began to complain early in the Johnson administration that more information should come from the President, especially about foreign affairs, Lippmann agreed that Johnson's custom of calling press conferences sporadically and on short notice was an unsatisfactory arrangement. But he said that every President had to adjust the conferences both to his own personality and to the current position of national and world affairs. There was no reason for Johnson to try to continue in the Kennedy style, he said. "I don't blame him for not trying to do what Kennedy did... Kennedy was a virtuoso. It would be like asking him [Johnson] to sing 'Tosca.'" His own solution, he said, would be to devote a third of each conference to carefully prepared answers to questions submitted previously. This would protect the President from talking about questions "that cannot be talked about wisely," he said, and keep him from "thinking out loud about the policies he has inherited from his predecessors." To ventilate the whole problem, Lippmann suggested that "it would be interesting if the White House has a press conference about press conferences . . ."

The trouble with the Johnson system was not that it failed to produce news, Lippmann said. "In fact, there is a torrent of news pouring out of the White House." But by making it difficult for reporters to see the President's subordinates and by failing to give adequate notice of the Presidential conferences, the administration was blockading specialized reporters capable of explaining the flood of news, Lippmann said. Then, sounding a little bored with the idea, he suggested that the President and the press set up a joint commission to study the problem of informing the people.[59]

Two years later, in the Spring of 1967, Lippmann said that the relations between the President and the press were, so far as he knew, the worst in history, and he placed all the blame on the President. In two long articles bristling with phrases like "Mr. Johnson is a pathologically secretive man," Lippmann analyzed "the credibility gap." The phrase, he said, was in the Victorian tradition of delicately referring to legs as limbs—"a polite little euphemism for deception," which, he refrained from saying explicitly, was itself a polite little euphemism for lying.[60]

The two Lippmann articles so irritated the President that at a White House dinner party for President Sunay of Turkey, Johnson, it was reported, "took a crack at one news commentator who 'is still with us' who had accused President Truman of 'arrogance and of wanting to play world policeman.'" At this, the report in the Washington *Post* continued, "The dinner guests laughed and one passed the word to another that President Johnson was hitting at one of his chief critics, Washington *Post* columnist Walter Lippmann."[61] In a "Today and Tomorrow" column two days later Lippmann said: "At the dinner for the President of Turkey on Monday evening at the White House, President Johnson referred to me as one who had in 1947 opposed military and financial aid to Greece and Turkey because I opposed the

Truman Doctrine. This is not true, and I am, therefore, reprinting in full the first article I wrote after the enunciation of the Truman Doctrine."[62]

The war of words between Woodley Road and Pennsylvania Avenue entranced the Washington press corps. Herblock, never respectful of presidential dignity, devoted a thousand words to it in the Washington *Post*. "If Lippmann were a less modest man," the cartoonist said, "the attention lavished on him by his chief of state would be enough to turn his head. And if he and Johnson had lived in the days of Thomas More and Henry VIII, he would have lost his head completely."[63]

The London *Observer,* in an article entitled "The Wit of LBJ," reported: "President Johnson is telling a nasty story, which he himself finds very funny, to visitors to the White House. The Lippmann in the story is Walter Lippmann, the distinguished columnist who is Johnson's most formidable critic on Vietnam.

"The story has to do with a lecturer at Columbia University who finds himself distracted by a girl student in a tight sweater bearing the words, 'Make Love Not War.' After the lecture, he asks her if in the future she can wear something less provocative, as she is spoiling everyone's concentration. The girl is shocked and says it is a purely political slogan: 'It certainly doesn't mean I'm an easy lay.' That evening the lecturer meets Lippmann and tells him about the episode. Lippmann listens very seriously and then asks, 'But what is an easy lay?' Next day the lecturer repeats Lippmann's reaction to his students, who listen very seriously and then ask: 'But who is Walter Lippmann?'

"Rude, crude and vindictive towards his critics: that's our Lyndon."[64]

If the *Observer* article was true—and the *Observer* is an extremely respectable newspaper with none of the taste for salacity that characterizes England's biggest Sunday paper, the *News of the World*—then the President unwittingly was paying Lippmann the not entirely dubious compliment of characterizing him as a fastidious and unworldly man.

In the "credibility gap" articles, Lippmann accused the President of "disrespect for free journalism." Describing the relations between the administration and the press as "unique," Lippmann said they differed "not only in degree but in kind from the normal tensions between responsible officials and free journalism."

The credibility gap could be traced back to Johnson's first press conference on December 7, 1963, Lippmann said, when the President began to practice "razzle-dazzle" with the budget in an attempt to create an image of himself as a thrifty man. The gap widened in 1965, Lippmann continued, when the President broke his campaign pledge and made the war in Viet Nam an American war. Since then, Lippmann said, "Mr. Johnson has persistently manipulated the news of war and peace. When he was escalating the war he has covered it with gestures about peace." The deception included "the fiction" created in the State Department in 1964, Lippmann said, about the absence of overtures from Hanoi to negotiate a settlement of war.

There were two other instances, Lippmann said, which may "have hurt Mr. Johnson more than any other. The first was his claim until the final hour of the Democratic Convention that he had not made up his mind about who would be his Vice-President in 1964. Even at the time no one believed this." The other instance, Lippmann said, was the sudden reversal of his decision to take a public part in the political campaign of 1966, and his attack on the press for having said he would do so.

The defense of secrecy offered by the President's press secretary, Bill D. Moyers, that until "the moment of decision" the President must "maintain his options," contained some "disturbing possibilities," as, Lippmann said, James Reston had pointed out. "In order to maintain the President's 'options,'" Lippmann said, "the Congress and the public are deprived of a right to deliberate on a course of action. In exactly this way the Nation has been committed to a big war about which nothing was debated and explained while the President's secretly chosen decision was handed down by fiat."

The customary tension between press and public officials, with the press ferreting out information and officials trying to keep it from them was "tolerable and workable," Lippmann said. But the rules of the game, he indicated—the rules prescribed in the First Amendment—had to be observed. The press had no "absolute and unlimited right . . . to publish anything and everything and at any time," he said. But neither was it permissible, he said, for "an elected official to use his official powers to manipulate the press . . . in order to erase opposition to the will of the leader."

The charge that the administration was unfairly attempting to

manipulate public opinion received the endorsement of the Freedom of Information Committee of Sigma Delta Chi, the 18,000-
member professional society of American journalists. The committee's report in November of 1967 accused the administration of
"deliberately misleading the public, press and Congress through
flat lies, through half-truths and through clever use of statistics
that distort." The President's press conferences, the report said,
were staged in a way to make it "unlikely that he will face...
consistent hard questioning. He has it well organized for a White
House snow job."[65]

Viet Nam was the main cause, for Lippmann, as it was for
millions of others, of the erosion of confidence and trust in
Johnson, but it was with obvious regret that the columnist could
no longer believe, as he had two and half years earlier, that
"President Johnson is by instinct, temperament, conviction and
experience a man for this season."[66]

A neutralization of South Viet Nam might have been possible
early in 1964, Lippmann said, but once Saigon had lost its own
war and the American bombing of the North had begun he saw
no hope for a favorable settlement. Suppose that a cease-fire could
be arranged, he said, and suppose that the United States, as it
promised to do, subsequently withdrew its troops. *"How will Mr.
Rusk know,"* he asked, *"that the whole revolutionary business will not
start up again when we are gone?* Since we cannot stop the revolution
even while we are there with our Army, Navy and Air Force,
how does Mr. Rusk intend to keep the revolution stopped permanently?"[67]

President Johnson, Lippmann warned, "will have to pay a heavy
price for the historical mistake of involving the United States
in a land war against Asians in Asia." His alternative, Lippmann
said, was to accept a grievous wound to his pride by settling for
less than victory or to risk expanding the war into a world war.
Hammering at the theme of futility, Lippmann wrote article after
article of warning, imprecation, and prophecy: increasing violence
in American cities, growing disrespect and contempt for America
abroad, the loss of the Presidency of the Republicans in 1968.[68]

When Red China's internal problems offered hope that Hanoi
could no longer count on Peking for substantial support, Lippmann feared that President Johnson would succumb to the temptation of trying "to squeeze a victory" over North Viet Nam. There

were two Johnsons, he said, or "two spirits wrestling within him. One is that of the peacemaker and reformer and herald of a better world. The other is that of the primitive frontiersman who wants to nail the coonskin to the wall, who wants to be the biggest, the best, the first, a worshipper of what William James called the bitch-goddess, success."[69]

In May of 1967 Lippmann said that he began to suspect that Hanoi, perhaps advised by Moscow, had become hopeful, because of American public opinion polls, that Johnson would not be re-elected. He said that "it is probable, I think, that Ho Chi Minh and his associates are determined not to negotiate with the men who have attacked and are destroying their country." Then Lippmann offered, very cautiously, the hypothesis that just as an end to the Korean War had to wait for a change of administrations, so the election of a Republican President "may well turn out to be the only solution now."[70]

(Nixon's policy on the Viet Nam War during his first three years as President was, in Lippmann's opinion, "acrobatic and absurd," pretending that South Viet Nam could win the war in spite of the withdrawal of United States troops. The American adventures into Laos and Cambodia were futile attempts to disguise the failure of the policy, he said, and the President's 1971 overture to Red China was, at least in part, a "great forward pass" designed to rescue him from the inevitable failure in Viet Nam.

(About the new China policy Lippmann was enthusiastic, believing that it corrected the old "colossal error" of treating Red China as an enemy. Only a "certified anti-Communist like Nixon" could have engineered the reversal, Lippmann said and predicted that it would be one of the administration's most significant accomplishments.)[71]

Proposing a new and, he admitted, "startling" new strategy for America in the Pacific, Lippmann suggested a withdrawal of American sea and air power to Australia and New Zealand. One objection to this he dismissed by saying: "The rhetorical claim that if we do not stand fast in South Viet Nam, we shall have to fight in Hawaii or even California seems to me a frivolous insult to the United States Navy." Another objection, that the United States could not wield as much influence from Melbourne as it could from Saigon, could be met, he said, by properly defining "influence." By substituting for "General Westmoreland and his firepower," trade agreements, cultural programs, diplomacy, and propaganda, Lippmann said, more meaningful and respectable influence could be exerted.[72]

And extraordinary dividends would accrue, he said—a reduction of the threat of war with China, diminishing our main conflict of interest with Russia, and restoring American respect in the court of world opinion. Best of all, the American people need no longer be "revolted and ashamed," he said, "by the spectacle of themselves engaged in a war where a big rich superarmed giant is trying to beat the life out of a dwarf."[73]

Although all wars are difficult to describe and explain, the war in Viet Nam, Lippmann said, was "especially difficult to report truly and objectively." In normal newspaper reporting, he said, the first rule is to interview everyone concerned with the event. But the war correspondent always, he said, "is in the position of being able to photograph only one side of the moon." So the reports on the progress of a war need to be taken skeptically, he said, except perhaps for eye-witness accounts of skirmishes etc. The essential and inevitable one-sidedness of war correspondence was aggravated in Viet Nam, he said, by the absence of large numbers of neutral observers who helped give perspective to World Wars I and II.

What was taking place on the other side of the front in 1917 and 1943, he said, was described by "newspapermen and diplomats and businessmen and clergymen and travelers from free and neutral countries bordering on the belligerents ... There are very few such people in this war." And so not much was known about the state of affairs in Viet Nam, he said, including the willingness of the Vietnamese to continue to endure the destruction of their land.

It was true, he said, that there seemed to be a consensus among correspondents about two facts: that American intervention prevented a victory for North Viet Nam and that a long guerrilla war in South Viet Nam was inevitable. The prospects of and the progress toward ending the guerrilla war and pacifying South Viet Nam, he said, "is probably the big story now. And this is a story which *can* really be reported because it is not, physically, impossible to investigate both sides of it."[74]

A little later when a great clamor arose because the New York *Times* published stories by Harrison Salisbury reporting from

Hanoi that American bombing of military targets in North Viet Nam had killed and wounded many civilians and destroyed many civilian homes, Lippmann defended Salisbury against charges that he had become "a tool of enemy propaganda."

"We must remember that in time of war," Lippmann said ironically, "what is said on the enemy's side of the front is always propaganda, and what is said on our side of the front is truth and righteousness, the cause of humanity and a crusade for peace. Is it necessary for us . . . to stoop to such self-deceiving nonsense?"

The reports of civilian losses in the bombings were news only because the New York *Times* printed them, Lippmann pointed out. *Le Monde* and other European newspapers published similar reports months earlier. After the Salisbury dispatches appeared, numerous news reports from Washington, quoted "defense authorities" and "reliable sources" as admitting that the bombings caused "extensive civilian damage in North Vietnam" but rejecting any implication that civilian targets were chosen deliberately.

The second indictment against Salisbury—that he reported what he was told by North Viet Nam Premier Pham Van Dong as well as what he described as an eyewitness—Lippmann dismissed by saying: "Of course a reporter in Hanoi will be told what the authorities in Hanoi wish him to believe." What was an English, a French, or a Japanese reporter told when he interviewed authorities in Washington? Lippmann asked. Was he, too, then to refrain "from reporting it and interpreting it as best he can"?[75]

Some other American journalists were not so kind to Salisbury. James Reston, his colleague on the *Times*, said that Salisbury violated the first principle of good reporting by reporting as fact what he was told as well as what he saw.[76] And the Pulitzer Prize advisory board, over the strenuous objections of Joseph Pulitzer, III, overruled the recommendation of its own judges that Salisbury be given the 1966 award for international reporting.[77]

The journalist's only true commitment, superior to all others, even to his loyalty to his country's government, Lippmann said, is his commitment to seek the truth and to report and explain it as he sees it. "In so far as he puts truth in the first place, he rises toward—I will not say into, but towards—the company of those who taste and enjoy the best things in life."

The desire for success, he said, embraces all the conflicts that arise to deter journalists who attempt to put truth in the first place. "The first and most evident of the conflicts," he said, "is between choosing, on the one hand, to publish whatever most easily interests the largest number of readers most quickly—that is to say, yellow journalism, and, on the other hand, to provide, even at a commercial loss, an adequate supply of what the public will in the longer run need to know . . .

"A second drama, in which contemporary journalists are involved, consists in their conflict between pursuit of the truth and their need and their desire to be on good terms with the powerful. For the powerful are perhaps the chief source of news. They are also the dispensers of many kinds of favor, privilege, honor and self-esteem. The most important forms of corruption in the modern journalist's world are the many guises and disguises of social-climbing on the pyramids of power . . ."

Another conflict arose, he said, from the "natural and human desire to say 'my country right or wrong.' " Most helpful to the journalist here, Lippmann said, were two guides for conduct. "One is to remember President Truman's advice that if you do not like the heat stay out of the kitchen. It is always possible to retreat into less hotly contested subject matter. The other rule is that if you believe you must go into the kitchen, keep an eye on yourself, keep asking yourself: are you sure you are still seeking the truth and not merely trying to win the argument?"

In the Great Society, Lippmann said, using the term in Graham Wallas' sense of big, complicated, urban, a free press is an "organic necessity" without which effective government cannot exist. Deprived of competitive reporting and editorial criticism, he said, both the legislative and the executive branches, no matter how elaborate their own intelligence services, operate in the dark. So the greatest peril to the press as a whole, he said, is monopoly, which reduces "the naked data" and the interpretation and analysis of the data that a pluralist society must have.[78]

After taking a long leave of absence in the Summer and Fall of 1966, Lippmann announced on May 25, 1967, that he would discontinue the regular "Today and Tomorrow" series. "The work of a Washington columnist," he said, "requires . . . constant and immediate knowledge, and it is only too obvious that the job should be done by men in the prime of their lives." Thirty-six years of "writing on a fixed schedule and at more or less fixed length," he said, was long enough. (Lippmann was then 77 years old.) "But as I do not mean to retire and to lapse into silence," he said, "I have been experimenting with new forms—with longer articles which cover a wider range of subject matter and can, if editors choose, to be broken up into a series of smaller pieces."[79]

Looking back on those 36 years, Lippmann could derive satisfaction from the fact that the correspondents whose ranks he was leaving regarded him as so preeminent among them that he, like the New York *Times,* had become *sui generis,* a Fifth Estate in the world of public affairs. In 1962 there were 634 correspondents working in Washington. In a sampling of the opinions of 242 of them about their work and their colleagues, 101 ranked Lippmann as "fairest, most reliable." Nobody else came close. Marquis Childs, who ranked second, received the accolade from 20 of his colleagues. Twenty-five years earlier, Lippmann ranked only third. Three times as many, then, put their trust in Raymond Clapper rather than in Lippmann. But those were the days of the New Deal, and, unlike their publishers and Lippmann, most correspondents admired it.[80]

The day Lippmann announced that he was writing his last regular column his colleague James Reston acclaimed him as "the greatest journalist of the present age . . .[who] lived the ideal of most thoughtful newspapermen." The notion that Lippmann was leaving Washington because of a feud with President Johnson was too absurd to believe, Reston said. "Walter Lippmann's career is too important to be discussed in terms of Lyndon Johnson's vicious vendetta." During Lippmann's 35 years as a columnist, Reston continued, "he has been vilified by experts . . . so the savage and cruel personal comments Johnson and others in the White House have made about him tell us more about them than they do about Lippmann."[81]

Lippmann believed that Johnson misled him, and others felt that the President played the role of coy deceiver in an attempt to woo the Great Pundit's favor. Johnson used to tell his friends, *Life* magazine reported, that "the great Lippmann marched by his side" and frequently said, "I had Walter Lippmann over today." Soon after John Kennedy was killed, the new President asked Lippmann how to deal with de Gaulle; and in 1965, when the President was composing a speech about Viet Nam to be delivered at Johns Hopkins, he talked with Lippmann for seven hours about what he should say, not so much because he valued the advice, some Washington correspondents suspected, but because he felt

that if he could keep Lippmann in line the intellectual establishment would march with him.[82]

But as the war escalated and Lippmann accused the President
of "the exploitation . . . of dead heroes" calls from the White House
ceased, and the President, whom Lippmann later called "personally unlikeable," began to tell visitors jokes about him and
to call attention to his mistakes in judgment.

Admitting his disaffection for the President, Lippmann himself
denied that he was leaving Washington because of it. "I'm not
leaving because of Lyndon Johnson," he said. "I wouldn't give
him that satisfaction. I stuck it out here through the McCarthy
era . . ." The decision to move to New York and to write at a
more leisurely pace had been considered for about two years,
he said. "We decided on this before Johnson went off the deep
end."[83]

Interviewed in the 17-room duplex cooperative apartment
which he purchased on Park Avenue and 85th Street in New
York, Lippmann said, "It's a matter of getting older." The Los
Angeles *Times* Syndicate, which had taken over distribution of
his column to more than 300 newspapers, announced that it was
renegotiating contracts for less frequent and longer articles, and
Newsweek said that during eight months of the year Lippmann
would continue his twice-a-month commentary.[84]

Given the choice that he and the voters had to make on November 5, 1968, it was predictable that Lippmann would support
Nixon, even though he had never before reposed confidence in
him. But his choice was not easy. With another option, Robert
Kennedy or perhaps even Eugene McCarthy versus Nixon, his
benediction might have gone the other way. And if Rockefeller
had won the nomination in Miami, it is doubtful that Lippmann
would have considered any Democrat his equal.

Lippmann refrained from "it might have been" post mortems
about Kennedy after the murder in Los Angeles. More than a
year before he predicted, incorrectly, that it was "unthinkable"
that Kennedy would campaign for the nomination unless Johnson
withdrew. When Kennedy began in March of 1967 publicly to
oppose the conduct of the war in Viet Nam, Lippmann said that
it signalled his bid for the Presidency in 1972. "A new generation
will be present then, and it is clear that Robert Kennedy cannot
be with it if he shrinks from the battle now." The reports that

Johnson was "furious" at Kennedy were understandable, Lippmann said, because the President was confronted with a tough,
professional, power-seeking Democrat—not "a voice crying in the
wilderness"—who had concluded that the only avenue to national
leadership was a flagrant break with the White House.[85]

But although Kennedy was closer to "the mainstream of the
Democratic Party" than the President or Humphrey, Lippmann
said, he could not afford to fight for the 1968 nomination. A
Johnson-Kennedy contest would wreck the party and favor "the
nomination and election of a right-wing Republican, perhaps
Nixon, perhaps Reagan," Lippmann concluded.[86]

Unlike Kennedy, whose "appetites are to be where the real
power is," Eugene McCarthy could afford to contest for the nomination, Lippmann said, because he had no prospect of winning
it. McCarthy's mission, he said, was to raise "a flag to which the
dissenting and the despairing can repair . . . they do not have
to win."

Declaring that the Johnson Administration had "corrupted and
undermined the faith of our people in their political system,"
Lippmann said that McCarthy was trying "to stop the rot" and
"pull the Democratic Party out of the disaster . . ." But though
McCarthy might help restore the party for leadership in the 1970's,
the only hope in 1968, Lippmann said, lay in "a rejuvenated
Republican Party." This was his conclusion nearly a year before
the election, when Rockefeller, John Lindsay, and Charles Percy
were considered to have a chance to be nominated.[87]

After Johnson announced that he would not run and death
removed Kennedy as a contender, Lippmann analyzed the prospects of a nation led by Humphrey and found them dismal.
Humphrey's problem, he said was Humphrey's own "high credu-
lity quotient—his endless capacity for becoming quickly and thoroughly persuaded." Excluded from the councils which made them,
Humphrey had opposed the decisions to escalate the Viet Nam
war in 1965, Lippmann said, but facing the possibility that Johnson
might drop him as his running mate in 1968, the Vice President
became a naive and enthusiastic propagandist for the war. "He
exclaimed, for example," Lippmann said, "that there was 'a tremendous opening here for realizing the dream of the Great Society
in the great area of Asia, not just here at home.' "

A man capable of such an "infatuated flight from reality," Lipp-

mann said, after absolving the Vice President of hypocrisy, would
be more worrisome to have in the White House than a devious,
old-fashioned politician who said one thing and did another.[88]
But in July of 1968 when Humphrey prepared a speech in which
he attempted to repudiate the Viet Nam war, Lippmann called
it "a somersault for political expediency" which might be offensive
to "the moral scruples of the voters." A propensity for the
expedient was a Nixon weakness, too, Lippmann observed, and
he appealed to the Republicans "to produce a candidate who
inspires sufficient confidence to unite and govern the nation."[89]

After the convention in Miami, Lippmann said that the Republicans "did their best for the Johnson-Humphrey Democrats . . .
Nixon and Agnew offer them their best, perhaps their only, chance
to win the election." The proceedings in Miami, he noted, "brought
many of the best newspapermen to a point where they tried to
laugh for fear that they might cry." Disclaiming prophecy, he
said that the Democrats would probably return the Republicans'
favor by nominating Humphrey, who would try but fail to dis-
sociate himself from the Johnson record and the disastrous war.[90]

The Republicans were cleverer than the Democrats, Lippmann
said after the phantasmagorical convention in Chicago. By choosing an island as the site of their meeting they avoided what he
called the need "to prove that a Democratic city government could
maintain law and order in a great modern city." In a rather cosmic
column, quoting a letter from Erasmus to Martin Luther, Lippmann described the plight of the voter as the election approached.
Everywhere men saw, he said, what Erasmus called "the irremedi-
able confusion of everything"—the authority of the family "shak-
en," the church "confused," the state losing "its sovereign power
over the loyalty of the citizen," the schools and universities in
"a deep uncertainty about the nature of truth." And in contrast
science and technology were promising freedom from disease and
drudgery, longer lives, new marvels in communication and trans-
portation—all to little avail culturally or spiritually.

Still attempting to make up his own mind about a candidate
to support, Lippmann said: "When my friends ask me what I
am going to do in November, I take refuge in the fact that it
is not necessary to make up my mind now in September." But
he was certain, he said, that both for the good of the country
and the good of the party the Democrats should be turned out.

Yet he was compelled to add: "All this would be true were it not that Nixon is, as they say, a 'pragmatist'—which means that he might do anything."[91]

A month before the election Lippmann made his "hard and dismal choice," telling the millions who followed him in *Newsweek* and in the infrequent "Today and Tomorrow" columns that "Nixon is the only one." The rationalization of the choice, or the logic of it, if that is a better term, showed Lippmann at the height of his form.

As President, neither Nixon or Humphrey could or would be unchanged, he said, and those who were asking whether Humphrey could inaugurate another New Deal or New Frontier, or whether Nixon could restore the tranquillity of the Eisenhower years, were seeking answers to old unanswerable questions. We must assume a new Nixon and a new Humphrey, he said, who would face foreign problems which were theoretically soluble and domestic problems which could not be solved in four years, or eight, or even perhaps in the span of a generation.

Admitting its fragility, he said he based his hope that Nixon would end the war in Viet Nam on Nixon's overriding ambition to be President for eight years. "I think Nixon's whole future will be staked on getting cease-fire and a self-respecting withdrawal of our land forces. That is the best I am able to hope for. But I see nothing better in Humphrey."

What he called "the reconstruction of the American environment" in order to redress the grievances and end the miseries of minorities would be impossible for "an indefinite term of years," he said, because there was no consensus on how to do it and a growing consensus against spending for it. Consequently, he said, there was the probability of revolutionary dissent and of a rising demand for its repression. Should the need for repression arise, it would be better for the conservatives to take the necessary steps, he said. "It would be a disaster, I think, if a man like Humphrey had to do what is against the whole grain of his nature." If reaction must come, he said, it would be better for the Democrats to be on the sidelines preparing "for the inevitable reaction against reaction."

Tagging Nixon as the preferable hatchet man against disorder was not necessarily an obverse compliment for Humphrey. The liberal mandate for "permissiveness and largesse" had at least

temporarily run out after 40 years, Lippmann said, and it "is
not surprising and it is not in itself deplorable" for there to be
a landslide movement toward "discipline and authority and self-
reliance." The United States had become "by far the most violently
disordered" of the world's advanced nations, Lippmann remarked
sadly. "And so I would say to my fellow liberals: do not shirk
the imperative priority of the restoration of security. Do not leave
the task of dealing with violence to those who do not believe
in the liberal and compassionate reforms of our society."

Nixon was not his first choice, he said, and the possibility of
Spiro T. Agnew as President ("not qualified by experience or
by education") was frightening. "But the coming popular verdict
does not seem to me intolerable." He truly believed, he said, that
there was a "new Nixon, a maturer and mellower man, who is
no longer clawing his way to the top . . . who has outlived and
outgrown the ruthless politics of his early days."[92]

After the election Lippmann said that there was little to rejoice
about except that the result "might have been so much worse"—
a Humphrey victory or a decision thrown into the House of Representatives. Everyone, including Humphrey, he said was "fortunate that he and his torn party do not have to form an Administration for a divided and confused country."

As for Nixon, Lippmann said that the new President faced
the bleak task of trying to teach the country that it is not "omniscient and omnipotent" as rather adolescently it had believed
itself to be. To govern successfully, Lippmann said, Nixon must
avoid three big mistakes—the mistake of continuing the land
war in Viet Nam and especially doing it with a drafted army;
the mistake of the Eisenhower Administration of permitting
obsolete orthodoxy to blight economic growth; and the mistake
of allowing domestic violence to escalate. "The future, as I see
it," he said, "is not bright with the promise of a new dawn. But
the dark night of disorder and disunity is not upon us."[93]

A summing up of Lippmann's views about the press and its
influence on society was provided in a three-hour colloquy he
conducted with a group of journalism graduate students at Columbia University shortly before his eightieth birthday in 1969. Lippmann's mood was somber, his comments skeptical and subdued.

Asked how the mass media could better educate the rulers and
the ruled to deal with a social environment revolutionized by sci-

ence and technology, he said that he did not know. He had lived in the midst of change, he said, "never really understanding it very well . . . not knowing what to do about it." Those who would educate either Congressmen or the masses must first re-educate themselves, he said. "We know what to do about a particular thing, but about the general situation we don't know. And the fact that we don't know is perhaps the beginning of wisdom."

It was true, he said, that good reporters in 1969 were "much more sophisticated and educated men than reporters were in 1922" when he published *Public Opinion*. But though they were less prone to view the world in terms of stereotypes and superficialities, he said, they, like everyone else, were unprepared for the chaotic events with which they had to deal.

He was still skeptical, as he had been in 1925, when he wrote *The Phantom Public*, about the capacity of public opinion to deal with complicated problems. The great dilemma of popular government, he said, was a simplistic electorate, anxious for absolutes, confronted with questions which defy absolute answers.

Perhaps journalism in general tended to oversimplify in order to satisfy a public demand, he said. "But broadcast journalism has not only a terribly simplifying effect, but a distorting effect, I think, because it makes everything more dramatic than it should be, more interesting, more amusing." For the problems of the prosaic world, he said, one must turn to prose in print. "You can get a smell of them [on television] . . . and then you can read about them . . ."[94]

In another interview shortly before his eightieth birthday Lippmann told Henry Brandon, associate editor of the Sunday *Times* of London, that newspapers are here to stay and that news columnists and analysts have become increasingly important. "People like Walter Cronkite and David Brinkley are excellent, really, but you can't live on what they give you."

Political journalism in the late 1960's might seem to be swinging to the right, Lippmann said, but he doubted that it was an ideological shift. Age and the ambition for personal success were the usual causes of conservatism, he said. "It's always safer to be conservative than not. You're much less on the defensive. You have much less to explain yourself for."[95]

One of Lippmann's greatest virtues has been a perversity against conforming to political and ideological trends. Aside from his sheer endurance, and probably responsible for it, one of the most remarkable things about him has been his openness of mind.

In the 1930's to the dismay of his old friends and in defiance of the intellectual fashion, he condemned Stalinism and the New Deal. In the late 1940's he opposed the Truman-Acheson hard line against Communist expansion. In the 1950's he sinned against the liberal establishment by supporting Eisenhower, though he won partial redemption by attacking Senator Joseph McCarthy and the brinkmanship of John Foster Dulles. In the 1960's and earlier he was cool toward enforced desegregation of the schools and total obedience to the one-man, one-vote rule. He admired John Kennedy though he did not regard Kennedy's accomplishments as President highly. He respected Lyndon Johnson and grew to distrust him. He distrusted Richard Nixon and came to support him.

One might argue that such legerdemain betokens adherence to the principle of expediency, which is usually considered unprincipled. But some rule or rules must govern the choices of the expedient. Seeking an "absolute" to explain Lippmann is a task which presumably would defy Lippmann himself and Drs. Freud, Jung, Brill, and Binger.

Superficially, a clue might be found in one of his favorite words—civility—which seemed to signify for him the suppression of acquisitive, combative, rebellious instincts. Very late in his life, Lippmann said when he was 82, he had come to believe that in addition to evolving the unique capacity to speak and to write man has also developed "an inherited code of civility" which teaches him that "nobody can exercise absolute power . . ."[96] For Lippmann the achievement of civility, or disinterestedness, was a relatively easy task. Talented, superbly educated, prosperous by inheritance and his own efforts, it was rather natural that he should wish to see in others the attributes which were desirable for him.

The rule of civility should govern, of course, the conduct of nations as well as men—walk softly and carry no sticks at all, or, if need be, only one big enough for self-protection. With this premise it is easy—probably too easy—to explain Lippmann's foreign policy, including his Anglophilia. The British had been greedy, but in learning to subdue their greed had become the most civilized of nations. The German appetite in 1914 was understandable until it became voracious. The aspirations of the Communists were tolerable, but their police state was barbarous. The punic treaty of Versailles made a German rebellion inevitable, but the Nazis' inhumanity and rapacity menaced the civilized Atlantic Community. A counter-strike nuclear arsenal is necessary for America, but the role of world-policeman is arrogant and brutal, besides being impossible.

The qualities of disinterestedness, moderation, and civility are admirable, but it is difficult for the underprivileged to adhere to them, since they are suited to curb impetuosity and hence to preserve the status quo. The absence of impetuosity in Lippmann, noted early by Mable Dodge Luhan and John Reed, and a little later by James Cain, provoked the criticism that his moral views lacked a sense of urgency and commitment.

As late as 1965, Christopher Lasch observed that it was possible for Lippmann to view the problems of education, civil rights, and urban decay "without any sense of crisis." Underlying Lippmann's "decency, sobriety, and reasonableness," which made him almost unique as a political analyst, there was, Lasch said, a sense of complacency.

The truly civilized man tends to be patrician, and, even if he is careful, a bit Pharisaical. Lippmann's distrust of mass rule and "the tyranny of the majority," his reliance on leadership for the solution of critical problems, seemed to signify, Lasch said, echoing the views of Archibald MacLeish a decade earlier, a surrender of "the will to solve our problems democratically."[97]

A democratic solution of problems, Lippmann emphasized in *The Public Philosophy*, is possible only in a society committed to democratic principles. Lippmann's own definition of those principles, especially as they touch on liberty of speech and press, set tighter limits on freedom of expression than some of his contemporaries believed compatible with democracy.

In 1925 when Justice Holmes urged freedom for Benjamin Gitlow, who had been convicted for urging proletarian revolution, Lippmann applauded in a *World* editorial, even though Holmes' opinion went so far as to say: "If, in the long run the beliefs expressed in proletarian dictatorship are destined to be accepted by the dominant forces of the community, the only meaning of free speech is that they should be given their chance and have their way."[98]

But in 1955 Lippmann explicitly proclaimed the view that the right to enjoy the free institutions of speech and press was reserved to those who adhere to the institutions. Those who do not adhere, especially Fascists and Communists, he said, ought to be silenced by due process of law, because, should they attain power, they would destroy the Bill of Rights. The opposite view, attractive to Holmes, Lippmann's old friend Zechariah Chafee, Jr., Alexander Meiklejohn, Justices Black and Douglas, did not appeal to him. Their belief that the First Amendment is as close to a political absolute as one can get he rejected. It was necessary, he concluded, to restrict men's words as well as their deeds, provided that the restraint or punishment was imposed by due process of law.[99]

Perhaps it is only curiously coincidental that Lippmann's first book about the press was entitled *Liberty and the News* rather than *Freedom of the Press*. As Meiklejohn and others have pointed out, the Bill of Rights sanctions abridgement of liberty but forbids abridgement of freedom. The Fifth Amendment provides for deprivation of life, liberty, or property with due process of law. There is no due process clause to dilute the First Amendment. The Supreme Court in the 1960's began to incline to the Meiklejohn rather than the Lippmann views, holding unanimously that speech or print devoted to public issues was not subject to abridgement. Although the court added a rider: that deliberate malice or reckless disregard of the truth was punishable as civil libel, it foreclosed state or federal sanctions against inflammatory expression.[100]

Criticism of government and government officials, provided it is free from personal malice and flagrant lies, seems now immune to punishment in the United States. But the big problem for the democratic journalist is not staying inside the ample tent of protection afforded by the courts. The journalist's dilemma lies in reconciling the risk of disclosure of what he knows or thinks he knows with what he conceives to be "the national interest." It is a dilemma which has driven some editors into retirement.

Contemporary journalists, in a world of dirty little cold wars, can no longer confidently repair to the noble standard erected for the press by the *Times* of London in 1852. "The first duty of the press," the *Times* declared, "is to obtain the earliest and most correct intelligence of the events of the time, and instantly, by disclosing them, to make them the common property of the nation ... The duty of the journalist is the same as that of the historian—to seek out the truth, above all things, and to present to his readers not such things as statecraft would wish them to know but the truth as near as he can attain it."[101]

Present-day journalists, particularly political correspondents like Lippmann, are to a far greater degree than ever before makers of history as well as historians. Besides helping to shape events, sometimes by flagrant participation in them, journalists are the repository of secrets, many of them dreadful, which they fear to share with their readers. "Newspapers shouldn't play God." But they do.[102]

Lippmann stated the problem clearly in a speech in 1965. "I have in mind, to begin with," he said, "the conflict between, on the one hand, the public's right to know, or it may be the public's curiosity to know, and, on the other hand, the need of the government to be able to deliberate confidentially before announcing a conclusion, and in certain circumstances, especially in its foreign relations, the government's right to a measure of secrecy and dispatch.

"The conflict is, I am inclined to believe, perennial in the sense that there is no abstract principle which resolves it."

But the problem of what the press does with the unkept secrets which come into its ken Lippmann seemed to brush aside, saying only that the conflict between the duty to seek the truth and loyalty to the country is "trying" and can be solved at times by "retreat into less hotly contested subject matter."[103] If the journalist uses this escape hatch, it is questionable whether he can, as Lippmann said he must, join the scientist and the scholar in placing "truth in the first place."

Predicating that truth, or disclosure, must at times be the handmaiden of national interest or security—that, as James Reston says, "the old principle of publish-and-be-damned ... can often damage the national interest"—presumes a theory about what the national interest is.[104]

The division of the world into competitive nation states is barbaric, Lippmann believed, but there is no prospect foreseeable by the most optimistic of men that national rivalries will end. The supreme interest must therefore be national survival, which entails the defense against attacks from within and without of a nation's political, social, and economic institutions.

In foreign relations, governments must operate from a position of strength. This means not just balance of power but favorable balance of power, alone or in concert with nations whose ideals are similar. In the short run, at least, the good of all mankind is best promoted by a balance of power favorable to the Atlantic Community, especially the United States and Britain, because in this community lies the world's best hope for freedom and justice and escape from misery, poverty, and exploitation.[105]

Specifically, Lippmann advocated for the United States a "blue water" strategy based on air and sea supremacy in the Atlantic and Pacific. Beyond the blue water, in Asia especially, he said, America has no vital interest to defend or be capable of defending. "What happens on the land—on the surface—in the Eurasian Continent is something we can negotiate about but not something which we can direct or govern." The boundary between the East and West in Europe was flexible, he said, but it must be achieved and maintained "without the presence of American infantry."

The true balance of power and the best hope of peace, Lippmann said, resided in America's nuclear arsenal, and the absolute essential was to make sure that nuclear power was really balanced. The virtue of nuclear weapons, he believed, was that "the facts of life" precluded either the Soviets or the United States from using them. It was possible, he said, that Russia might attempt a nuclear strike against China, but even this could not provoke total war, because neither country would successfully invade the other. China as a threat to America or to world peace he discounted, and he urged that the United States be absolutely neutral in the conflicts between China and Russia.

The money spent defending the national interest from foreign interference need not interfere with the development of domestic programs to promote the general welfare, Lippmann believed. "The United States could and can afford guns and butter," he said. But the guns should command and defend only "the common homeland of western civilization," and the butter should not include marmalade. "The country is fed up," he said, "... with inflationary promises."

President Nixon's approach to social welfare—a guaranteed minimum annual income—was inherently sound, he said, and he doubted that crash programs for social walfare would be effective. It was rather foolish, he said, to talk of diverting the billions spent on space exploration to social projects, because neither the Congress nor the taxpayer could agree on what the projects should be.[106]

For more than sixty years—from *A Preface to Politics* through *The Public Philosophy* and in later columns and interviews—Lippmann struggled with the problem of educating the masses to govern themselves. In his eighties he was still struggling with it, working on a book which he said would deal "with the problem of the ungovernability of mankind in our era and why and how and whether and what."[106] Judging from what seemed to be his mood, it will not be an optimistic book, nor will it offer any panaceas for solving the problems which beset the citizen, the politician, the statesman, or the journalist.

NOTES

CHAPTER I

1. "Socialism at Harvard," by Walter Lippmann, *Harvard Illustrated,* March 1909, p. 137.

2. "Too Great Expectations," Lippmann column in *Newsweek,* Jan. 13, 1969. p. 11.

3. "Re Lamont on Lippmann," letter from Harrison Reeves in *New Masses,* Nov. 30, 1937, p. 19.

4. *The Fourth Branch of Government,* by Douglass Cater. Houghton Mifflin Company. Boston. 1959. pp. 98–100.

5. "Walter Lippmann on Manchester," Washington *Post,* April 18, 1967. Also see "The Legend of Kennedy," Nov. 22, 1967. (A "Today and Tomorrow" column.)

6. "Walter Lippmann: Pundit and Prophet," by Richard H. Rovere, *Flair,* January 1951, pp. 36–37, 118–120. "Washington: Walter Lippmann Goes Home," by James Reston, New York *Times,* May 26, 1967.

7. "Walter Lippmann: The Philosopher as Journalist," by Louis J. Halle, *New Republic,* Aug. 3, 1963, pp. 17–20.

8. *The Crossroads of Liberalism,* by Charles Forcey. Oxford University Press. New York. 1961. pp. 94–104.

9. "View from Olympus," by John Crosby, *Seminar,* December 1968, p. 15.

10. *Walter Lippmann and His Times,* ed. by Marquis Childs and James Reston. Harcourt, Brace and Company. New York. 1959. pp. 21–36. *Walter Lippmann A Study in Personal Journalism,* by David Weingast. Rutgers University Press. New Brunswick. 1949. pp. 3–11.

11. The information about New York newspapers in the 1890's comes from *The News and America,* by Edwin Emery. Prentice-Hall. Englewood Cliffs, N. J. 1962. pp. 486–487, and from "Annals of Crime—The Case of The Scattered Dutchman," by A. J. Liebling, *New Yorker,* Sept. 24, 1955, pp. 50–103. Determining exact circulation figures before 1914, when the Audit Bureau of Circulations was organized, is difficult.

12. *The End of the World,* ed. by James W. Barrett. Harper and Brothers. New York. 1931. pp. 116–120.

13. *Walter Lippmann and His Times*, pp. 30–36.

14. "A Footnote to Santayana," by Walter Lippmann, *Saturday Review of Literature*, Dec. 7, 1929, p. 513.

15. *Harvard Crimson*, April 27, 1935. Quoted in *Copey of Harvard*, by J. Donald Adams. Houghton Mifflin Company. Boston. 1960. "Harvard—1910," by Walter Lippmann, *Harvard Monthly*, April 1910, pp. 43–45.

16. "Harvard in Politics: A Problem in Imperceptibles," by Walter Lippmann, *Harvard Monthly*, December 1909, pp. 95–98. "In Defense of the Suffragettes," by Walter Lippmann, *Harvard Monthly*, November 1909, pp. 64–67.

17. "The Discussion of Socialism—Politics and Meta-Politics," by Walter Lippmann, *Harvard Illustrated*, April 1910, pp. 231–232.

18. "A Preface to Lippmann—2. Education of a Commentator," by John Mason Brown, *Saturday Review*, May 7, 1954, p. 60.

19. *The Letters of Lincoln Steffens*, ed. by Ella Winter and Granville Hicks. Harcourt, Brace and Company. New York. 1938. p. 637.

20. *The Autobiography of Lincoln Steffens.* Harcourt, Brace & World. New York. 1958. (Originally published in 1931.) pp. 592–597.

21. "A Man with a Flashlight Mind," by Beverly Smith, *American*, September 193.

22. "An Open Mind: William James," by Walter Lippmann, *Everybody's*, December 1910, pp. 800–801.

23. *The Crossroads of Liberalism*, pp. 102–103, 327–328.

24. "George R. Lunn and the Socialist Era In Schenectady," by Kenneth E. Hendrickson, Jr., *New York History*, January 1966, pp. 22–39.

25. "Schenectady the Unripe," by Walter Lippmann. New York *Call*, June 9, 1912.

26. "An Unripe Criticism," by Morris Hillquit, New York *Call*, June 16, 1912.

27. "The Shrewdly Good," by Walter Lippmann, New York *Call*, June 23, 1912.

28. "A Bold Plan," by Upton Sinclair, New York *Call*, Sept. 15, 1912.

29. "Two Months in Schenectady," by Walter Lippmann, *Masses*, April 1912, p. 13.

30. *Walter Lippmann and His Times*, p. 36.

31. *Walter Lippmann—A Study in Personal Journalism*, p. 11. Also see *Saturday Review*, May 7, 1954, p. 60.

32. "Walter Lippmann—The Career of Comrade Fool," by Ernest Sutherland Bates, *Modern Monthly*, June 1933, pp. 266–274.

33. *A Preface to Politics*, by Walter Lippmann, Macmillan Company. New York. 1933. (Originally published in 1913.) pp. 16, 54, 56, 282, 287.

34. "Walter Lippmann III. Obfuscator de Luxe," by Amos Pinchot, *Nation*, July 19, 1933, pp. 67–68.

35. *A Preface to Politics*, pp. 34–52, 83, 106. *The Crossroads of Liberalism*, pp. 109–113, 326.

36. *A Preface to Politics*, pp. 194–197.

37. *The Crossroads of Liberalism*, pp. 105–108.

38. *A Preface to Politics*, pp. 277–278.

39. "A Presidential Joker," by Walter Lippmann, *Everybody's*, February 1912, p. 244.

40. *Drift and Mastery*, by Walter Lippmann. Mitchell Kennerley. New York. 1914. pp. 80–81.

41. *Movers and Shakers*, Vol. 3 of *Intimate Memories*, by Mabel Dodge Luhan. Harcourt, Brace and Company. New York. 1936. pp. 23, 43, 68, 120.

42. "Up in Mabel's Room," by Clifton Fadiman, *New Yorker,* Nov. 21, 1936, pp. 108–110.

43. *Movers and Shakers,* p. 119.

44. "Ickes Declares the Columnists are Calumnists," New York *Herald Tribune,* April 12, 1939.

45. *The Improper Bohemians,* by Allen Churchill. E. P. Dutton and Company. New York. 1959. p. 37.

46. *Movers and Shakers,* pp. 257–258.

47. *John Reed—The Making of a Revolutionary,* by Granville Hicks. Macmillan Company. New York. 1936. p. 174.

48. *Movers and Shakers,* pp. 319–331.

49. "The White Passion," by Walter Lippmann, *New Republic,* Oct. 21, 1916, pp. 293–295.

50. *Movers and Shakers,* pp. 87–93. *The Improper Bohemians,* pp. 43–52.

51. *The End of American Innocence,* by Henry F. May. Alfred A. Knopf. New York. 1959. pp. 303–313.

52. *Movers and Shakers,* pp. 188–212.

53. *Ibid.,* pp. 96–113.

54. *Ibid.,* pp. 117–122.

55. *The Improper Bohemians,* pp. 54–55. *Movers and Shakers,* pp. 142, 235–241.

56. *The Improper Bohemians,* pp. 57–58.

57. "A National Diagnosis," by Walter Lippmann, *Everybody's,* February 1913, pp. 247–248. "The Greatest Question," by Walter Lippmann, *Everybody's,* April 1914, pp. 502–504. "A Key to the Labor Movement," by Walter Lippmann, *Metropolitan,* September 1914, pp. 16, 52–53.

58. *Movers and Shakers,* p. 298.

59. *John Reed,* pp. 172–174.

60. "Legendary John Reed," by Walter Lippmann, *New Republic,* Dec. 26, 1914, pp. 15–16.

61. John Reed's *The Day in Bohemia,* in which the verses about Lippmann appeared, was privately printed in 1913. It is reprinted in *Movers and Shakers,* pp. 172–185.

62. *Movers and Shakers,* p. 298.

63. *John Reed,* p. 225.

64. *Movers and Shakers,* pp. 432, 485–487.

65. *Yankee from Olympus,* by Catherine Drinker Bowen. Little, Brown and Company. Boston. 1944. pp. 385–387.

66. *The Holmes-Einstein Letters,* ed. by J. B. Peabody. Macmillan Company. London and Toronto. 1964. pp. 102, 136–137, 205, 281.

67. "Oliver Wendell Holmes," a "Today and Tomorrow" column, Jan. 14, 1932.

68. "What is Science," review in the *Nation* of Lippmann's *Drift and Mastery.* Jan. 7, 1915, 21–22.

69. "Mr. Rockefeller on the Stand," by Walter Lippmann, *New Republic,* Jan. 30, 1915, pp. 12–13. "The Irresponsible Rich," by Walter Lippmann, *Metropolitan* April 1915, pp. 43–44.

70. *The Good Society,* by Walter Lippmann. Little, Brown and Company. Boston. 1938. pp. ix–x.

71. *The Stakes of Diplomacy,* by Walter Lippmann. Henry Holt and Company. New York. 1915. p. 10.

CHAPTER II

1. *Philosopher's Holiday,* by Irwin Edman. Viking Press. New York. 1938. p. 236.
2. "Notes for a Biography," by Walter Lippmann, *New Republic,* July 16, 1930, pp. 250–252.
3. *The Crossroads of Liberalism,* p. 176.
4. "The Nation and The New Republic," by Beulah Amidon, *Survey Graphic,* January 1940, pp. 21–26.
5. "Independence in Newspapers," *World* editorial, May 3, 1929.
6. "Public Opinion—Liberals," *Time,* Nov. 13, 1939, pp. 21–22.
7. Talk by Lippmann at 50th anniversary dinner of *New Republic* in Washington, March 5, 1964. Text published in *New Republic,* March 21, 1964, p. 14.
8. "The Old New Republic," review by Norman Podhoretz of *The Face of Five Decades:* Selections from Fifty Years of the *New Republic,* in the *New York Review of Books,* April 8, 1965, pp. 18–20.
9. "The Faith of Broadway," by Walter Lippmann, *New Republic,* Nov. 28, 1914, pp. 19–20. "The Lost Theme," by Walter Lippmann, *New Republic,* April 15, 1916, pp. 258–260. "An Angel Barks Up the Wrong Tree," letter from Leo Stein to *New Republic,* April 29, 1916, pp. 349–350. "Freud and the Layman," by Walter Lippmann, *New Republic,* April 17, 1915, pp. 9–10. "Scandal," by Walter Lippmann, *New Republic,* April 24, 1915, pp. 297–299.
10. "Law and Order," by Walter Lippmann, *Metropolitan,* August 1915, pp. 32, 37. "Books and Things," by Walter Lippmann, *New Republic,* Aug. 7, 1915, p. 24.
11. "That Soft Pedal," by Walter Lippmann, *Harvard Illustrated,* February 1915, pp. 219–221.
12. New York *Times,* July 2, 1936.
13. *The Stakes of Diplomacy,* p. 5. *The Crossroads of Liberalism,* p. 224.
14. *The Influence of War on Walter Lippmann 1914–1944,* by Francine C. Cary. State Historical Society of Wisconsin. Madison. 1967. pp. 12–19.
15. *The Stakes of Diplomacy,* pp. 20–25.
16. "Uneasy America," by Walter Lippmann, *New Republic,* Dec. 25, 1915, pp. 195–196. "Washington Notes," by Walter Lippmann, *New Republic,* Jan. 15, 1916, pp. 278–279.
17. *The Stakes of Diplomacy,* pp. 54–57.
18. "Insiders and Outsiders," by Walter Lippmann, *New Republic,* Nov. 13, 1915, pp. 35–36. "Leadership and 'Misrule by the People,'" by Charles Forcey, *New Republic,* Feb. 21, 1955, pp. 13–16.
19. *Fighting Years,* by Oswald Garrison Villard. Harcourt, Brace, and Company. New York. 1939. p. 361.
20. "Notes for a Biography," *New Republic,* July 16, 1930, pp. 250–252.
21. *The Influence of War on Walter Lippmann,* pp. 30–31.
22. Diary of Col. Edward M. House and Woodrow Wilson Papers, quoted in *The Influence of War on Walter Lippmann,* pp. 28–29 and in *The Crossroads of Liberalism,* pp. 266–267.
23. "America's Part in the War," by Walter Lippmann, *New Republic,* March 10, 1917, pp. 29–30. House Diary, March 9, 1917, quoted in *The Influence of War on Walter Lippmann,* pp. 34–35.
24. "Who Willed American Participation?" *New Republic,* April 14, 1917, pp. 308–310.

25. House Papers, April 3 and 12, 1917, quoted in *The Influence of War on Walter Lippmann,* pp. 37–39.

26. "Facts Demanded on Coast Danger," New York *Times,* Feb. 15, 1942.

27. Lippmann letter to House, Oct. 17, 1917, in House Papers. (Yale Collection.)

28. "Walter Lippmann to Aid Baker," New York *Times,* May 30, 1917. "All Labor Disputes Go to New War Board," New York *Times,* Aug. 11, 1917.

29. *At the Paris Peace Conference,* by James T. Shotwell. Macmillan Company. New York. 1937, pp. 3–4. *The Intimate Papers of Colonel House,* ed. by Charles Seymour. Houghton Mifflin Company. Boston and New York. 1938. Vol. III, pp. 170–171.

30. Lippmann letters to House, June 16, Aug. 9, Aug. 15, Sept. 2, 1918, in House Papers.

31. House letter to Lippmann, in House Papers, Oct. 2, 1918.

32. Wilson to House, Aug. 31, 1918, in Wilson Mss., 2nd series, Library of Congress, quoted in *The New Radicalism in America (1889–1963),* by Christopher Lasch. A. A. Knopf. p. 221.

33. "Drop News from Sky on All Army Fronts," New York *Times,* Nov. 1, 1918. "Germans Impressed by Our Propaganda," New York *Times,* Nov. 9, 1918.

34. *Walter Lippmann A Study in Personal Journalism,* p. 17. *Intimate Papers of Colonel House,* Vol. III, p. 152; Vol. IV, p. 153.

35. Lippmann to House, Nov. 7, 1918, in House Papers.

36. "Walter Lippmann," *United Nations World,* May 1947, p. 80.

37. *Willard Straight,* by Herbert Croly. Macmillan Company. New York. 1924. p. 544.

38. Lippmann to Newton D. Baker, June 9, 1919, in Baker MSS, Library of Congress.

39. Lippmann to House, July 19, 1919, in House Papers.

40. *The Crossroads of Liberalism,* pp. 288–292. "Notes for a Biography," *New Republic,* July 16, 1930, pp. 250–252.

41. "Unrest," by Walter Lippmann, *New Republic,* Nov. 12, 1919, pp. 315–322. "Urges Staff of Experts—Walter Lippmann Proposes Formation of a Body to Aid Legislators," New York *Times,* April 12, 1919. Also see "What Must We Do To Be Saved?" editorial in New York *Times,* April 14, 1919, referring to Lippmann as "respectably radical."

42. *Reporting The Wars,* by Joseph J. Mathews. University of Minnesota Press, Minneapolis. 1957. pp. 155–158, 176–188.

43. "The Basic Problem of Democracy—I. What Modern Liberty Means," by Walter Lippmann, *Atlantic Monthly,* Nov. 1919, pp. 616–627.

44. "Publicity at Moscow," a "Today and Tomorrow" column, Dec. 22, 1945. "Stop, Look and Listen," May 1, 1951.

45. "The World We're In, an interview with Walter Lippmann by Ronald Steel," *New Republic,* Nov. 13, 1971, p. 20. Also see the Washington *Post,* Oct. 10 and 12, 1971, for Steel's interview with Lippmann.

46. *The Phantom Public,* by Walter Lippmann. Harcourt, Brace and Company. New York. 1925. pp. 38–39.

47. *The Public Philosophy,* by Walter Lippmann. Little, Brown and Company. Boston. 1955. (The edition quoted was published by Mentor Books, New York, in 1956.) pp. 23–24.

48. "A Test of the News," by Walter Lippmann and Charles Merz, *New Republic,* Aug. 4, 1920, pp. 1–42.

49. *Liberty and the News,* by Walter Lippmann. Harcourt Brace and Howe. New York. 1920. pp. 9–11, 65–66, 25–68, 69–104.

50. "The Press in an Age of Controversy," by James Russell Wiggins, *Quill,* April 1969, p. 11.

51. *Legal Control of the Press,* by Frank Thayer. Foundation Press. Brooklyn. (4th Edition.) 1962. pp. 223–225.

52. Review of *Liberty and the News,* New York *Times,* March 21, 1920.

53. "What to Do About News Juggling," by W. J. Ghent, *Review,* May 29, 1920, p. 571.

54. "Democracy and a Free Press," by Henry Litchfield West, *Bookman,* Oct. 1920, pp. 116–121.

55. "See Red Hysteria in Sedition Curb," New York *Times,* Feb. 29, 1920.

56. "A Test of the News," *New Republic,* Aug. 24, 1920, pp. 1–42.

57. "Lippmann at 77 Cuts Down Pace," New York *Times,* May 26, 1967. "Pulitzer, 1958," New York *Times,* May 6, 1958.

58. "On Criticism of the Press," a "Today and Tomorrow" column, March 27, 1947.

59. " 'A Test of the News': Some Criticisms," *New Republic,* Sept. 8, 1920, pp. 31–33. "Filtering the News," *New Republic,* Sept. 15, 1920, pp. 61–62. "Lippmann at 70," by Louis M. Lyons, *Nieman Reports,* January 1960. pp. 22–23.

60. "What Is Wrong With the Newspapers?" by Walter Lippmann, *Vanity Fair,* February 1921, pp. 36, 96. *The United States and World Affairs—1931,* by Walter Lippmann and W. O. Scroggs. Harper and Brothers. New York. 1932. pp. 7–8.

61. "Public Opinion," by John Dewey, *New Republic,* May 3, 1922, pp. 286–288.

62. "From Public Opinion to Public Philosophy," by Heinz Eulau, *American Journal of Economics and Sociology,* July 1956, pp. 439–451.

63. *Public Opinion,* by Walter Lippmann. Macmillan Company. New York. 1922. (The edition quoted was published by Penguin Books, New York, in 1946.) pp. 10, 11.

64. *Ibid.,* p. 236.

65. *The Public Philosophy,* pp. 18–19.

66. *News Editing and Display,* by Charles H. Brown. Harper and Brothers. New York. 1952. pp. 272, 275, 283. *Introduction to Mass Communications,* by Edwin Emery, Phillip Ault and Warren Agee. Dodd, Mead and Company. New York. 1965. pp. 89, 95, 158, 274.

67. *Public Opinion,* p. 258.

68. *Ibid.,* pp. 266–267.

69. *Ibid.,* pp. 269–270.

70. *Ibid.,* p. 271.

71. "The Job of the Washington Correspondent," Lippmann's address to National Press Club on his 70th birthday, *Atlantic,* January 1960, pp. 46–49. A slightly expanded version was published in *Nieman Reports,* October 1959, pp. 20–22, under the heading "Walter Lippmann's Birthday Address to the National Press Club."

72. "Fact Finding and Steel," a "Today and Tomorrow" column, July 21, 1959.

73. *Public Opinion,* p. 275.

74. *Ibid.,* pp. 301–302.

75. "Public Opinion and Democracy," by Ernest Gruening, *Nation,* July 6, 1922, pp. 97–98.

76. *Dangerous Estate,* by Francis Williams. Longmans, Green and Company. London. 1958. pp. 288–289.

CHAPTER III

1. *The World of Swope,* by E. J. Kahn, Jr. Simon and Shuster, New York. 1965. p. 273.

2. "The Press Today, VII. What's Wrong with the World," by Oswald Garrison Villard, *Nation,* June 25, 1930. p. 724.

3. "Two Revolutions in the American Press," by Walter Lippmann, *Yale Review,* March 1931. pp. 439–440.

4. "The End of the *World,*" by James M. Cain, *New Freeman,* March 11, 1931. pp. 611–612.

5. "Washington: Walter Lippmann Goes Home," by James Reston, New York *Times,* May 26, 1967.

6. Letter from Herbert Bayard Swope in *Saturday Review,* March 17, 1945. p. 15.

7. Cain, *op. cit.,* pp. 611–612.

8. *The End of the World,* ed. by James W. Barrett, pp. 32–34.

9. Review by Bruce Bliven of Lippmann's *Men of Destiny, Atlantic,* November 1927, pp. 60–61.

10. *Memoirs, Sixty Years on the Firing Line,* by Arthur Krock. Funk and Wagnalls. New York. 1968. pp. 61–63, 72.

11. "The Life and Death of the *World,*" by Allan Nevins, *Saturday Review,* March 14, 1931. p. 663.

12. *The World the Flesh and the Messrs. Pulitzer,* by James W. Barrett. Vanguard Press. New York. 1931. pp. 60–61.

13. *The World of Swope,* pp. 246–247.

14. Foreword by Lippmann to *Highlights,* by Rollin Kirby. Published by William Farquhar Payson, New York. 1931. pp. xiii–xv.

15. "Leftover Liberal," *Time,* March 20, 1939, p. 42. (On the retirement of Kirby from the *World-Telegram.*)

16. "A Free Press," editorial by Lippmann in the *World,* Jan. 3, 1927.

(Henceforth in the notes the Lippmann editorials will be identified by title and date only.)

17. "Pride of Opinion," *World,* April 28, 1927.

18. "By Decree of Mr. Coolidge," *World,* May 19, 1927.

19. "Calvin Coolidge Says," *World,* July 2, 1930. *Calvin Coolidge—The Quiet President*, by Donald R. McCoy. MacMillan Company. New York. 1967. pp. 399–402.

20. "Piano v. Bugle," article in *Time,* March 30, 1931, p. 24, mentioning Hoover's relationship with the *World.*

21. "Clear and Present Danger," *World,* June 10, 1925. For a discussion of the "clear and present danger" test, see *Freedom of Speech: The Supreme Court and Judicial Review,* by Martin Shapiro. Prentice-Hall, Inc. Englewood Cliffs, N. J. 1966. pp. 46–75.

22. "The Special Privilege of a Judge," *World,* Feb. 18, 1926. For Supreme Court decisions limiting power of judges to punish for contempt of court, see Bridges v. California, 314, U.S. 252 (1941); Pennekamp v. Florida, 328, U.S. 331 (1946); and for the "men of fortitude" reference Craig v. Harney, 331, U.S. 367 (1947).

23. "Reflections on the Browning Case," *World,* Jan. 28, 1927. For a discussion of newspaper treatment of the Browning, Hall-Mills and other celebrated trials during the 1920's, see *Jazz Journalism,* by Simon M. Bessie. E. P. Dutton & Co., Inc. New York. 1938. Also see New York *Times'* Index 1920–1927. For

an explanation of the *Times'* policy toward the trials, see *The Story of the New York Times, 1851–1951*, by Meyer Berger. Simon and Schuster. New York. 1951. pp. 257–259.

24. "On Regulating Earl Carroll," *World*, July 11, 1930.

25. "Objections to Censorship of the Theater," *World*, Feb. 17, 1931.

26. "Columnists on Parade," by Margaret Marshall, *Nation*, April 23, 1938. p. 464. For the reference to Lippmann as Puritan see "A Preface to Lippmann. 1. Philosopher-Journalist," by John Mason Brown. *Saturday Review*, April 24, 1954. p. 38.

27. "Obscenity and the Tariff," *World*, March 20, 1930. "Invocation" in *The Selected Verse of Ogden Nash*. The Modern Library. New York. 1945. pp. 22–23.

28. "Censorship," *World*, March 11, 1927.

29. *Ulysses*, by James Joyce. Random House. New York. 1934. p. x.

30. "Morals for Profit," *World*, April 2, 1930.

31. "No Red Hysteria," *World*, March 12, 1930.

32. "Louisiana: Note on the Defense of Free Institutions." A "Today and Tomorrow" column, Feb. 5, 1935.

33. "A Question of Honor," *World*, Dec. 23, 1927. (Editorial on Klan parade in New York.) "The Right to Parade," *World*, May 22, 1928. (Another editorial defending the rights of the Klan.)

34. "Shrinking Lindy," *World*, June 7, 1929.

35. "The Test of a 'Liberal Judge,' " *World*, May 24, 1930.

36. "For the *Herald Tribune*," *World*, Aug. 11, 1928.

37. "Injustice and the Newspaper," *World*, Nov. 16, 1926. (On the Aiken, S. C., lynching.)

38. *Walter Lippmann and His Times*, p. 81.

39. *Protest: Sacco-Vanzetti and the Intellectuals*, by David Felix. Bloomington. Indiana University Press. 1965. p. 12.

40. "Justice in Massachusetts," *World*, April 12, 1927. "Justice Not Yet Done," *World*, April 20, 1927. "The Prejudices of Judge Thayer," *World*, May 6, 1927. "The Verdict of the Law," *World*, Aug. 5, 1927. "An Appeal to Gov. Fuller," *World*, Aug. 6, 1927. "Is This Due Process of Law?" *World*, Aug. 9, 1927. "Mercy," *World*, Aug. 10, 1927. "A Respite," *World*, Aug. 11, 1927. "Insurance Against the Possibility of Irrevocable Error," *World*, Aug. 12, 1927.

41. *Heywood Broun*, by Dale Kramer. Current Books, Inc. New York. 1949. p. 168.

42. "Threats and Irritation," *World*, Aug. 13, 1927.

43. *Protest: Sacco-Vanzetti and the Intellectuals*. p. 177.

44. *Heywood Broun*. pp. 178–179.

45. *The World of Swope*. pp. 271–272. *Heywood Broun*. pp. 181–182.

46. "Patriotic Service," *World*, Aug. 24, 1927.

47. "The End of the *World*," by James M. Cain. *New Freeman*, March 11, 1931. p. 612.

48. "Aftermath," *World*, Aug. 26, 1927.

49. "A Preface to Lippmann. 3. Reason in an Age of Unreason," by John Mason Brown. *Saturday Review*, May 8, 1954, p. 47.

50. "It Seems to Me," by Heywood Broun. New York *World-Telegram*. Nov. 18, 1937.

51. "Biochemistry—Walter Lippmann and the Sex Life of Bugs," *Time*, Sept. 17, 1965. p. 95.

52. *It Seems to Me*, by Heywood Broun. Harcourt, Brace and Company. New York. 1935. "Horses With Their Hair Down," pp. 282–284.

53. *Ibid.,* "Mr. Hearst and Mr. Lippmann," pp. 278–281.

54. *Heywood Broun,* p. 140.

55. "It Seems to Heywood Broun," *Nation,* May 16, 1928, p. 532.

56. "It Seems to Heywood Broun," *Nation,* May 9, 1928, p. 557. Also see "Heywood Broun," editorial in *Nation,* May 16, 1928, defending Broun and criticizing the *World,* p. 553.

57. *Heywood Broun.* pp. 192, 299–300.

58. "Lippmann Abridged," *Time,* Nov. 14, 1932. p. 20.

59. *The Essential Lippmann,* ed. by Clinton Rossiter and James Lare. Vintage Books. New York. 1965. p. xiii.

60. "The Life and Death of the *World,*" by Allan Nevins. *Saturday Review,* March 14, 1931. p. 663. *Walter Lippmann and His Times.* pp. 78–79.

61. *The World The Flesh and the Messrs. Pulitzer.* pp. 73, 85.

62. "A Visit with Walter Lippmann," by William Atwood, *Look,* April 25, 1961, p. 106.

63. *Citizen Hearst,* by W. A. Swanberg. Bantam Books. New York. 1963. p. 469.

64. "Probe to the Bottom," *World,* Dec. 17, 1927. "Mr. Hearst's Defense," *World,* Dec. 22, 1927.

65. *The End of the World,* pp. 24, 145, 178–180.

66. "Lippmann Will Travel," New York *Times,* Feb. 27, 1931.

67. "Lippmann Urges the Liberal Spirit," New York *Times,* March 26, 1931.

68. "The Press and Public Opinion," by Walter Lippmann, *Political Science Quarterly,* June 1931, pp. 161–170.

69. "Two Revolutions in the American Press," by Walter Lippmann. *Yale Review,* March 1931, pp. 433–441.

70. "The Thirst for Information," speech by Jenkin Lloyd Jones, editor of Tulsa *Tribune,* to the National Newspaper Promotion Association, in Phoenix, Ariz., May 2, 1960.

71. "Can Journalism Be Taught?" by Alfred Friendly, *Reporter,* Jan. 7, 1960, pp. 34–36. See also Lippmann's comments on journalism teaching and on the Nieman Foundation in "Lippmann is 70; 500 Join Tribute," New York *Times,* Sept. 24, 1959. Lippmann's notes and the typescript of his after-dinner talk to teachers of journalism at Columbia are in the collection at Yale, labelled "date undetermined." A reference in the talk to the Rhinelander divorce case would seem to date it in 1926 or 1927.

72. New York *Times,* April 3, 1921.

73. "The Enormously Civilized Minority," by Walter Lippmann, *Vanity Fair,* March 1928, pp. 39, 120.

74. "The New Machiavelli," by Walter Lippmann, *New Republic,* May 31, 1922, pp. 12–14. (Lippmann's analysis of Mencken.)

75. "Katzenjammer," review by Mencken of Lippmann's *The Phantom Public,* *American Mercury,* January 1926, pp. 125–126.

76. *The Phantom Public,* pp. 13–15, 65, 68, 70.

77. *Walter Lippmann and His Times.* pp. 205–206.

78. *Men of Destiny,* by Walter Lippmann. Macmillan Company. New York. 1927. pp. 100–106.

79. *American Inquisitors,* by Walter Lippmann. Macmillan Company. New York. 1928. pp. 4–6, 10–13, 45–46, 95–96. Also see "The Ordeal of General Ike," by David F. Schoenbrun, *Harper's,* October 1952, p. 29.

80. "Court Ends Arkansas Darwinism Ban," New York *Times,* Nov. 13, 1968.

81. *A Preface to Morals,* by Walter Lippmann. Macmillan Company. New York. 1928. pp. 16–19.

82. "Mover and Shaker: Walter Lippmann as a Young Man," by Heinz Eulau, *Antioch Review*, Fall 1951, p. 312.

83. *A Preface to Morals*, pp. 64–65.

84. *Ibid.*, pp. 268–270, 287.

85. "Modern Stoicism," review by Irving Babbitt of *A Preface to Morals, Forum*, July 1929, pp. x–xiv. "Enduring the Truth," review by George Santayana of *A Preface to Morals, Saturday Review*, Dec. 7, 1929, pp. 512–513.

CHAPTER IV

1. "Lippmann to Write for *Herald Tribune*," New York *Times*, March 28, 1931. See also "Topics of the *Times*," same issue.

2. "To Mr. Lippmann," editorial in New York *Herald Tribune*, Sept. 8, 1931.

3. "Magical Prosperity," the first of the "Today and Tommorrow" columns, syndicated by the *Herald Tribune*, Sept. 8, 1931.

(Henceforth in the notes the columns will be identified only by title and date.)

4. "Help for those Who Need it," Oct. 21, 1931.

5. "Agenda for Recovery," April 20, 1935.

6. "Lippmann Tells of Necessity for Private Relief," headline above text of Lippmann speech, New York *Herald Tribune*, Sept. 24, 1935.

7. "Lippmann Assails Patman Bonus Bill," New York *Times*, May 15, 1935.

8. *Heywood Broun*, p. 73.

9. *Conversations with Walter Lippmann*, transcriptions of Columbia Broadcasting System Correspondents' interviews with Lippmann, 1960–1965. Little, Brown and Company. Boston. 1965. pp. 115, 220–221.

10. "Walter Lippmann," by Allan Nevins, New York *Herald Tribune*, Sept. 11, 1932.

11. Communication to author from George Cornish, July 1971.

12. *New Yorker*, Oct. 1, 1932.

13. "Walter Lippmann Looks at the Political Scene," by William Allen White, New York *Herald Tribune* Book Section, Oct. 23, 1932.

14. "The Candidacy of Franklin D. Roosevelt," Jan. 8, 1932.

15. "Walter Lippmann, the Career of Comrade Fool," by Ernest Sutherland Bates, *Modern Monthly*, June 1933, pp. 266–274.

16. *The Crisis of the Old Order*, by Arthur M. Schlesinger, Jr. Houghton Mifflin Company. Boston. 1957. pp. 98, 291, 362.

17. "Roosevelt and Smith," *World* editorial, Oct. 3, 1928.

18. "Roosevelt, Smith and Baker," Feb. 12, 1932.

19. "The Nomination of Roosevelt," July 4, 1932.

20. "One Voter's Choice," Oct. 7, 1932.

21. "Democracy and Dictatorship," Feb. 24, 1933. "Has Congress Abdicated?" May 3, 1933.

22. "The President's Task. III. Enterprise and the New Deal," Oct. 12, 1933.

23. "The Burden of the Complaint," Aug. 15, 1935. "Emergency Over, Time Has Come for Roosevelt to Return Blanket Powers to Congress," report in New York *Herald Tribune*, Aug. 21, 1935, of Lippmann speech on National Broadcasting Company network.

24. "The Frustration of Debate," Jan. 4, 1936.

25. "At the End of The Campaign," Oct. 31, 1936.

26. "The Voter's Choice," Sept. 8, 1936. Also see New York *Herald Tribune* editorial, "Lippmann for Landon," same date.

27. *Conversations with Walter Lippmann,* pp. 18–19.

28. "Landon and the National Union," Sept. 10, 1936. Estimates of the number of unemployed in 1936 differed greatly. The Republicans claimed eleven million were still out of work. Democratic spokesmen cited figures as low as five million. See, e.g., New York *Times,* Oct. 23, 1936, and Nov. 24, 1936.

29. *The Method of Freedom,* by Walter Lippmann. Macmillan Company. New York, 1935. pp. 36–47.

30. "At the End of the Campaign," Oct. 31, 1936. *Walter Lippmann, A Study in Personal Journalism, pp. 69, 73, 76. Interpretations: 1933–1935,* by Walter Lippmann. Macmillan Company. New York. pp. 286–290.

31. *The Politics of Upheaval,* by Arthur M. Schlesinger, Jr. Houghton Mifflin Company. Boston. 1960. pp. 399–401.

32. "Newspapers and the N.R.A.," Nov. 15, 1933. "Lippmann Advises Publishers to Refuse Code when Nira Ends," New York *Herald Tribune,* Jan. 17, 1935.

33. "It Seems to Me," by Heywood Broun, New York *World-Telegram,* Jan. 23, 1935.

34. "Newspaper Blood Money," *Christian Century,* Feb. 6, 1935, pp. 166–168.

35. *Newsroom Problems and Policies,* by Curtis D. Mac Dougall. Macmillan Company. New York. 1941. pp. 536–537.

36. "The Wagner Labor Bill," March 28, 1935.

37. "Lippmann Protests Against American Newspaper Guild Political Views," New York *Times,* July 22, 1937. See also New York *Herald Tribune* for "Guild Policies Are Challenged by Lippmann," "Guild Officers Held Betrayers by Lippmann," and "Guild Members Held Not Bound by Its Politics."

38. "It Seems to Me," by Heywood Broun, New York *World-Telegram,* Aug. 24, 1933.

39. *Heywood Broun,* p. 275, pp. 299–300.

40. "Let Colonel Lindbergh Alone," April 6, 1932.

41. "The Departure of the Lindberghs," Dec. 28, 1935.

42. "The Hauptmann Case," April 7, 1936. "Text of Address by Lippmann to Newspaper Editors' Society," headline over text of Lippmann speech, in New York *Herald Tribune,* April 19, 1936. "Editors of U.S. Assail Seizure of Telegrams," New York *Herald Tribune,* April 19, 1936.

43. "National Bar Adopts Standards to Curb Release of Crime News," New York *Times,* Feb. 20, 1968.

44. "Case at Ipswich Assizes," Oct. 29, 1936. "A King's Marriage," Dec. 8, 1936. "The Love and Duty of a King," Dec. 10, 1936.

45. "Elucidator," review of *The Good Society,* and a summary of Lippmann's career, in *Time,* Sept. 27, 1937, pp. 45–48.

46. "Mrs. Lippmann Sues Columnist," Associated Press report, Oct. 19, 1937, in New York *World-Telegram.* "Mrs. Byrne Armstrong Weds Walter Lippmann," New York *Herald Tribune,* March 27, 1928.

47. "Lippmann in New Form," announcement that Lippmann would end the regularly scheduled column and move to New York. *Newsweek,* June 5, 1967, p. 64.

48. "Walter Lippmann: the debacle of a mind," review by Corliss Lamont of Lippmann's *The Good Society,* in *New Masses,* Nov. 2, 1937, p. 23.

49. "Re Lamont on Lippmann," letter from Harrison Reeves to *New Masses,* Nov. 30, 1937, p. 19. Also see in same issue on same page, "Reviewer Lamont

Replies," and "Lippmann as Social Lion," letter from Reeves to *New Masses,* replying to Lamont, Dec. 28, 1937, p. 19.

50. "A Word of Advice—The Bribe of a Bauble," editorial in New York *Journal,* Oct. 12, 1938; Philadelphia *Inquirer,* Sept. 21, 1938.

51. "Notes on the Freedom of the Press," April 25, 1936. *Conversations with Walter Lippmann,* pp. 161–162.

52. "The Rise of Personal Government in the United States," speech by Lippmann at Johns Hopkins University, published in *Vital Speeches of the Day,* May 1, 1937, pp. 419–423.

53. "Lippmann and the Court," by Max Lerner. *Nation,* Feb. 27, 1937, p. 230.

54. "The Right People," by Heywood Broun. *New Republic,* Sept. 29, 1937, pp. 203–204.

55. "Legislative Inquisition," March 5, 1936.

56. *The Politics of Upheaval,* pp. 322–323.

57. "Notes on the Freedom of the Press," April 25, 1936.

58. "Liberty and Its Many Champions," Dec. 11, 1937.

59. "The New Deal and the Press," May 10, 1938.

60. "The Power of the Press Is Not Waning," article by Percy B. Scott, based on interview with Lippmann, in *American Press,* December 1963, p. 1.

61. "Shop Talk at Thirty," by Marlen Pew. *Editor & Publisher,* Sept. 26, 1936, p. 48. Also see, for publishers' support of Republicans and correspondents' preference for Democrats, *The Opinionmakers,* by William L. Rivers. Beacon Press. Boston. 1967. pp. 177–178. And see "Politicians and The Press," by William B. Dickerson, Jr., in *Editorial R search Reports,* Sept. 2, 1964, pp. 655–659.

62. "Freedom of the Radio," June 22, 1934.

63. "Concerning Radio News," Sept. 14, 1939.

64. "On Going Abroad," Aug. 14, 1937.

65. *The Good Society,* pp. x–xii, 107–109.

66. "Liberalism in a Vacuum," review by John Dewey of *The Good Society* in *Common Sense,* December 1937, pp. 9–11.

67. "Walter Lippmann's Evolution," by Louis J. A. Mercier, *Commonweal,* Aug. 4, 1939, pp. 348–350.

68. "Authors and Humanism," by Warren A. Smith, *Humanist,* October 1951, p. 199.

69. "Lippmann Agonistes," review by Max Lerner of *The Good Society* in the *Nation,* Nov. 27, 1937, p. 589.

70. "Walter Lippmann," review by James Truslow Adams of *Interpretations 1931–1932,* a collection of "Today and Tomorrow" columns edited by Allan Nevins and published by the Macmillan Company in 1932. The Adams review appeared in *Saturday Review,* Jan 7, 1933, pp. 361–362, and White's comments in the New York *Herald Tribune* book section Oct. 23, 1932.

71. Review by Clifton Fadiman of *The Method of Freedom* in the *New Yorker,* June 9, 1934, pp. 92–94.

72. *The Method of Freedom,* pp. 107–109.

73. *The Good Society,* p. 230.

74. *The New Imperative,* by Walter Lippmann. The Macmillan Company. New York. 1935. pp. 34–35.

75. "An Open Letter to Walter Lippmann," by Edmund Wilson in the *New Republic,* Nov. 11, 1931, pp. 344–345.

76. Letter from Henrik Willem van Loon in the *New Republic,* Dec. 2, 1931, pp. 73–74.

77. "Walter Lippmann. I. The Great Elucidator," first in a series of four articles by Amos Pinchot, *Nation,* July 5, 1933, pp. 7–10. Also see "A Man with a Flashlight Mind," by Beverly Smith, *American,* September 1932.

78. "Walter Lippmann. IV. On Democracy," by Amos Pinchot, *Nation,* Aug. 2, 1933, pp. 126–131. "Walter Lippmann. III. Obfuscator de Luxe," by Amos Pinchot, *Nation,* July 19, 1933, pp. 67–70.

(In a column in *Editor & Publisher,* July 22, 1933, p. 44, Marlon Pew defended Lippmann against Pinchot's criticism. A note on the Yale Collection index card for the column states: "On the occasion of Mr. Lippmann's visit to the collection in March, 1938, he stated that Mr. Pinchot had expressed a wish that he had never written the articles in the *Nation* and that he apologized to W.L.")

79. *Modern Monthly,* June 1933.

80. "This Is Where We Came In," by John Riddell, *Vanity Fair,* Sept. 1933, p. 35. "Walter Lippmann, Our Humpty Dumpty," by Herbert Mead, *American Criterion,* Dec. 1935, pp. 3–5. "Columnists on Parade," by Margaret Marshall, *Nation,* April 23, 1938, pp. 464–467. "Personal Journalists," by Silas Bent, *Saturday Review,* Dec. 12, 1936, p. 4.

81. "Elucidator," *Time,* Sept. 27, 1937, p. 47. Also see "About the Author of Today and Tomorrow," *Copy,* Spring 1937.

82. "The Nation's Columnists Divide in Great Debate on American War and Peace," *Life,* April 24, 1939, p. 24. "The Fortune Survey. X. Pundits' Progress," *Fortune,* January 1940, p. 92. *Collected Poems of Kenneth Fearing.* Random House. New York. 1940. p. 97.

CHAPTER V

1. "U.S. Editorial Pages Gain in Influence"—report by Phillip Schuyler of interview with Lippmann in *Editor & Publisher,* June 29, 1944, p. 8.

2. "The Burning of the Books," May 12, 1933.

3. "The Defense of the World Court," Feb. 2, 1935.

4. "Disentanglement in Europe," Oct. 17, 1936. "American Rearmament," Jan. 8, 1938. "Senator Nye Grows Older," May 7, 1938. "The Road to American Security," Oct. 3, 1939.

5. *The Influence of War on Walter Lippmann,* pp. 132–135.

6. "An Estimate of American Public Opinion about Foreign Affairs," March 23, 1939.

7. "The Nation's Columnists Divide in Great Debate on American War and Peace," *Life,* April 24, 1939, pp. 24–25.

8. *The Influence of War on Walter Lippmann,* pp. 142–143. "The Necessary Plan of American Defense," May 14, 1940.

9. "Issues and Men," by Oswald Garrison Villard, *Nation,* May 25, 1940, p. 654.

10. *Forty Years with Berenson,* by Nicky Mariano. Alfred A. Knopf. New York. 1967. p. 268.

11. "Knox Pledges Speed-Up," New York *Times,* Aug. 11, 1940.

12. "Facts Demanded on Coast Danger," New York *Times,* Feb. 15, 1942.

13. "The Generation That Was Duped," June 15, 1940.

14. "From the Compiègne Armistice to the Philadelphia Convention," June 25, 1940.

15. "The Meaning of Willkie," June 26, 1940. "Black Tuesday in Philadelphia," June 27, 1940.

16. "The Willkie Tidal Wave," June 29, 1940.

17. "The Political Consequences of Willkie's Nomination," July 2, 1940.

18. "The Two Conventions," July 20, 1940.

19. "Mr. Willkie's Campaign," Aug. 27, 1940.

20. "On the Strength of Democracy," Nov. 5, 1940.

21. "Mr. Roosevelt's Mandate," Nov. 7, 1940.

22. "The Colliding Opinions," July 31, 1941.

23. "The Country in Peril," May 17, 1941.

24. "Everybody's Business and Nobody's," April 10, 1941.

25. *U.S. Foreign Policy: Shield of the Republic,* by Walter Lippmann. Little, Brown and Company. Boston. 1943. pp. ix–xiii.

26. "Submitted in Evidence," Feb. 2, 1942.

27. "Mr. Hull Returns to Congress," Nov. 18, 1943. Also see comments by Lippmann in *Atlantic,* May 1945, p. 131.

28. "F.D.R. and the Press," Oct. 15, 1942.

29. "War Information," June 16, 1942.

30. "Something Off My Chest," March 14, 1942.

31. *The Coming of the New Deal,* by Arthur M. Schlesinger, Jr. Houghton Mifflin Company. Boston. 1959. pp. 199–201, 208–209, 221–225. *The World of Swope,* pp. 381–385. For the Lippmann columns on devaluation, see *Interpretations: 1933–1935.* pp. 155–183. In his *Memoirs,* pp. 164–165, Arthur Krock gives a different version of Lippmann's involvement. Summarizing a conversation with James M. Cox, one of the American delegates, Krock says Cox told him that Lippmann, Moley and Keynes wrote the statement which Roosevelt repudiated. Krock does not mention their writing, with Swope's help, the interpretation of the repudiation.

32. "Secrecy and Accountability," Oct. 20, 1942. "The Cult of Incompetence," June 24, 1942.

33. "Information for Newspapermen," July 11, 1942.

34. "On Discussing War Plans," July 30, 1942. "U.S. Editorial Pages Gain in Influence," *Editor & Publisher,* July 29, 1944, p. 8.

35. "Missing Clews," Oct. 23, 1943.

36. "International Freedom of the Press," Dec. 23, 1943.

37. *U.S. War Aims,* by Walter Lippmann. Little, Brown and Company. Boston. 1944. pp. 149–151.

38. "A Capitalist Paper On Sale in Moscow, But Only to Aliens," New York *Times,* April 14, 1968.

39. "Hot Spot at Hot Springs," April 17, 1943.

40. "The Propaganda That Backfired," July 10, 1943.

41. "Letter from Washington," by Richard H. Rovere, *New Yorker,* June 23, 1956, pp. 68–80.

42. "The Yalta Papers I," March 31, 1955.

43. "Roosevelt Will Devote Profits From Books to 'Public Purpose,'" New York *Times,* March 2, 1938. "The Sale of Official Opinions," March 3, 1938. For a continuing account of the controversy over the sale of the Roosevelt papers see New York *Times Index* for 1938 and 1939 under the heading "Roosevelt, Franklin D.—Publications."

44. "Mirror of the Spirit," Feb. 25, 1943.

45. "Report from Europe," Nov. 30, 1944.

46. "On U.S. Propaganda," May 22, 1947. "The Voice of Mr. Borgia," June 1, 1948.

47. "Plausible Nonsense," Dec. 6, 1945.

48. "Mr. Roosevelt and a Fourth Term," April 18, 1944.

49. "Henry Wallace," July 11, 1944.

50. "After the Two Conventions," July 25, 1944.

51. "Governor Dewey in Foreign Affairs," Oct. 21, 1944.

52. "The Election: One Man's View," Nov. 2, 1944.

53. *Julius Caesar,* Act III, Scene 2.

54. *Further Poems of Emily Dickinson.* Little, Brown and Company. Boston. 1929. p. 119.

55. "On Senator Lodge," New York *World,* Oct. 25, 1924. For a discussion of the obituarist's problem ("when you write a man's obituary, you become his advocate") see "Obits: 1945," by A. J. Liebling, in *The Best Of A. J. Liebling.* Methuen. London. 1965. pp. 174–181.

56. "The President as Strategist," April 7, 1945.

57. "Roosevelt Is Gone," April 14, 1945.

58. "President Truman," April 17, 1945.

59. "The Press at San Francisco," *Life,* May 4, 1945, p. 43.

60. "San Francisco?" April 13, 1945.

61. "At the Golden Gate," April 26, 1945.

62. "Monday's Showdown," May 3, 1945.

63. "High Politics at San Francisco," May 8, 1945.

64. "High Politics at San Francisco," May 12, 1945.

65. "Mr. Truman's Foreign Policy," May 29, 1945.

66. "The Broken Field," Sept. 29, 1945.

67. "Our Allies and Japan," Sept. 27, 1945.

68. "Mr. Acheson's Remarks," Sept. 22, 1945.

69. "The Rise of the United States," Sept. 20, 1945.

70. "Washington Background—The Home of the Walter Lippmanns," *House and Garden,* June 1944, pp. 42–43.

71. "Walter Lippmann: Pundit and Prophet," by Richard H. Rovere, *Flair,* January 1951, pp. 36–37, 118–120. "The Press—The Man Who Stands Apart," *Time,* Dec. 22, 1958, pp. 48–49.

72. "A Preface to Lippmann," by John Mason Brown, *Saturday Review,* April 24, 1954, pp. 9–11, 36–38. *Walter Lippmann and His Times,* p. 226.

73. "Personality," *Time,* May 26, 1952, p. 43.

74. "Walter Lippmann Is Opposed to Wage Theory of Enough Money to Buy Food," editorial in *United Mine Workers Journal,* April 15, 1943, p. 9.

75. "Behind the Columns," by John Janney, *American,* January 1940, pp. 34–35, 118–119.

76. "Pundit in a Penthouse," by Barbara Giles, *New Masses,* Sept. 10, 1940, pp. 11–12.

77. "Impossible Interviews—No. 16: Walter Lippmann vs. Walter Winchell," *Vanity Fair,* April 1933, p. 33.

78. "This Is Where We Came In," by John Riddell, *Vanity Fair,* September 1933, pp. 41, 44.

79. "Fair and Warmer," by Corey Ford, *Colliers,* Aug. 31, 1940, p. 41.

80. "Walter Lippmann," by Fred Rodell, *American Mercury,* March 1945, pp. 263–273.

81. *The Influence of War on Walter Lippmann,* pp. 160–161.

82. "Power Politics," review in *Time* of Lippmann's *U.S. Foreign Policy,* pp. 98–103. "Policy for Survival," review by Edward Meade Earle in *Saturday Review* of *U.S. Foreign Policy,* June 12, 1943, pp. 5–6, 19–20. Review in *Newsweek* of *U.S. Foreign Policy,* June 21, 1943, pp. 96–98.

83. *U.S. Foreign Policy,* pp. 147–152, 161–177.

84. *U.S. War Aims,* pp. vii, 73–95, 131–132, 191–195.

85. "Modern Thucydides," review by Lippmann of *The Gravediggers of France,* by Pertinax, in *Key Reporter,* Winter 1944–45, p. 3.

CHAPTER VI

1. "A Columnist Is an Editorial Writer," by Walter Lippmann, *Quill,* March 1951, pp. 6, 12.

2. "U.S. Editorial Pages Gain in Influence," *Editor & Publisher,* June 29, 1944, p. 8.

3. *The Reporter's Trade,* by Joseph and Stewart Alsop. Reynal & Company. New York. 1958. pp. 5–6.

4. "Cole Presses Talks to Settle the Newspaper Strike," New York *Times,* May 10, 1966. "15 Area Papers Get Lippmann and Alsop Columns," New York *Times,* Dec. 13, 1966. "Suicide in Manhattan," *Newsweek,* May 15, 1967, p. 89.

5. "A Bit of Theorizing," April 30, 1953.

6. "The Wayward Press—Death on the One Hand," by A. J. Liebling, *New Yorker,* March 28, 1953, p. 104.

7. "How Did We Get Here?" June 17, 1954.

8. "On Criticism of the Press," March 27, 1947.

9. "On the Television Problem," April 2, 1951.

10. "Fulbright and Kefauver," March 29, 1951.

11. *Walter Lippmann and His Times,* p. 230.

12. "Television and the Conventions," Aug. 30, 1956.

13. "The Young Criminals," Sept. 7, 1954.

14. "Sadism in the Movies," Oct. 5, 1954.

15. "The TV Problem," Oct. 27, 1959.

16. "The Administration and TV," Jan. 5, 1960.

17. "Television and the Press," March 3, 1960.

18. "It Looks Like a Way Out of the Wasteland," by Walter Lippmann, Washington *Post,* May 7, 1967.

19. "Mr. Truman's Press Conference," Oct. 12, 1946.

20. *Kennedy and the Press,* edited and annotated by Harold W. Chase and Allen H. Lerman. Thomas Y. Crowell Company, New York. 1965. p. XI.

21. "An Idea for the Democrats," Oct. 18, 1948. "The Will of the People," Oct. 25, 1948.

22. *Marshall Field III,* by Stephen Becker. Simon and Schuster. New York. 1964. pp. 384–386.

23. "Disorder at the Top," April 1, 1948. "To Change Horses," April 19, 1948. "One Night's Work," July 19, 1948.

24. "The Victory of Roosevelt's Party," Nov. 4, 1948.

25. "On U.S. Propaganda," May 22, 1947. "The Many Voices of America," Dec. 27, 1951.

26. "Help Wanted," *Newsweek,* Sept. 28, 1959, p. 112. "Abolish the Voice of America," April 27, 1953.

27. "The Dies Committee," Jan. 11, 1940.

28. "The Spy Investigation," April 17, 1948.

29. "Senators and Scientists and Secrecy," May 23, 1949.

30. "End This Disorderly Conduct," June 14, 1949.

31. "Acheson and McCarthy," May 2, 1950.

32. "McCarthy and the Constitution," May 9, 1950.

33. "Mr. Smith Fixes the Future," June 11, 1951.

34. "The New Loyalty Policy," Feb. 5, 1953.

35. "Brownell and McCarthy," Dec. 15, 1953.

36. "The Parting of the Ways," Feb. 23, 1954. "The McCarthy-Stevens Affair," March 1, 1954.

37. "Our National Obsession," March 25, 1954.

38. "The President and the Press," April 26, 1954.

39. "The Sound of the Trumpet," March 22, 1954.

40. "Eisenhower and the Constitution," March 23, 1954.

41. *Senator Joe McCarthy,* by Richard H. Rovere. Harcourt, Brace and Company. New York. 1959. pp. 164–167. *Days of Shame,* by Charles E. Potter. Coward-McCann, Inc. New York. 1965. pp. 14–23. "The Untold Story of McCarthy's Fall," by Richard H. Rovere, *New York Review of Books,* Oct. 28, 1965, pp. 3–5.

42. "Nightmare in Washington," May 3, 1954.

43. "A Better Day," Dec. 27, 1954.

44. "Stevenson and the Democrats," March 31, 1952. *Conversations with Walter Lippmann,* p. 4.

45. "The Ordeal of General Ike," by David F. Schoenbrun, *Harper's,* October 1952, p. 29.

46. "The Eisenhower Movement," March 17, 1952.

47. "Mr. Lippmann's Encyclical," editorial in *Freeman,* April 7, 1952, pp. 423-424.

48. "Eisenhower's Week," June 9, 1952.

49. "The Importance of the Campaign," Oct. 16, 1952.

50. "The Nixon Affair," Sept. 25, 1952.

51. "A Mighty Majority," Nov. 6, 1952.

52. *Mandate for Change,* by Dwight D. Eisenhower. Doubleday and Company. New York, 1963. p. 233. Also see *Walter Lippmann: Philosopher-Journalist,* by E. L. and F. H. Schapsmeier. Public Affairs Press. Washington, D.C. 1969. pp. 122–123.

53. "The Election Explained," Nov. 3, 1952.

54. "Total War and Co-existence," June 18, 1951.

55. "Ehrenburg and the Fourth of July," July 4, 1946.

56. "Stalin and Dulles," Dec. 30, 1952.

57. "On Talking About Talking," Nov. 19, 1953.

58. "The Voices of the President," Feb. 12, 1953.

59. "Tuesday's Show," May 19, 1955.

60. "The Oppenheimer Case," April 15, 1954. "Disorderly Government," June 3, 1954. "The Oppenheimer Case," June 7, 1954.

61. "Politics and Eggheads," April 26, 1966.

62. "Injustice off the Cuff," Jan. 17, 1955.

63. *Kennedy and the Press,* p. 163.

64. "Election Issues," Sept. 28, 1954.

65. "Eisenhower Now and in '56," June 30, 1955.

66. "Walter Lippmann—Pundit and Prophet," by Richard Rovere, *Flair,* January 1951, pp. 36–37, 118–120. "The People, Yes—and No," review by Richard Rovere of Lippmann's *The Public Philosophy* in the *New Yorker,* Feb. 19, 1955, pp. 114–119.

67. "A Preface to Lippmann," by John Mason Brown, *Saturday Review,* May 8, 1954, pp. 12, 46–48.

68. "The Alternative," by Archibald MacLeish, and "A Rejoinder," by Walter Lippmann, *Yale Review*, June 1955, pp. 481–500.

69. *The Public Philosophy*, pp. 78–84, 132–133.

70. *Walter Lippmann and His Times*, pp. 219–221.

71. "From Public Opinion to Public Philosophy: Walter Lippmann's Classic Reexamined," by Heinz Eulau, *American Journal of Economics and Sociology*, July 1956, pp. 439–451.

72. *The Selected Letters of Bernard Berenson*, by A. K. McComb. Houghton Mifflin Company. Boston. 1964. pp. 280–281.

CHAPTER VII

1. *Chicago Race Riots*, by Carl Sandburg. Harcourt, Brace and Howe. New York. 1919. pp. iii–iv.

2. "The Mounting Crisis in Education," May 20, 1954.

3. "The Powell Amendment," Feb. 2, 1956.

4. "The Miss Lucy Case," Feb. 9, 1956.

5. "Mr. Faulkner's Letter," May 8, 1956.

6. "Faubus and Beyond," Oct. 3, 1957. "Law Without Policy," Aug. 26, 1958.

7. "Defaulting Politicians," Aug. 28, 1958.

8. "Tragedy and Outrage," March 16, 1965.

9. "On Seeing It Through," June 4, 1963.

10. "Thoughts on Wednesday Morning," Aug. 29, 1963.

11. "The Negroes' Hopes Are a War Casualty," by Walter Lippmann, Washington *Post*, Aug. 20, 1967.

12. "The Race Report," *Newsweek* column, March 25, 1968, p. 19.

13. "Eisenhower Consents," March 2, 1956.

14. "The Doctors and the Presidency," June 21, 1956.

15. "Eagerbeaverism," July 3, 1956.

16. "Truman and Stevenson," Aug. 14, 1956.

17. "Chicago and San Francisco," Aug. 23, 1956.

18. "Eisenhower Versus the Democrats," Oct. 2, 1956.

19. "Suez and Eisenhower," Oct. 16, 1956.

20. "The Election and the Crisis," Nov. 8, 1956. "The Main Question," Oct. 9, 1956.

21. "The Sherman Adams Affair," June 24, 1958.

22. "Mr. Dulles and the Press," Aug. 27, 1957.

23. "Rumors and Denials," Dec. 31, 1957.

24. "The Portent of the Moon," Oct. 10, 1957. "The Fundamental Challenge," Jan. 2, 1958.

25. "The Unheeded Alarms," Aug. 21, 1958.

26. "The Propaganda Contest," Jan. 21, 1958.

27. "Testing Pro and Con," April 10, 1958.

28. "The Escape from Reality," April 3, 1958.

29. "Diplomacy Vs. Publicity," Oct. 16, 1958.

30. "Dulles: A Tribute," May 26, 1959.

31. "Khrushchev on TV," June 4, 1957.

32. "Truman and Eisenhower," Aug. 27, 1959. "On Summitry," Sept. 3, 1959.

33. "The Road Show," Sept. 24, 1959. "Saturation Coverage," by Benjamin Bradlee, *Reporter*, Oct. 29, 1959, pp. 32–34.

34. "The Spy Plane," May 10, 1960. "The Spy Business," May 12, 1960. "The U-2 in Paris," May 17, 1960.
35. "First of All," May 19, 1960. "What Next?" May 24, 1960.
36. "The Fulbright Inquiry," June 2, 1960.
37. "The CIA Affair," Feb. 21, 1967.
38. "Intelligence and Dirty Tricks," Feb. 23, 1967.
39. "Mr. Katzenbach's Committee," Feb. 28, 1967.
40. "Mr. K. and the Democrats," June 9, 1960.
41. "It's Like Playing Chess," May 31, 1960.
42. "The Job of the Washington Correspondent," speech by Lippmann, printed in *Atlantic,* January 1960, pp. 46–49, and in *Nieman Reports,* October 1959, pp. 20–22.
43. *Walter Lippmann and His Times,* pp. 23, 162–166, 187–188, 222–224.
44. "A Columnist and His Mistakes," *Newsweek,* Sept. 28, 1959, pp. 112–113.

Chapter VIII

1. "Defeatism," Feb. 9, 1960.
2. "This Year's Elections," Nov. 18, 1958.
3. "The Political Doldrums," Dec. 24, 1959.
4. "Stevenson and Kennedy," April 14, 1960.
5. "Kennedy," July 12, 1960.
6. "Some Political Notions," Dec. 31, 1959.
7. "Kennedy and Johnson," July 17, 1960.
8. "The Aborted Campaign," Sept. 13, 1960.
9. "The TV Debate," Sept. 29, 1960.
10. "The Two Men," Oct. 18, 1960.
11. "The Religion Issue," Sept. 20, 1960.
12. "A Visit With Walter Lippmann," by William Atwood, *Look,* April 25, 1961, p. 102.
13. "Is Kennedy Elected?" Dec. 8, 1960.
14. *Look,* April 25, 1961, p. 102.
15. "The President and the People," March 7, 1961.
16. *Conversations with Walter Lippmann,* pp. 40–41.
17. "Al Smith," Oct. 7, 1944.
18. *A Thousand Days,* by Arthur M. Schlesinger, Jr. Houghton Mifflin Company. Boston. 1965. pp. 719–725.
19. "The Columnists JFK Reads Every Morning," *Newsweek,* Dec. 18, 1961, p. 65. *With Kennedy,* by Pierre Salinger, Doubleday and Company. Garden City. New York. 1966. p. 120.
20. "To Ourselves Be True," May 9, 1961.
21. "The Rule of Law," June 22, 1961.
22. *With Kennedy,* p. 253.
23. *A Thousand Days,* pp. 825–827.
24. *With Kennedy,* pp. 271–279.
25. *Thirteen Days,* by Robert F. Kennedy, W. W. Norton and Company. New York. 1969. pp. 94–96, 107–109.
26. "On The Cuban Question Today," Feb. 12, 1963.
27. *With Kennedy,* p. 261.
28. "Walter Lippmann on Managed News," *Newsweek,* April 15, 1963, p. 23.
29. "Progress Without Crisis," Jan. 10, 1963.

30. *A Thousand Days*, pp. 629–630.

31. "A Muddle of Words," Feb. 28, 1961.

32. *New Yorker*, Feb. 17, 1962, p. 52.

33. "Journey on Television," *Time*, July 18, 1960, pp. 38–40. "Today and Tomorrow on TV," by Robert Lewis Shayon, *Saturday Review*, July 23, 1960, p. 34.

34. *Conversations with Walter Lippmann*, p. x.

35. "An Hour with Walter Lippmann," *Progressive*, August 1961, p. 14.

36. "The Warren Report," Sept. 29, 1964.

37. "The Long Post-Mortem," Dec. 1, 1966.

38. "Walter Lippmann on Manchester," Washington *Post*, April 18, 1967.

39. "The Legend of Kennedy," Nov. 22, 1967.

40. "Murder Most Foul," Nov. 26, 1963.

41. "The Transfer of Power," Dec. 3, 1963.

42. "The Unfinished Business," Nov. 28, 1963. "On Continuing," Dec. 5, 1963.

43. "Government Unworkable," Dec. 10, 1963.

44. "The Vice-Presidency," April 23, 1964.

45. "The Kennedys and the Johnsons," March 24, 1964.

46. "Low-Level Campaigning," March 10, 1964.

47. *Conversations with Walter Lippmann*, pp. 154–156.

48. "The Republican Struggle," June 16, 1964.

49. "The Coming Campaign," July 16, 1964.

50. "A Virtual Despair," Aug. 4, 1964.

51. "A Choice," Aug. 28, 1964.

52. "On Warmongering," Sept. 24, 1964.

53. "His Last Ploy," Oct. 27, 1964.

54. "Extremism and Consensus," Nov. 12, 1964.

55. "Faithful Public Servant," July 2, 1964.

56. "Walter Lippmann on Our Problem in Viet Nam," *Newsweek*, Sept. 28, 1964, p. 23.

57. "Walter Lippmann on the All-Purpose Myth," *Newsweek*, May 24, 1965, p. 23.

58. "Walter Lippmann on the Misconceived War," *Newsweek*, June 6, 1966, p. 19.

59. "Concerning the Presidential Press Conference," Feb. 24, 1964. "Two Most Eminent and Strikingly Different Columnists," by John K. Jessup, *Life*, May 7, 1965, pp. 40–41. "Walter Lippmann on the Presidential Press Conference," *Newsweek*, March 1, 1965, p. 17.

60. "The Credibility Gap—I," March 28, 1967. "The Credibility Gap—II," March 30, 1967.

61. "President Sunay Learns Moon Is Slightly Mod," Washington *Post*, April 14, 1967.

62. "Personal Privilege," April 16, 1967.

63. "The Other Other War," by Herblock, Washington *Post*, May 14, 1967.

64. "The Wit of LBJ," London *Observer*, Nov. 12, 1967.

65. "SDX Committee Says LBJ Uses Lies to Mislead Public," Birmingham (Ala.) *News*, Nov. 13, 1967.

66. "A Man for This Season," Nov. 3, 1964.

67. "Walter Lippmann on the Vietnamese War Today," *Newsweek*, Sept. 13, 1965, p. 17.

68. "Walter Lippmann on the President's Hard Decision," *Newsweek*, Jan. 17, 1966, p. 13. "The Shifting Political Winds," June 16, 1966.

69. "Walter Lippmann on the Temptation of Lyndon Johnson," *Newsweek*, Feb. 27, 1967, p. 21.

70. "An Insoluble War?" May 2, 1967.

71. "The World We're In, an interview with Walter Lippmann, by Ronald Steel," *New Republic*, Nov. 13, 1971, pp. 18–21.

72. "The Case for U.S. Pullback to Australia," by Walter Lippmann, Washington *Post*, Oct. 22, 1967.

73. "War Affronts Conscience," Dec. 7, 1967.

74. "Reporting from Vietnam," Dec. 27, 1966.

75. "Harrison Salisbury in Hanoi," Jan. 10, 1967.

76. Reston's criticism of Salisbury was made during a press conference at the University of Alabama on March 17, 1967.

77. "The Prize Flap," *Newsweek*, May 15, 1967, p. 89.

78. "On the Importance of Being Free," speech by Lippmann to International Press Club in London, published in *Encounter*, August 1965, pp. 88–90.

79. "Personal Explanation," May 25, 1967.

80. "The Washington Correspondents After 25 Years," by William L. Rivers, *Columbia Journalism Review*, Spring 1962, pp. 4–10.

81. "Washington: Walter Lippmann Goes Home," by James Reston, New York *Times*, May 26, 1967.

82. "The Presidency—The Oval Office vs. the Attic, by Hugh Sidey, *Life*, May 19, 1967, p. 44 B.

83. "Farewell to Washington," *Time*, Jan. 6, 1967, p. 36. "Leaving the Scene," *Newsweek*, Jan. 9, 1967, p. 39.

84. "Walter Lippmann Buys Co-Op," New York *Times*, March 2, 1967. "Lippmann at 77 Cuts Down Pace," New York *Times*, May 26, 1967.

85. "Who Killed Cock Robin?" March 9, 1967.

86. "Walter Lippmann on 1968 in the Crystal Ball," *Newsweek*, March 13, 1967, p. 31.

87. "Walter Lippmann on Eugene McCarthy's Mission," *Newsweek*, Dec. 18, 1967, p. 25.

88. "Walter Lippmann on the Credibility Quotient," *Newsweek*, July 15, 1968, p. 19.

89. "Walter Lippmann on the Return of the Native," *Newsweek*, July 29, 1968, p. 7.

90. "Walter Lippmann on Between Miami and Chicago," *Newsweek*, Aug. 26, 1968, p. 15.

91. "Walter Lippmann on the Dismal Choice," *Newsweek*, Sept. 23, 1968, p. 23.

92. "Walter Lippmann on the Hard Choice," *Newsweek*, Oct. 7, 1968, p. 27. "Nixon Is the Only One," Oct. 7, 1968. "Walter Lippmann on the American Predicament," *Newsweek*, Oct. 21, 1968, p. 27. "Walter Lippmann on Order and Justice," *Newsweek*, July 1, 1968, p. 19.

93. "Walter Lippmann on Nixon Wins," *Newsweek*, Nov. 18, 1968, p. 37.

94. "On Understanding Society—Walter Lippmann," *Columbia Journalism Review*, Fall 1969, pp. 5–9.

95. "Talk with Walter Lippmann, at 80, About This 'Minor Dark Age,' " by Henry Brandon, New York *Times* Magazine, Sept. 14, 1969, p. 140.

96. "The World We're In, an interview with Walter Lippmann, by Ronald Steel," *New Republic*, Nov. 13, 1971, p. 23.

97. "Walter Lippmann Today," review by Christopher Lasch of *Conversations with Walter Lippmann*, in *New York Review of Books*, Dec. 9, 1965, .pp. 24–26.

98. Gitlow v. U.S. 268 U.S. 652.

99. *The Public Philosophy*, pp. 101–102.

100. *Free Speech and Its Relation to Self-Government*, by Alexander Meiklejohn. Harper and Brothers. New York, 1948. pp. 38–56. New York *Times* v. Sullivan, 376 U.S. 254.

101. *Times* of London, Feb. 6 and 7, 1852, quoted in *Dangerous Estate*, by Francis Williams, pp. 7–9.

102. *The Kingdom and the Power*, by Gay Talese. World Publishing Company. New York and Cleveland. 1969. pp. 4–5, 7, 18, 23, 116, 317, 474. "Newspapers Shouldn't Play God," by Herbert Brucker, *Saturday Review*, Jan. 1, 1955, pp. 9–10, 67–69.

103. "On the Importance of Being Free," speech by Lippmann printed in *Encounter*, August 1965, pp. 89–90.

104. *The Artillery of the Press*, by James Reston. Harper & Row. New York. 1967. pp. 21–39.

105. *Walter Lippmann's Philosophy of International Politics*, by Anwar H. Syed. University of Pennsylvania Press. Philadelphia. 1963. pp. 333–340.

106. "Talk with Walter Lippmann at 80," New York *Times* Magazine, Sept. 14, 1969, pp. 134–135. "Lippmann, at 80, Is Still the Concerned Man," New York *Times*, Sept. 24, 1969.

INDEX